Praise for *The Tarot Architect*

"Duquette's *Tarot Architect* masterfully unveils the code and engineering of consciousness through the lens of western magical traditions. With this book you will design a precise blueprint for a perfect working model of the cosmos, the tarot becoming your compass and your building blocks. Through brilliant synthesis of Qabalistic and Hermetic principles, meditative practices, and ritual work, this groundbreaking text transforms abstract esoteric principles into practical tools. This is an indispensable tarot grimoire that is both accessible and profound. The serious student of Western Mystery traditions is going to cherish this text."

—Benebell Wen, author of *I Ching, the Oracle* and *Holistic Tarot*

"Lon Milo Duquette shares deeply valuable insights into Qabalistic and Hermetic principles of tarot in his trademark fun, approachable way. *The Tarot Architect* is a must-read for anyone interested in getting more from their work with tarot."

—Maevius Lynn, Thelemic author and teacher

"*The Tarot Architect* is a game-changer for tarot enthusiasts ready to take their practice to the next level."

—Theresa Reed, the Tarot Lady, author, *Tarot: No Questions Asked*

T0383219

THE TAROT
Architect

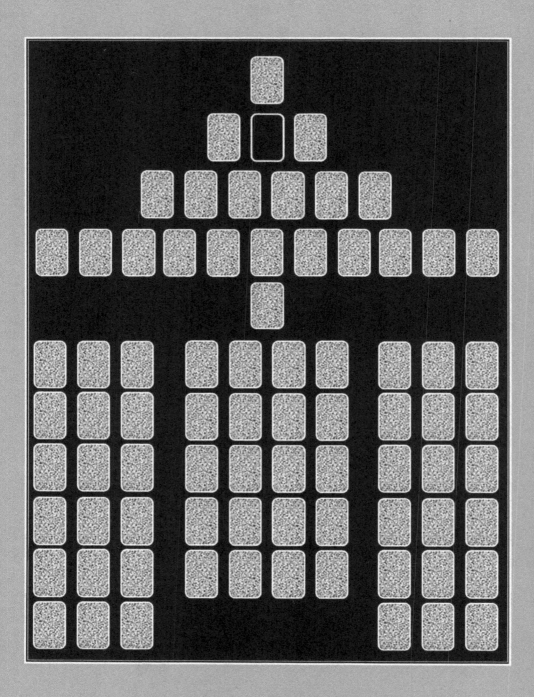

THE TAROT
Architect

How to Become the Master Builder
of Your Spiritual Temple

Lon Milo
DuQuette

Foreword by **MARY K. GREER**

WEISER BOOKS

This edition first published in 2025 by Weiser Books, an imprint of
Red Wheel/Weiser, LLC
With offices at:
65 Parker Street, Suite 7
Newburyport, MA 01950
www.redwheelweiser.com

ISBN: 978-1-57863-854-3

Library of Congress Cataloging-in-Publication Data
Names: DuQuette, Lon Milo, 1948- author. | Greer, Mary K. (Mary Katherine), writer of foreword.
Title: The tarot architect : how to become the master builder of your spiritual temple / Lon Milo
DuQuette; foreword by Mary K. Greer. Description: Newburyport, MA: Weiser Books, 2025. | Includes
bibliographical references. | Summary: "This book is a transformative journey into the arcane world of tarot
that guides you through the depths of tarot with a unique blend of scholarship and humor, transforming
your understanding of self and universe alike. You will discover how to interact with the cards and
learn simple ritual exercises designed to activate and integrate the spiritual forces resident in each card,
enriching your practice and igniting your spiritual evolution"-- Provided by publisher. Identifiers: LCCN
2024054053 | ISBN 9781578638543 (trade paperback) | ISBN 9781633413528 (ebook) Subjects: LCSH:
Tarot. Classification: LCC BF1879.T2 D8699 2025 | DDC 133.3/2424--dc23/eng/20250111
LC record available at https://lccn.loc.gov/2024054053
Cover design and art by Sky Peck Design
Interior illustrations by Lon Milo DuQuette and rendered for publication by Iris Rebecka Johnston
Typeset in Times New Roman

Printed in the United States of America
IBI
10 9 8 7 6 5 4 3 2 1

I invoke thee, I A O, that thou wilt send H R U,
the great Angel that is set over the operations of this
Secret Wisdom, to lay his hand invisibly upon these consecrated
cards of art, that thereby we may obtain true knowledge of hidden
things to the glory of thine ineffable Name. Amen.

The author wishes to thank Rebecka Johnston
for polishing and repairing the tarot images and in-text images.

This work is lovingly dedicated to
~ Rachel Pollack ~
August 17, 1945–April 7, 2023

Contents

Book I
Laying the Foundation

Book II
Creating Your Own Deck

Foreword

I had to laugh when I read about Lon building houses of cards when he was young, because I live in a house of cards! Every room of my house has bookshelves and tables stacked with card decks—specifically tarot cards—and books, oodles of books on tarot. Not a one of them will do for you what this book promises if you follow the practices Lon DuQuette describes.

Who is this book for?

It is for those who desire a set of seventy-eight cards that serve, not just as pieces of cardboard, but as vital forces embodying the mystery and magic of the universe within and without. Such a set can be used to both mirror and manipulate one's own experience and even the world around one. It serves as the key that unlocks the ability to create change in accord with will.

The mechanism focuses on magical correspondences initiated by the late 19th-century Hermetic Order of the Golden Dawn. You'll become familiar with this one system (and some variations within it) that seeks to integrate numbers, astrology, color, sound, geometry, letters, the qabalistic Tree of Life, and more, with the supernatural realms and denizens aligned with the tarot. If you choose to undertake this journey, you will be richly rewarded.

Few people have explored the underlying dynamics among the qabbalistic and tarot correspondences to the extent that Lon DuQuette has. And fewer still have managed to distill these to their most essential, yet mysterious, natures that can be understood simply via mundane, everyday explanations. More importantly, Lon has given those who choose to work with the disarmingly simple practices and meditations in this book the ways to experience consciously living in the magical universe that exists within and all around you. If this sounds grandiose, it is, but it is also entirely possible, as working through this book will demonstrate.

Working with the Tarot Correspondences

Since the late 1960s, as I began my serious exploration of the various tarot decks and systems for working with the tarot, I was astonished to discover how many different esoteric and magical schemes had been ascribed to them. While the varied systems have continued to intrigue me, I feel the knowledge found in the Golden Dawn, OTO, Thelema, and later the Builders of the Adytum (B.O.T.A.) correspondences are the most fully developed for practicing that form of magic that ultimately seeks the knowledge and conversation with one's Holy Guardian Angel. A lofty goal—yet one that is within reach of anyone who gives themselves over to the work.

Over the years, I have seen Lon present his qabalistic tarot framework for beginning and advanced students many times in workshops. He's always been able to introduce a year's worth of complex material in a matter of hours. This book will take a bit longer as you need to put what you learn into practice. It carries Lon's teachings even further as he has masterfully honed and refined the material to make it accessible to everyone and transformative when used with the meditative and attunement practices.

A Memory Palace

Any deck you choose to work with or create for yourself according to Lon's instructions serves as a framework for a memory palace for your inner work.

In a world before photocopy machines and computers, and in which even access to books and paper was limited, a practice of visualizing a sequence of familiar places (loci) was established. In such a place one deposited outlandish, multisensory images reminding one of any set of items. It works for memorizing shopping lists, vocabulary, formulas and their sequences, and lines of poetry or speeches. The Greeks wrote about this extensively, and the method flourished during the medieval and Renaissance periods. It was soon discovered that operating within such a highly charged multisensory and multidimensional mental environment was conducive to working with the forces or energies (and need I say gods or spirits) that lie beyond the physical plane. The so-called Art of Memory, as it can be related to tarot, is discussed in depth by tarot scholar Robert O'Neill,

> The reader who has labored through the preceding chapters on
> 15th century concepts of magic should not be scandalized by the

associations of the Art of Memory and magic. In a culture where spiritual things are more real than material ones, calling something to memory makes that thing real and existing. The memory art thus provided a mechanism for the manipulation of the nonmaterial. And purposeful manipulation of the nonmaterial isn't a bad definition of magic! (www.tarot.com/tarot/robert-oneill/art-of-memory)

Where the Universe and We Touch

This book creates more than just a memory palace consisting of seventy-eight loci. Lon is here introducing you to an inner realm of great potential and majesty that has the power to transform you and your relationship to the living universe. As Lon so eloquently puts it, "When universal influences such as these touch human consciousness, human consciousness eventually touches back and intuitively demands, as it were, ever more perfect evolutionary adjustments to the initial influence." This is the purpose of temple work.

These exercises will take you out of the simple realm of the mind and imagination—as wondrous as they are—and imprint the information and understanding at the physical level of your senses and even into the cells of your body. In place of a so-called palace Lon has us build a temple out of tarot cards involving as many senses as possible so that we can experience and even manipulate the lines of force and energy that connect all parts of creation.

For decades I thought working with the Cube of Space was an overwhelmingly impossible task. And then, following Lon's suggestions, I was able to experience being at the center of an elemental Big Bang; and then a cube of planetary trumps engulfed me while scintillating lights and forces of zodiacal energy surrounded me. Suddenly it all made sense! But is it practical?

Bringing It Back Down to Earth

Lon speaks of reality as a shuffled deck. Tarot author Rachel Pollack and I used to read all seventy-eight cards in less than five minutes as demonstration readings for students in our classes. As Lon reveals, each card is a building block that is an essential component of that moment's edifice within us and a "narrow window of space-time" peering into the universe. When we do a reading with ten or three or even one of these shuffled seventy-eight cards, we are attempting to make sense of the most accessible or relevant part of us in that moment's edifice. Or we can choose to work with any card by deliberate choice to activate its specific force within. Yet all the cards in reality exist so as to vibrate together as parts of a whole, and that is what this book will teach you. Don't worry; this will all become clear as you read Lon's explanations and learn to make a house of cards into a temple and that temple into a place and source of vitality and understanding.

In addition to the twenty-two Trumps, the mixed dualities in the Chinese hexagram correspondences can be matched by a blend of Hindu tattwas in an understanding of the Court Cards. I was taught long ago by poet Diane di Prima to walk through the tattwa color-shapes into other realms, while Lon has helped me explore those who inhabit these realms more fully. The "small cards" (2–10) of the Minor Arcana form a planetary-beaded circlet of everyday experiences, which we can traverse with more understanding of our place in the whole.

May this journey upon which you are embarking bring you personal understanding and help in the enlightenment of all beings.

—Mary K. Greer, author of *Archetypal Tarot:*
What Your Birth Card Reveals about Your Personality, Path, and Potential
April, 2024

A Job Offer

You're nothing but a pack of cards!
—ALICE THROUGH THE LOOKING GLASS

Have you ever tried to build a house of cards?

As a bored youngster growing up in small-town Nebraska, I spent many a sweltering summer's day attempting to assuage my ennui with a deck of playing cards. Constructing a house of cards on the living room carpet promised to be less challenging to my indolent brain than playing solitaire and less physically demanding than repeatedly rolling off the couch to scoop up the cards I had failed to fling into a hat.

Erecting a house of cards requires a cool head, a keen eye, a steady hand, and, of course, far too much time on one's hands. My designs were mind-numbingly unimaginative. Most of the time I simply tried to form a few two-card A-frames or three- or four-card boxes to somehow create a relatively stable ground floor. I'd then managed to lay a few more cards on top to form a roof. When I was lucky, I could duplicate the same process to build a second floor. Occasionally, I could get my house of cards three or four stories high.

Constructing a house of cards requires luck and an instinctual sense of balance in order to reach higher than two or three levels before a draft, a swish of a cat's tail, or a poorly timed sneeze brings it all tumbling down—like the proverbial house of cards we all know so well. For centuries this expression of a *house of cards* has been used to describe any scheme that is ill-conceived or disorganized—a design so poorly planned and precarious that it is doomed to unravel the moment it meets the slightest breath of resistance or unforeseen developments.

On the other hand, the house of cards that is the subject of this book is anything but a poorly conceived and shoddily erected structure. Indeed, once we are armed with just a modicum of understanding, any deck of tarot cards becomes a powerful magical instrument, a mirror to our own soul, a seamless reflection of the scaffolding of the mind of God, a miniature working model of the cosmos, an oracle of the gods.

This little book has been written to provide you with that modicum of understanding and offer you a chance for a little on-the-job training.

A Job Offer

Don't laugh! It's a very good job—one with limitless prospects for advancement. You might even end up marrying the boss's kid and eventually becoming the boss yourself.[1]

The job comes with an impressive title: "master builder" of the most important edifice in the universe—a magical temple fashioned with such divine perfection that, once constructed and consecrated by your wisdom and understanding, it will vibrate like a cosmic tuning fork finely calibrated to the master note of the Music of the Spheres. Furthermore, if you play your cards right, the drone of that great vibration will set *your consciousness* oscillating in pure sympathetic resonance with the sweet symphony of life and creation.

A Perfect Working Model of the Cosmos?

I've been throwing around the phrase *perfect working model of the cosmos* as if I were suggesting that the cosmos is currently functioning in perfect working order. Make no mistake: That's exactly what I'm suggesting. No matter what you may believe to the contrary, the cosmos is, was, and forever shall be humming along perfectly! And *you* are not only a cog in the divine mechanism; you are in fact the perfect reflection of the whole darn machine.

"You old fool!" I hear some of you say. "That's the most naive thing I've ever heard! My universe is most certainly *not* in perfect working order. If I'm the reflection of the universe, then this universe must really be in bad shape!"

Considering all the injustices, environmental collapses, pandemics, social inequities, political upheavals, wars, genocides, ecological catastrophes, and mass extinctions we are surrounded by, our neighborhood universe certainly looks very screwed up. But just because we are currently unable to perceive how the cosmos is functioning in perfect order doesn't mean it *isn't*.

"The fault, dear Brutus, is not in our stars, but in ourselves."[2]

It is our woefully inadequate powers of perception that are to blame. As Goethe's Faust points out, "The world of spirits is not shut away; Thy sense is closed; thy heart is dead!"[3]

Allow me to quickly illustrate using a deck of tarot cards.

Objective "Reality" Is a Shuffled Deck

Usually, when you unseal a brand-new deck of tarot cards, you find them arranged in a sequential manner: the twenty-two Trumps (0–21), then the Aces, Court Cards, and Small Cards of the four suits—all in a tidy, consistent order. This fresh-from-the-factory, perfectly arranged deck could be viewed as representing the way things truly are in the universe.

When you shuffle that pristinely ordered deck, though, you aren't shuffling the universe . . . you are shuffling *yourself* and the clouded perspective from which your defective powers of perception are currently obliging you to see and interpret your existence and what you mistakenly believe is objective reality.

We view the seamless operating dynamics of the infinitely stable and beautiful universe as if through shattered eyeglasses that pervert and distort every image until our life appears to be a chaotic pile of confusing rubble.

So how did our glasses get broken?

We broke them ourselves. We grind them under our heels with every step we take in our futile attempts to run away from ourselves. We twist and warp them as we vainly struggle in Sisyphean futility against what appears to be unyielding forces of nature and the laws and principles that govern the behavior of matter and energy in this narrow window of space-time we're attempting to make sense of.

We have *dis*-attuned our ears from the Music of the Spheres and, like Samson, have brought the illusionary house of cards down upon ourselves.

Building Blocks

Each wafer-thin tarot card is in truth a solid and perfectly squared stone[4] that, when set into place by the hand of the master builder, forms an essential component of the cathedral of existence itself. The seventy-eight cards are the foundation, the supports, the walls, the ceilings, the buttresses, the doors, the windows and ornamentations. But, most importantly, they are the building blocks of the temple of *you* and *me* and every holographic shard of conscious existence.

Do you think I'm exaggerating? Do you think I'm being overly romantic or spiritually naive? After all, you might remind me, tarot is only *a pack of cards*: seventy-eight lifeless pieces of illustrated cardstock. But are they really lifeless?

They are—and they'll remain lifeless until something magical intervenes to bring them to life. That magical something is *you*. And you are the only one who can perform this great miracle of resurrection.

That is, of course, if you choose to accept the *job offer*.

INTRODUCTION

What to Expect

You do not learn tarot. Tarot teaches you.

—Rabbi Lamed Ben Clifford

I f you fancy yourself a "fortune teller" or if you just casually read cards for yourself or others, you're probably amazed at how often tarot cards respond to questions or personal issues with uncannily accurate insights and synchronicities. What is it about these seventy-eight pieces of colored cardstock that transform relatively ordinary people into drooling mystics and surprisingly talented soothsayers?

Many tarot readers tell me they actually sense a conscious life and a palpable spiritual force resident in the cards, an intelligence that not only answers questions but often seems to ferret out unspoken issues lurking behind the queries we think we are making. This is such a common phenomenon that overly superstitious dabblers often get spooked and never want to touch the cards again.

There are very good reasons why tarot seems to trigger psychic responses in so many who choose to seriously work with it as part of their spiritual practice. This little book is intended to first demonstrate how and why tarot is the perfect reflection of the cosmos and the objective universe we live in and then help you install this perfection within yourself so you may come to a better understanding of what an awesome cosmic entity you really are.

A Magic Tool

Tarot has been the most important tool in my magical workshop for over a half century. What started as a colorful and amusing adjunct to my study of

Hermetic Qabalah and ceremonial magick has become the very cornerstone of my temple.

I am by no stretch of imagination the most knowledgeable tarot scholar in the world, nor do I claim to be a supernaturally talented reader of the cards. What I believe I do have to offer—and what I hope to share with you—is a basic practical understanding of the following:

- How tarot fits within the arts and sciences of the Western magical traditions

- How the cards can serve as the picture book of the Hermetic Qabalah

- How, when tarot's qabalistic dynamics become absorbed and installed within your own psychic structure, the cards can become powerful tools of self-transformation and self-realization

For forty years it has been my pleasure and privilege to *teach* the magical applications of tarot to students and practitioners around the world. My workshops, courses, and study programs have evolved over the years and are now distilled in this book into what I hope will be for you a practical manual of study and practice.

- *Yes*. I will offer a bit of background information about the genesis of tarot and its importance within Western magic and mystery traditions. (For this, I've relied on the input and guidance of colleagues whose formal scholarship concerning the objective history of tarot far eclipses my own.)

- *Yes*. I will briefly discuss several important fundamentals of Hermetic Qabalah to give you a working familiarity with a few of Qabalah's sacred *Numbers* and the twenty-two *Letters* of the sacred Hebrew alphabet and how tarot can be employed as the living embodiment of those Numbers and Letters.

- *Yes*. I will, occasionally (in sidebar messages) ask you to focus on specific tarot cards as you read the text to encourage you to get out your cards and actually *do* things with them rather than just *read* about them.

- *Yes*. I will occasionally present specific meditations and homework assignments that may include certain chants, vocal intonations, and magical visualizations that utilize cards in various ways to help you attune to the specific spiritual frequencies and forces resident in each. These exercises and meditations are the most important feature of this book and should not be omitted or practiced half-heartedly. They are the means by which the framework of your house of cards will organically form within your own consciousness.

- *Yes*. You will learn the unique colors and basic symbolism of each of the seventy-eight tarot cards as well as simple ritual exercises designed to *activate* and *integrate* the spiritual forces resident in each individual card.

- But perhaps the most important feature this course—if you choose to join in the fun—is you will be given the opportunity to build your own *house of cards* by creating, customizing, and magically charging your own complete deck of tarot cards.

The Tarot of "You"

Early in 1974 I enrolled in a Tarot Fundamentals correspondence course offered by the Builders of the Adytum (B.O.T.A.).[1] The centerpiece of the course was the requirement that each student paint or in some other way color a complete set of the twenty-two Trump cards. We were provided a tableau of the uncolored line-drawing images of the B.O.T.A. cards[2] printed out on firm cardstock. Each week the instructional monographs contained coloring instructions, meditations, and detailed information to intimately acquaint the student with the cards. Each card took me two weeks to complete, but when the project was finished, I was someone else. I realized that I had undergone a true and profound initiation.

This is the kind of experiential initiation I wish for you to experience. Of course, we won't be using the B.O.T.A. card forms. Instead, you will be working with the *Tarot of Ceremonial Magick* (Magical Omaha, *magicalomaha.com*), a magical deck that I designed and my artist-wife Constance-Jean DuQuette rendered in the late 1980s.

Embedded throughout the pages that follow you will find all seventy-eight full-size uncolored and unfinished images that you will be encouraged to color yourself and personalize with your own additional images or alterations.[3]

In addition to the simple line drawings of iconic tarot images appropriate to each card, each unfinished card is already labeled with the appropriate *number*, *title*, *calendar dates*, *planetary and zodiacal* assignments, and the *names* and *sigils* of important *angels* and *spirits* traditionally associated with the card.

The aim is to create, as much as possible, your own unique deck. You are, of course, free to use or ignore any of these more magical features. You may even wish to design your own card images entirely from scratch. In fact, I think it would be wonderful if you did! But I am also hoping you will take advantage of the head start these artistic and educational exercises will offer you as you study and install the essence of the cards within your psychic self.

I will help you as much as possible by providing tables that outline the appropriate qabalistic color scales for each card and suggestions for additional images, devices, or magical symbols that have for centuries been traditionally associated with each card.

But I can't do the magic for you. The *magic* must be entirely your own!

How Seriously Do You Want to Take This Project?

You can use colored pencils or pens to work directly on the pages of this book. But, if you seriously think you might like to end up with a workable deck, you will find a file of single-page reproductions of each of the seventy-eight blank card forms on my website (*londuquette.com/books.php*) that can be printed on inexpensive cardstock. That way you'll be able to cut out a finished set of cards without damaging the book.

Sound like a lot of work?

Yes! It *will* be a lot of work. But it will also be a lot of fun. And once you start, I can almost guarantee the project will immediately take on a magical life of its own. More importantly, *you* will take on a new magical life of *your* own.

Think you aren't a talented artist?

So what! Art is art. Just roll up your sleeves and start. Your efforts, no matter how comically clumsy or breathtakingly exquisite, will serve to magically consecrate your deck as only you can do. The magick of your focused *will* and your evolving understanding of the unique virtues of each card will serve to awaken within you and the cards the divine forces and resident spirits.

I do hope you will choose to play along and follow the simple step-by-step instructions, practice the easy meditations, and then allow the angels of your newly lubricated magical imagination—and your hidden artistic genius—to do the rest. You'll not only be creating a priceless personal magical treasure; you'll be performing the Great Work of building the Magick Temple of Tarot within yourself, in your own psyche and within your own soul!

And after all, your soul is the only place in the universe where this sacred house of cards will fit.

IMPORTANT NOTICE

In order to immediately begin the various exercises presented in this book, it will be helpful for you to have at hand:

- A full tarot deck. Any standard seventy-eight card deck of tarot cards that contain:

  - twenty-two Trump cards

  - four suits that represent Wands, Cups, Swords, and Disks

- A pitch pipe or some instrument or device to determine specific musical notes

BOOK I

Laying the Foundation

The path once laid the journey is inevitable.

CHAPTER 1

The Building Code

Tarot is a wheel, a mandala revealing the mechanics of creation.
Each card has its place upon the great wheel; from the inscrutable
Zero of the Fool to the dense materiality of the Ten of Disks.

—*TAROT OF CEREMONIAL MAGICK*[1]

Chances are you are already somewhat familiar with tarot. You might even be a professional reader or seasoned occultist for whom tarot plays an important role in your spiritual practices. If so, you probably own at least one commercially produced deck you currently feel comfortable using for your personal meditations and divinatory practices. If so, good!

You'll want to have a deck of tarot cards at hand as you read and study this book.

I travel with two decks that I use for my personal, on-the-road magical operations (yes, I said magical operations) and for readings for others. The two decks are:

1. My own *The Tarot of Ceremonial Magick*[2] (the deck my wife Constance and I created in the late 1980s and that for the last thirty years has been my deck of choice)

2. The Crowley-Harris *Thoth Tarot*[3]

On occasions when neither of my preferred decks are available, I'm quite comfortable using the classic Smith-Waite,[4] B.O.T.A.,[5] Golden Dawn,[6] or *any* pack that happens to be at hand. Why am I not fussier about what deck I use? Because, after over a half century of working with tarot, I've come to the realization that the magic of tarot isn't in the cards but in myself.

You, however, won't need fifty years to make your cards magic. In fact, *any* tarot deck will become a powerful magical tool in your hands the moment you recognize it as such. I have written this little book to help you do precisely that while giving you the opportunity to understand, organize, and systematically install each card in its proper place within your own psyche. By doing this, you will cast a true and powerful spell upon both yourself *and* the cards—a spell that will awaken within you the host of universal spiritual forces that live just beneath the painted surface of each and every card in the pack.

Qabalah

Every standard seventy-eight-card deck,[7] no matter how awesomely beautiful or whimsically silly the artwork may be, is by virtue of its *fundamental structure* genetically[8] linked to all other decks by a golden thread of the shared harmonies of numbers. These numbers aren't merely mathematical factors or abstractions; they are living entities: dynamic instruments of consciousness that are working hard right now in your life and in the universe around you. From microsecond to microsecond, these celestial numbers maintain the fabric of space-time and are perpetually creating, sustaining, and destroying universes and existences.

Numbers are the programming code of the creation and continuity of existence itself, and *Qabalah*[9] is one name for this master code. Qabalah provides the building code for your house of cards, and tarot's seventy-eight cards are, in turn, the educational flash cards of Qabalah. In order for you to transform *any* deck into a powerful magical instrument, you'll need to be familiar with just a couple fundamental principles of this marvelous spiritual science.

You might be thinking all this sounds like it's going to be pretty dull stuff. You might even be tempted to skip ahead in the book and just start coloring your own cards. Of course, you're free to do that. It's your book (I hope). But I also hope you will hold off until you've read on and absorbed a little basic information that will acquaint you and attune you to the *building code*.

Don't worry. It won't take long. I'll make the lessons short and digestible. In fact, because I *myself* am the laziest tarot qabalist in the world, I'll limit our discussion to a quick overview of just three essential *working tools*:

Working Tool 1: The Tetragrammaton: יהוה, *Yod Heh Vav Heh*
(the Great Name of God)

Working Tool 2: The Tree of Life

Working Tool 3: The Cube of Space

CHAPTER 2

Working Tool 1
The Tetragrammaton

יהוה

Figure 1.
"God is a Four-Letter Word."
Yod Heh Vav Heh.

our is a very big number in Qabalah and tarot. The *Lesser Arcana* of tarot is made up of *four* suits. Each suit contains *ten*[1] Pip Cards (Ace–Ten), and *four* Court Cards: Knight, Queen, Prince, and Princess.[2]

Why four?

God only knows!

I'm not trying to be disrespectful. I mean this literally: Only *God* knows!

Let's start by admitting to ourselves that *nobody*—not you, nor me, nor the wisest old Qabalist—is capable of wrapping our meat brains around the transcendent concept of an *Absolute Singularity*—you know—that THING everyone tries to stuff in a heavenly box and call "God."

Oh sure! We can argue about it and fight wars and kill each other over whose imaginary supreme singularity is better than the other guy's, but the best any of us can do is rattle off a bunch of *omni-* adjectives like *omnipresent, omnipotent, omniscient, omni-this* or *omni-that*. Or we clumsily try to describe God as being all-powerfully strong, immeasurably *one-like,* or transcendently *singular,* or infinitely *eternal,* or everlastingly *wall-to-wall-ish.*

In order for the ancient philosopher qabalists to kick-start the process of hypothesizing about the nature of a divine singularity, they poured themselves a shot of espresso and embarked upon a little thought experiment. They rolled up their sleeves and rolled out their sacred scriptures[3] for inspiration. What first caught their attention was a brand-new name of God—a four-letter name. This new name didn't appear anywhere in Scripture until the sixth chapter of the Book of Exodus[4] when this particular God blew everyone's mind by parting the Red Sea just in time to save Moses and the Children of Israel from Pharaoh's pursuing army.[5]

The name of this scene-stealing God is spelled יהוה, Yod Heh Vav Heh. The ancient qabalists concluded if a wonderworking God who actually does dramatic stuff like this has a four-letter name, the power and character of this God must be encapsulated in every letter of its name.

A Four-Part Singularity

And so they began their qabalistic deliberations by assuming God is a four-part[6] singularity, each part characterized by one of the letters of its name. They then commenced to speculate, bicker, meditate, debate, ruminate, squabble, pontificate, and argue about what particular powers and qualities each of the four parts would theoretically need to possess in order to create the universe and hold existence together.

What they came up was the basic formula of the Tetragrammaton: יהוה, Yod Heh Vav Heh.

Sidebar 1

PLEASE DO THIS NOW!

Take your four **Aces**. Kiss[7] each of them and lay them down in a vertical column. Starting at the top:

- Ace of Wands (Yod)
- Ace of Cups (Heh)
- Ace of Swords (Vav)
- Ace of Disks (Heh)

Just casually glance upon these four cards from time to time as you read the following.

Here are just a few of the concepts that reveal the basic fourfold structure of the cosmos and our house of cards. You might want to put a bookmark at this page because it is likely you will be referring to these four-part attributes again.

Four Qabalistic Worlds

Each of the four letters of the Tetragrammaton represents one of four Qabalistic Worlds or layers of existence superimposed one upon another.

Yod: י—Atziluth—the Archetypal World (God's Will)

- World of *gods* or specific facets or *divine qualities*

Heh: ה—Briah—the Creative World (God's Love)

- World of *archangels*, executors of the *divine qualities*

Vav: ו—Yetzirah—the Formative World (God's Mind)

- World of *angels*, who work under the direction of *archangels*

Heh: ה—Assiah—the Material World (God's Creation)

- World of the *spirits*, who focus the specialized duties of their ruling *angel* to infuse matter and energy—you and me

Four Parts of the Soul

Because, according to qabalistic and biblical traditions, human beings are made in the image of God, that must mean that you and I are walking, talking miniature replicas of יהוה, Yod Heh Vav Heh, and possessed of four *Parts of the Soul* that reflect the four Qabalistic Worlds:

Yod: י—Chiah[8]—the *Life Force*

- The Chiah is the Life Force itself. It is our true identity, which, ultimately, is pure reflection of the Supreme Consciousness of deity.

Heh: ה—Neshamah—the *Soul-Intuition*

- The Neshamah is the part of our soul that transcends our thinking processes. (For example, when a mother intuitively senses when her child is in danger, it is because the mother's Neshamah reaches beyond the physical body and is not bound by space and time.)

Vav: ‎ו—Ruach—the *Intellect*

- The Ruach is the part of our soul that monopolizes our attention to such a degree that we identify ourselves completely with the thinking process.

Heh: ‎ה—Nephesh—the *Animal Soul*

- The Nephesh is the primitive level of consciousness we share with the animal, plant, and mineral kingdoms. Our Nephesh manifests most obviously in our instincts, appetites, emotions, sex drive, and survival mechanisms.

Four Elements, Tarot Suits, and Court Cards

Finally, all layers of ‎יהוה, Yod Heh Vav Heh, consciousness crystallize in the objective reality around us as the four[9] elements (*Fire, Water, Air, and Earth*). These elements, and the characteristic qualities and powers they embody, find comfortable homes and employment opportunities in every pack of tarot cards as the four *Suits,* and the four *Court Cards* within each suit.

Yod: ‎י—Suit of Wands—Fire

Heh: ‎ה—Suit of Cups—Water

Vav: ‎ו—Suit of Swords—Air

Heh: ‎ה—Suit of Disks—Earth

The Court Cards of each suit serve as a miniature subset ‎יהוה, Yod Heh Vav Heh, and share a comfortable fourplex inside their Ace.

Yod: ‎י—Fire—Wands—Knights

Heh: ‎ה—Water—Cups—Queens

Vav: ‎ו—Air—Swords—Princes

Heh: ‎ה—Earth—Disks—Princesses

Yod Heh Vav Heh is most obviously at work in tarot's Lesser Arcana, but its formula permeates every nook and cranny of existence and every room of our house of cards. However, before we move on, I need to point out something especially magical about the second or final ה Heh in the great four-letter name of God.

Cosmic Spark Plug—The Second Heh Is Special

יהוה, Yod Heh Vav Heh, is a *four*-letter name, but it is comprised of only *three* Hebrew letters. The fourth and final letter, ה Heh, is repeated. This implies a special status to the final Heh. It also implies a special status to everything the final Heh represents, including the Court Card Princesses:

The lowest Qabalistic World, *Assiah,* is special.

The lowest Part of the Soul, *Nephesh,* is special.

The lowest element, *Earth,* is special.

The lowest tarot suit of *Disks* is special.

The lowest Court Card, *Princesses,* are special.

Right now, this curious little tidbit of information might not seem very significant, but it is very important. I want you remember it because, like the spark plug in an internal combustion engine, it is the feature that makes this working tool work.

The special status of the final ה, Heh, as *lowest of the low* links it directly to the *highest of the high:* the all-important *fifth* element of Spirit (which we will talk more about in Book II). Spirit is the magical magnetism that attracts and *pulls* the four elements together in various combinations and proportions to form the material universe, while at the same time keeps them *pushed* apart so that everything just doesn't turn into mush!

In the Lesser Arcana of tarot, the element Spirit is represented by the four Aces, which are paired with their Princesses (the Earth Court Cards) like the Ouroboros snake with its tale in its mouth. This is why the Court Card Princesses are called "Thrones of the Aces."

The final ה serves as a cosmic *spark plug* that detonates at the end of a stroke cycle of an exhausted creation to trigger the beginning of a new one.

Heh, and all the concepts Heh embodies, keeps the motor of existence perpetually running . . . perpetually existing.

But now, before we turn our attention to the magic of our second working tool, I want you to take a moment to practice a very simple meditation that will help you attune yourself to the dynamics of יהוה, Yod Heh Vav Heh.

Please don't skip this brief meditation. In fact, do it as often as you can until it becomes second nature.

Meditation 1

יהוה

Yod Heh Vav Heh
Four Worlds in a Chair

1. Be seated comfortably in a chair. Clap four times (4-4-4-4), and gaze for a moment upon the *Ace of Disks*.

2. *Close your eyes,* and take two or three cleansing breaths.

3. *Open your eyes,* and touch the chair upon which you are seated. Feel it. Recognize it as a material object. Look at it. Knock on it. Smell it if you can. Engage all your senses to acknowledge the objective existence of the chair. Say to yourself, *This chair is made for my physical body to sit upon. It is a material object made from other material objects for the purpose of supporting my body and the bodies of all who rest upon it. This particular chair and everything else in this room exists in the* Material World—*the world of Assiah. This chair exists in the tarot world of* **Disks**—*the world of the final* ה *Heh of* יהוה, *Yod Heh Vav Heh.*

4. Clap four times (4-4-4-4), and gaze for a moment upon the *Ace of Swords*.

5. *Close your eyes,* and try to re-create the image, the sound, and the smell of the chair in your mind's eye and memory. Bring its form clearly to life in your imagination, its colors, its shape. Say to yourself, *The pattern for this particular chair exists as an* idea *in the* Formative World *of Yetzirah. The nonmaterial design for this particular chair exists in the tarot world of* **Swords**, *the world of* ו *of* יהוה, *Yod Heh Vav Heh.*

ה

6. *Open your eyes.* Clap four times (4-4-4-4), and gaze for a moment upon the *Ace of Cups.*

7. *Close your eyes,* and consider for a moment just why people need chairs: all chairs, any chairs, couches, stools, benches. Recognize the fact that in your mind you are *creating the patterns* for every kind of seating device in the world that functions to get people off their feet to allow their bodies to rest. Say to yourself, *The general need for chairs of any kind to exist is in the* Creative World *of Briah; the need for* all seating devices *in general exists in the tarot world of the suit of* **Cups**, *the world of the first* ה Heh *of* יהוה, *Yod Heh Vav Heh.*

ו

8. *Open your eyes.* Clap four times (4-4-4-4), and gaze for a moment upon the *Ace of Wands.*

 Close your eyes, and simply think of the generic concept of *Rest:* objects at rest; rest for people; rest for animals, plants, and machines; rest from labor; rest after play, rest after sex, rest from strife; rest from activity; rest from consciousness; light resting from darkness; darkness resting from light; Death resting from Life; Life resting from Death; oblivion as rest from existence itself. Say to yourself, *The universal need for all things to occasionally rest exists in the* Archetypal World *of Atziluth and the tarot world of* **Wands**, *the world of* י Yod *of* יהוה, *Yod Heh Vav Heh.*

9. *Open your eyes,* look once more at your chair, and say out loud:

 Yod: י—Wands—Atziluth—The general cosmic concept of rest

Heh: ‎הֵ—Briah—Cups—The general need for resting devices for the human body

Vav: ‎וֹ—Yetzirah—Swords—Mental pattern for this specific chair

Heh: ‎הֵ—Assiah—Disks—This particular material object chair

10. Clap four times (4-4-4-4), and end the meditation by thinking how every*thing* you see around you in your everyday world exists in Assiah, the world of Disks, and is the *visible* result of three *invisible* layers of reality: Yetzirah, the world of Swords; Briah, the world of Cups; and Atziluth, the world of Wands.

———————

CHAPTER 3

Working Tool 2: The Tree of Life and the Sepher Yetzirah

The Tree of Life is probably the most recognizable image associated with the qabalistic foundations of tarot. Figure 2 on the following page is just one of many examples of how modern and traditional qabalists choose to arrange and illustrate several fundamental and profound cosmological concepts.

This particular tree is generally patterned on versions commonly used in the late 19th century by adepts of the *Hermetic Order of the Golden Dawn,* and later taught by Paul Foster Case's *Builders of the Adytum* (B.O.T.A.) and Aleister Crowley's A∴ A∴. For our purposes I believe it is the most convenient version because it is compatible with most other modern texts concerning hermetic Qabalah and esoteric tarot.

We'll discuss more about that in the pages that follow, but for the moment, let's learn where all this information came from.

The Sepher Yetzirah

Qabalah is not a book. There are, however, many classic texts that comprise traditional qabalistic literature. Many are ponderously thick, and beginning students often find them hopelessly obscure. I'm sure you'll be happy to learn that we'll only be focusing on the opening words of one tiny (but extremely important) booklet, the *Sepher Yetzirah* (the *Book of Formation,* or the *Book of Creation*).[1]

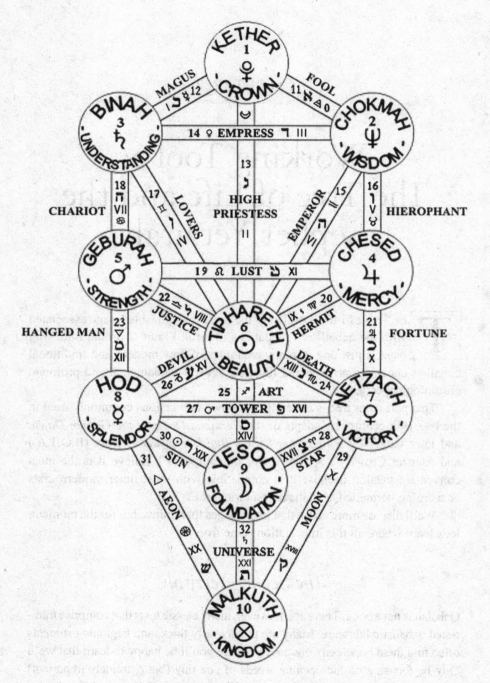

Figure 2. The Tree of Life
Thirty-Two Mysterious Paths of Wisdom, Ten Sephiroth, and Twenty-Two Paths

Jewish qabalists ascribe authorship of the Sepher Yetzirah to the biblical patriarch Abraham (but I don't think many of them actually *believe* that). However, the Sepher Yetzirah is arguably the oldest philosophical treatise written in Hebrew and the most ancient and revered document of esoteric Judaism.[2]

Please don't think you need to be Jewish, or believe in the biblical God, or indeed follow any religion's God or gods in order to make tarot and Qabalah meaningful to you. In fact, you don't need to subscribe to any particular belief system, supernatural wonder story, prophet, philosophy, or salesperson in order to become a world-class qabalist or tarot master.

In the Beginning

The Sepher Yetzirah starts out by introducing us to a very different and highly abbreviated version of the biblical story of creation. I'm a very lazy guy, so I've gone a step further and ruthlessly abbreviated the story even more by distilling it down to fifty-three carefully chosen words that offer a concise table of contents to both the Greater and Lesser Arcanum of the tarot.

God created existence and the Universe with the aid of

Three helpers:
Numbers, Letters, and Words, in
Thirty-Two Mysterious Paths of Wisdom.

They consist of
Ten Sephiroth[3] (Emanations) out of Nothing,
and
Twenty-Two Letters.

God divided the Twenty-Two Letters into Three Divisions:
Three Mothers (Fundamental Letters),
Seven Double Letters, and
Twelve Simple Letters.

The *Numbers* and *Letters*[4] of the *Thirty-Two Mysterious Paths of Wisdom* are organized and illustrated on the Tree of Life, where the Numbers are represented as the ten circles (sephiroth or emanations) and the Letters are represented as the twenty-two paths that connect the sephiroth. (See Figure 2.)

It doesn't take a *tarorocket* scientist to see how the ten numbered Pip cards of each suit might fit nicely on the ten sephiroth of the Tree of Life and how the twenty-two Trump cards can serve as the twenty-two connecting paths. As a matter of fact, if you look carefully at Figure 2, you will see all Thirty-Two Paths of Wisdom clearly numbered. (The ten sephiroth are numbered 1–10, and the connecting paths are numbered 11–32.)

This Tree of Life is the preliminary floor plan for your house of cards, so you'll want to know your way around it pretty well. Let's start by looking a little closer at the ten Numbers.

The Ten Numbers

The ancient qabalists wanted to discover more about יהוה and the four letters of the Name of God, so they started to play around with the number four. First, they put it under their mathematical microscope and observed that $1 + 2 + 3 + 4 = 10$. Naturally they concluded that the number Four conceals number Ten and Ten reveals Four. Obviously, Ten is a fundamentally important number and offers the qabalists a more detailed way to go crazy thinking more about Four and יהוה.

The ten *Numbers* mentioned in the Sepher Yetzirah are represented on the Tree of Life as the *ten circles* symbolizing ten *sephiroth* or *emanations out of nothing*. Each numbered sephirah represents a specific level (frequency) of divine consciousness. Taken together, all ten sephiroth represent the entire spectrum of consciousness (from the *Godhead* of number One down to the *yourhead*[5] of number Ten).

The ten numbered Pips of each tarot suit are characterized by spiritual qualities and natures unique to each of these ten landmark frequencies of divine consciousness. As I mentioned earlier, qabalistic tradition holds that you and I are *made in the image of God*, so each of us (if we could relax and accept our divine birthright) is already functioning as a miniature version the divine singularity. We all come factory-equipped with all ten levels of divine consciousness just waiting for us to tune them up, gas them up, turn the key, and head out on the *return-to-godhead highway*.

Triads

On the Tree, the ten Numbers are arranged in *three triads*. The top triad is *upward*-pointing; the second triad (being the reflection of the top triad) is *downward*-pointing, as is the third triad.

Dangling precariously from the bottom of the three triads is sephirah number Ten, which hangs alone, looking like a lonely afterthought of creation or a low-level attempt to be an echo of an echo of an echo of number One (sort of like a crystallized miniature facsimile of the divine singularity).

Just like the final Heh ה of the Tetragrammaton, number Ten is a very special player on the Tree of Life team. As a matter of fact, it is the most important component of *your* house of cards, because, as you will discover, Ten and the final ה of the Tetragrammaton are the *you* that you currently mistakenly believe is *you*.

NUMBER ONE (KETHER—GODHEAD)

We'll soon learn the names of all ten sephiroth, but for the moment let's talk about the top sephirah (number One). It's called Kether (the Crown) and represents the absolute singularity that we can't think about very easily; in tarot terms, Kether/One is the *Ace* of each of the four suits and represents the omni-everything consciousness of Godhead itself. In actuality, Kether is the only *true* sephirah. All the other sephiroth exist merely as twinkles in the eye of Kether. In house of cards terms, "All the tarot cards of the Lesser Arcana exist merely as twinkles in the eyes of the four Aces."

But hang on—where did number One and our Aces come from in the first place?

In order to answer that question, we need to chat about *Nothing*.

ZERO

Recall that the Sepher Yetzirah tells us that number One and all the Numbers and Letters came "out of Nothing." For the tarot qabalist, *Nothing* is *something* very important indeed! As a matter of fact, if we could pause and play a double-negative word game, we could say . . . "*Nothing* came before One! *Nothing* is more important than One! *Nothing* created One! *Nothing* is greater than One! *Nothing* is more powerful than One! *Nothing* is holier than number One!"

In the Greater Arcana, we have two cards (the first and final Trumps) that try to represent this important Nothing: Trump 0, *The Fool*, and Trump XXI, *The Universe*.

These two cards are quite literally the Alpha and Omega (or in Hebrew, the *Aleph* and *Tav*) of tarot. Each represents a different kind of Nothing: the Nothing that comes *before* Anything and the Nothing that comes *after* Everything.

TRUMP 0—THE FOOL

Many modern tarot decks (especially Qabalah-based decks) place the Fool at the beginning, as the first trump; but it isn't labeled #1. The Fool is Key 0 and positioned at the start of the Trump sequence. The Fool represents the mysterious Zero *out of which* number One (and subsequently everything else that follows) leaps *into existence* at the *beginning* of the creation cycle.

At the other end of the Trump sequence of cards is the other important Zero.

TRUMP 21—THE UNIVERSE

The zodiacal belt (or stylized ring) that appears at the center of most versions of the Universe card represents the mysterious Zero *into which* the completely manifested universe dances back *out of* at the *end* of the creation cycle.

The adventure between these two Zeros is a cosmic odyssey told by the twenty Trumps that stretch between the Fool and the Universe. It is also the personal initiatory journey of you and me and every monad of evolving consciousness.

Qabalists have a name for this Nothing: *Ain Soph*. In fact, they teach that it takes the development of three kinds of Nothing[6] in order for number One to finally get itself squeezed out of the puckered aperture of negativity and into existence.

Obviously, these are mind-bending musings that are intended to drive serious qabalists a little crazy (in a socially acceptable way). So before we move on from the subject of nothings, I'll digress just long enough to whisper this sweet nothing in your ear:

[Cue the celestial harp music.]

Someday, when you've sweetly awakened to a particular level of illumination, and as you near the climactic conclusion of all your incarnational escapades, you (and all the *yous* you ever thought were you) will be left with (and as) *Nothing*.

That *Nothing* is *Something Wonderful*. It is the *Something* you really *are*.

THE TREE OF TAROT PIPS

Because there are ten tarot Pips (the Ace and nine Small Cards) in each of the Lesser Arcana's four suits, we can easily see how they all comfortably fit on the Tree of Life. Technically, there are only nine Small Cards (2–10) per suit, and they all live inside their Ace. (See Figure 4.)

Just as all the sephiroth are merely descending frequencies of the consciousness of number One, all the numbered Small Cards represent descending and decaying aspects of their respective Aces.

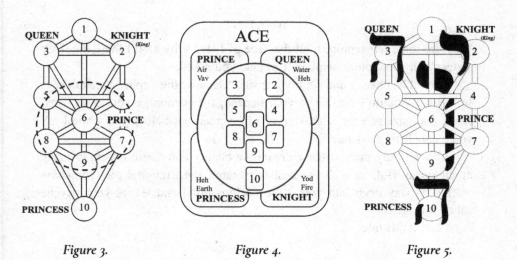

Figure 3.   Figure 4.   Figure 5.

The four Court Cards of each suit are also little יהוה, Yod Heh Vav Heh, subdivisions living inside their Ace. (See Figure 4.) The **Knight** represents the dynamics of number **Two** on the Supernal Triad and the **Queen** number **Three**. The **Prince** is centered in number **Six**, but his full principality includes the *entire macro*cosmic neighborhood of all **six sephiroth (Four–Nine)**. The **Princess** (like Malkuth) represents *micro*cosmic number **Ten**. (See Figures 3 and 5.) We will soon learn more about the special status of the Court Cards.

The Aces, Small Cards, and Court Cards are aspects of the ten sephiroth, and their planetary, elemental, qabalistic characteristics and divinatory meanings are determined in large measure by where they find themselves living on the Tree of Life.

Sidebar 3

PLEASE DO THIS NOW!

Build a Disk Tree of Life. Take the **Ace of Disks** along with the **Two** through **Ten of Disks**. Kiss them, and arrange the ten cards out in front of you in Tree of Life order. Just casually look at this Disk Tree of Life from time to time as you read the following.

WHY TEN?

Why are there *ten* sephiroth on the Tree of Life? Why aren't there nine? Or sixteen? Or some other number? I'm glad you asked.

I could be cheeky and simply answer, "Because the Sepher Yetzirah says so." But I wouldn't do that to you. Instead, I'll encourage you to sit back, relax, and gaze at your Disk Tree of Life spread out before you while I tell you a qabalistic *fairy tale*.

Like all fairy tales, it has a dreamlike quality that doesn't seem to make much sense. But, as with the best fairy tales, the irrational plot somehow worms its way deep into your subconscious mind and leaves your psyche subtly changed.

I call it this tale:

The Tree of Life

or

How Ten Kinds of Everything Came Out of Nothing Because the Great God What-It-Is Started Thinking about Itself— A Fairy Tale for Babes and Sucklings

Once upon a . . . *before-there-was-time*[7] . . .

God (whom we will call the great **What-It-Is**) brooded blissfully alone in the boundless sea of its Absolute Absoluteness.

Figure 6.

Because great What-It-Is was so absolutely singular, it had no need to be aware of the condition of its own self-existence. Why bother? After all, in order for great What-It-Is to even begin speculating about itself, it would first need to arouse itself from its state of seamless singularity and create some kind of internal *reflection* to ponder. Such an audacious disturbance would radically unsettle its smooth[8] condition of singularity and create an artificial *second state*—one that could accommodate *two* ideas:

(1) a *knower*

(2) a *something* for the *knower* to *know*

For reasons the wisest sages dare not speculate, great What-It-Is persisted in its desire to know itself. It voluntarily shattered its infinite smoothness and projected upon the center of itself its own reflection, thereby begetting a *second* condition.

Voilà! Great What-It-Is became self-aware. Number Two was born.

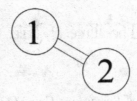

Figure 7.
The Wrong of the Beginning.
"Oh! That's what I am!"

"Oh! *That's* what I am!" great What-It-Is shouted. And for the first time it heard the echo of its own voice and realized the presence of a "that" along with its "I am."

Melancholy qabalists call this moment "The Fall" or "The Wrong of the Beginning."

But that's not where the beginning ends. Because simultaneously, along with the birth of number Two, a *third* condition instantly popped on the scene. This brand-new third condition was not the Self *or* the Reflection but the *Knowledge* or *Recognition* that there is a difference between the voice and the echo, between the "I am" and the "That."

The third condition is the *realization* that the One is not the Two.

"O! *That's* what I Am! But *That's* not Me!"

Now Number One was no longer a simple, uncomplicated singularity. Number One was now a Trinity Unit—a **"Supernal Triad."**

1. Number One, the *Self*

2. Number Two, the reflection—the *Not-Self*

3. Number Three, the knowledge or realization that the *Not-Self* is not the *Self*

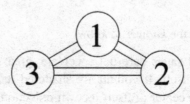

Figure 8.
The Supernal Triad
Number One Thinking about Itself.
"Oh! That's what I Am! But That's not Me!"

THE SUPERNAL TRIAD

Qabalists call the triad of One-Two-Three the *Supernal Triad*. Technically, the Supernal Triad isn't three separate numbers but a single unit of three conditions. One, Two, and Three are too abstract and transcendently codependent to qualify as ordinary numbers or levels of existence or levels of consciousness. There isn't even room for a *here* or a *there* in the Supernal Triad, but only facets or qualities of an infinite singularity, a bubbling pool of pure potentiality. This is why for tarot readers the Aces, Twos, and Threes all seem to be wonderfully strange and profound and often a bit inscrutable.

Consider your Ace, Two, and Three of Disks as an example:

The *Ace of Disks* is the Root of Earth (or the *tendency* to be Earth), but Earth as an elemental concept doesn't actually make its definable *appearance* until it tries to think about itself. Its reflection is the *Two of Disks* (Change) where it becomes recognizably present. Furthermore, Earth doesn't actually start *functioning* as Earth until the *Three of Disks* (Work).

The Aces, Twos, and Threes of the other suits develop in the same way.

Sidebar 4

PLEASE DO THIS NOW!

Clear your table and take the **Aces** and the **Twos and Threes** of *all four suits*. Kiss them, and lay them out as four side-by-side Supernal Triads: one for Wands, one for Cups, one for Swords, and one for Disks. Take a moment to casually observe the relationships of images and titles between the cards. No need to overthink or analyze too much . . . just observe as you think about what we've just said about the Supernal Triad, and as you read the following.

The Supernal Triad is as mysterious as the Holy Trinity; In fact, the Supernal Triad *is* the Holy Trinity. It is the supreme singularity—God trying to think about itself. And while the Supernal Triad is as it were the *mother* of what will be creation, it is not *creation* itself.[9] Our limited brains are forced to think of the Supernal Triad as somehow existing in an imaginary state of pure potentiality, in a nondimensional gelatinous state of preexistence.

For *creation* (as we commonly understand the word) to actually manifest—in order for our familiar cosmos of quantifiable matter and energy to exist in time and space—in order for there to be elbow room for gods and archangels, angels, powers, principles, planets, stars, forces and elements, and birds and bees—in order for *existence to exist*, the Supernal Triad as a single *unit* must reflect itself.

Just as Number One didn't actually go anywhere when its reflection was projected as Number Two, the Supernal Triad never stops being the Supernal Triad and doesn't *go* anywhere. But its *reflection* passes as it were through a looking-glass *Abyss* to create a three-part *echo* of itself.[10]

Just as I don't *go* anywhere when I give a certain flat-dimensional life to my ruggedly handsome reflection in the bathroom mirror, so too a *Second Triad* of Four-Five-Six takes on a semblance of life as the *below-the-Abyss* reflection of the Supernal Triad.

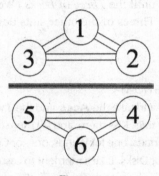

Figure 9.

Sidebar 5

PLEASE DO THIS NOW!

Take the **Fours, Fives, and Sixes** of *all four suits*. Kiss them, and lay them out to form *four* side-by-side Second Triads: one for Wands, one for Cups, one for Swords, and one for Disks. Take a moment to casually observe the relationships of images and titles between the cards. Observe how the number Four cards reflect the dynamics of the number Twos; how the number Five cards reflect aspects of the number Three; and how the number Sixes reflect the singularity of the Aces. No need to overthink or analyze too much . . . just observe as you read the following.

And, just as the Supernal Triad's Number Three was formed the instant Number Two came into being, a *Third Triad* of Seven-Eight-Nine was instantly created along with the Second Triad.

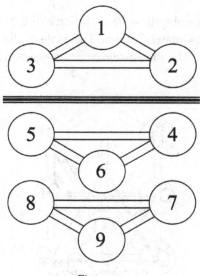

Figure 10.

Sidebar 6

PLEASE DO THIS NOW!

Take the **Sevens, Eights, and Nines** of *all four suits*. Kiss them, and lay them out to form four side-by-side Third Triads: one for Wands, one for Cups, one for Swords, and one for Disks. Take a moment to casually observe the relationships of images and titles between the cards and how they relate to the two triads above them. No need to overthink or analyze too much . . . just observe as you read the following.

THE MACROCOSM AND ITS SEVEN HEAVENLY HIERARCHIES

The Second and Third Triads below the Supernal Triad are considered the *macrocosm*,[11] or the Greater Cosmos. It's probably easiest for us to think about the macrocosm as being seven layers of heaven.

The doctrine of a stratified heaven has been proffered in one form or another by religions great and small for thousands of years. Our hardworking Tree of Life is perhaps the simplest way for us to start to wrap our meat brains around the subject.

In fact, this area (sephiroth 4–9) of the Tree of Life is technically called the *macro*cosm, or the Greater Cosmos. This is the realm of the classic planetary spheres symbolized by the *hexagram* or six-pointed *Star of David*.

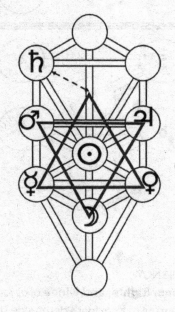

Figure 11.
The Hexagram. Symbol of the Macrocosm

Each sephirah of the macrocosm is a self-contained vibratory mini-world ruled by a specific god.[12] Each sephirah's god (or divine facet of the singularity) rules a specialized team of attending *archangels*, *angels*, *spirits*, and *intelligences*, all of whom reflect in various degrees their god's unique style and personality, quirks, and characteristics as they tirelessly execute their particular god's specialized responsibilities in the universe.

You might ask how we can possibly know the style and personality quirks and characteristics of the gods of each sephirah. You'd be surprise to know you are already hardwired with the answer.

Various spiritual traditions assign a vast array of names and biographical histories to the macrocosmic gods and hierarchies of spirits. Myths of many different cultures spanning millennia are often uncannily similar. The medieval Jewish kabbalists became extremely well-organized and anal-retentive about the whole thing and even assigned mathematically compatible alphanumeric[13] Hebrew names for all the various aspects of deity and their heavenly support staff.

What has all this to do with tarot? I'm glad you asked. The simple answer is this: All of these divine forces, archangels, angels, spirits, and mathematical harmonies and resonances represented by the sephiroth of the Tree of Life are alive and comfortably resident in the *Small Cards* of every tarot deck. They make each card its own self-contained universe, populated by a hierarchy of specialized spiritual qualities and forces.

Is it any wonder that each tarot card is formally named "Lord" of this or that as if to announce that each card is a living spirit-personage with its own personality, powers, skills, talents, and peculiar set of divinatory meanings? The better we understand exactly what and who is living in our cards, the better *we* will be able to reflect and arrange those same perfect harmonies and resonances within ourselves.

PLANETARY SPHERES OF THE MACROCOSM

The Western Mystery traditions generally view the macrocosmic heavens in terms of the seven classic planetary spheres known to us by the Roman names of the Greek Olympian gods who for millennia have taken up archetypal residency in the consciousness of Western civilization. When we project these gods onto the sephiroth of the Tree of Life's macrocosm (Figure 11), we see them as the following:

4 **Chesed** (Mercy), the sphere of **Jupiter**

5 **Geburah** (Strength), the sphere of **Mars**

6 **Tiphareth** (Beauty), the sphere of the **Sun**

7 **Netzach** (Victory), the sphere of **Venus**

8 **Hod** (Splendor), the sphere of **Mercury**

9 **Yesod** (Foundation), the sphere of the **Moon**

But that's only six. What about the *seventh* planet, *Saturn?*

Where is Saturn hiding on the macrocosmic hexagram of planetary spheres?

Saturn *does* have a home on the Tree of Life, but as you can see in Figure 11 on page 26, Saturn isn't exactly playing on the same macrocosmic playground as the six other planetary spheres. Saturn's sphere is above the Abyss as sephirah 3 in the predimensional Supernal Triad. What gives?

Please forgive me for digressing for a moment while I try to explain.

———————

ANOTHER DUQUETTE DIGRESSION—MYSTERY OF SATURN

Remember what I said a few pages back about the Fool card and the Universe card representing two very important kinds of Zero? Well, the Universe card does even weirder stuff, because in the tarot it is required to do double duty[14] by representing *both* the special element Earth *and* the special planet Saturn. All this specialness earns Saturn *two* very important places on the Tree of Life (see Figure 12):

1. The Universe card (and ת Tav, the Hebrew letter assigned to the Universe card) joins sephirah 10 (the *micro*cosm) to sephirah 9 to the rest of the *macro*cosmic tree.

2. And the Sphere of Saturn is also Binah, sephirah 3 up in the Supernal Triad itself.

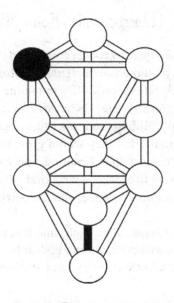

Figure 12.
Sphere of Saturn: 3 Binah
Path of 𐤕 Tav: Saturn/Earth Path joining 10 to 9

Why does Saturn—supposedly one of the so-called planetary spheres—qualify for such an exalted position way up there in the rarified atmosphere of the Supernal Triad? After all, Binah (3) is above the level of the other *macro-cosmic* planetary spheres. It's also above the Abyss, on the other side of the mirror that separates the Ideal and the Actual.

The quick answer is this: because Saturn is *not* your ordinary planetary sphere. Saturn resonates as a primeval rumbling from deep within the recesses of our unremembered dreams, from the almost Lovecraftian primordial womb of the chaotic Old Ones.

Saturn isn't even a god: Saturn is a *Titan!* And the Titans came before the tidy, balanced, orderly dimensional cosmos of the Olympian gods. Saturn is, in fact, *King of the Titans.*

A Macrocosmic Fairy Tale

Once upon a time before-there-was-a-Second Triad . . .[15]

Saturn, from his predimensional Titan's throne at Number Three, believed it was his imperial responsibility to maintain the status quo of his wild-west kingdom of preexistence. He became a classic paranoid king and feared that if any of his children were ever to escape the sealed three-part singularity of the Supernal Triad they would grow up and kill and dethrone him (just like he did to his father Uranus in an earlier fairy tale).[16] If a next-generation child were to escape, a new kind of below-the-Abyss objective universe would pop into existence, and the party would be over for the roughneck Titans.

To prevent that from happening, each time Saturn's wife Rhea (or Ops) presented him with another newborn little god-to-be, Saturn just popped the baby in his mouth like a cocktail onion and swallowed it whole. Problem solved.

The first baby snack was Artemis, who if given the chance would have made the perfect macrocosmic Moon goddess; then twins, Hermes (Mercury) and sweet baby Aphrodite (Venus); then radiant little Apollo (Sol); and finally, hot and spicy baby Ares (Mars).

Just so long as Saturn kept swallowing his young, a manifest macrocosmic creation was put on hold. Anything that could potentially become a thing remained undigested in Saturn/Binah's dimensionless belly—in a suspended state of precreational potentiality.[17]

This version of the myth goes on to tell how Rhea eventually got tired of this nonsense and decided enough was enough! When it came time for her to deliver the next baby (Zeus/Jupiter), she tricked old Saturn by serving up a buttered stone wrapped in a tortilla slathered in a vomit-inducing rancid salsa. While Saturn was choking down his hard-rock burrito, Rhea secretly spirited the child away across the Abyss border to the newly formed Second Triad, where she enrolled him in a posh boarding school with a centaur headmaster.

A new *fourth* sephirah, Chesed (Mercy), became the permanent address of Zeus/Jupiter, "first god" below the Abyss. Because number Four is actually the *first* manifested number in the new *dimensional* world, Zeus looked around and said, "Wow! I must be the self-begotten God of creation, because I don't see anyone else in this dimension!"

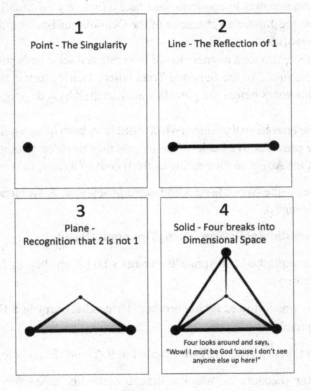

1

Point - The Singularity

2

Line - The Reflection of 1

3

Plane -
Recognition that 2 is not 1

4

Solid - Four breaks into
Dimensional Space

Four looks around and says,
"Wow! I *must* be God 'cause I don't see
anyone else up here!"

Figure 13.
The Macrocosm (and Dimensional Existence) is created when
Four breaks free of the Supernal Triad.

Naturally Jupiter believed himself to be the first *anything* there ever was and felt pretty privileged and exceptional, never realizing that his very existence was the result of a three-part predimensional dance up in the Supernal Triad Ballroom.

The Greeks have a name for this smug, insecure, and somewhat clueless "first" god below the Abyss: Demiourgos, a god who mistakenly believes it is the self-begotten creator and the only god-king in town.

The Romans called their Demiourgos Jupiter and Jove. And the Hebrews (silently) called it . . . are you ready for it? יהוה, *Jehovah.*

Zeus, Jupiter, Jehovah, Amoun, Woton, and many other father-figure gods are attributed to Number Four (Chesed) and share many fatherly, fickle, and jealous characteristics in common. Just take a look at your Small Card Fours and see how the Jupiterian character of the Demiourgos is exemplified in each of the four worlds.

But let's return for a moment to our fairy tale and see what's still happening up in Vomitorium 3 of the Supernal Triad where Titan Saturn is still seriously ill and on his knees before the porcelain altar of the Abyss disgorging previous meals.

First, he heaved up that stone (which must have been quite a relief); then out popped the previous five babies. One by one they tumbled through the newly torn veil of the Abyss landing safely as fresh gods of a shiny new macrocosm:

- First came Ares/**Mars**, who landed in sephirah **5**, **Geburah** (Strength).

- Then slid Apollo/**Sun** into **6**, **Tiphareth** (Beauty).

- Then splashed out Aphrodite/**Venus** who set up shop in **7**, **Netzach** (Victory).

- She was followed by her brother Hermes/**Mercury** in **8 Hod** (Splendor).

- And finally, Artemis/**Luna** landed in **9**, **Yesod** (Foundation).

Zeus/**Jupiter** (because he was the first to make his appearance below the Abyss) set up his throne in **4**, **Chesed** (Mercy) and convinced himself and his five siblings that he was their king.

Now I'm sure real mythologists will be appalled at my vulgar retelling of this classic tale. But from a qabalistic tarot point of view this is pretty much the essence of the story. And it's a story that's very important to our understanding of the Small Cards because the classic qualities, talents, vices, and virtues that characterize the powers and personalities of the seven gods of Olympus contribute major influences on the spiritual nature and divinatory meanings of each of the Small Cards.

In a very real sense, the six-pointed *Star of David* macrocosm sprang from the mouth of Binah/Saturn/sephirah 3. But near the bottom of the Tree of Life, Saturn as the Universe card serves another role equally important: that of reversing the process.

The Sepher Yetzirah assigns the Hebrew letter ת Tav to Saturn, and on the Tree of Life Tav is the mysterious *Path* that joins the *micro*cosm (10) to the *macro*cosmic group (9-8-7-6-5-4). (See Figure 12.)

I guess now might be a good time for us to briefly discuss the *micro*cosm, the Pentagram of the elements, and the all-important sephirah 10 on the Tree of Life. We could even say that the microcosm is the essential load-bearing material that is spread *beneath* the foundation of the house of cards.

10: THE MICROCOSM—CLIMAX OF THE DESCENT INTO MATTER

Figure 14.
Malkuth
The Microcosm Pentagram of the Elements

In the same way the *six-pointed* hexagram symbolizes the *macro*cosm, the *five-pointed* pentagram symbolizes the *micro*cosm and sephirah 10, Malkuth (the Kingdom), which dangles at the very bottom of the Tree of Life.

We can think of Malkuth as the crystallized material universe. On a more personal level, it is also the confused, unbalanced, conflicted, fragmented, deluded, befuddled, anesthetized, fearful, insecure, sleepwalking/clown-show consciousness that is *my head* and *your head.* But let's not be too hard on ourselves. Our confused, unbalanced, conflicted, fragmented, deluded, befuddled, anesthetized, fearful, insecure, sleepwalking/clown-show heads have something very magical up their sleeves.

Sephirah 10 is *"the climax of the descent of Spirit into Matter"*[18]—where the invisible becomes visible, where spirit becomes matter, where heaven manifests as earth, and where God, the great What-It-Is, manifests as the physical universe and you and me.

Most importantly, sephirah 10 is the one-and-only place in the entire universe where all the living sediment of the heavenly powers and principles finally settles. All the forces of light and energy and consciousness resident in the three triads above it lie *entombed and sealed* in an alchemical petri-dish sepulchre of elemental matter.

But, is it not said the Tomb is also a Temple of Initiation?[19]

It is the profoundest of cosmic ironies that the divine power does not reach perfection until it hits the "rock" bottom of the cosmos: sephirah 10, Malkuth, the element Earth, the Tens and the Princesses of tarot. All creation remains imperfect until the moment of entombment for the simple reason that until this dark nadir is reached, the grand experiential adventure of existence remains incomplete. Until it reaches Malkuth, the Self is not yet endowed with the entire spectrum of the light of consciousness—from Spirit to Matter—from the highest high to the lowest low.

No other sephirah besides 1 has what Malkuth/10 has. Trapped in the microcosmic muck of 10 are tiny bits of the DNA code of absolutely *everything*—the full spectrum of light, energy, and consciousness. Malkuth is the *only* sephirah on the whole Tree that possesses this full set of genetic material—enough to *clone* a fresh new Number One and literally trigger a new Big Bang.

Malkuth's unique position as the manifest culmination of an old creation makes sephirah 10 the *only place* from which a brand-new cycle of creation can be resurrected. To quote a venerable qabalistic axiom:

> *Kether (1) is in Malkuth (10) and Malkuth (10) is in Kether (1) only after a different manner.*

The Emerald Tablet of Hermes also says it pretty well:[20]

> *What is above is like what is below, and what is below is like that which is above. To make the miracle of the one thing.*

So give each Pip Ten and the Court Card Princesses some serious respect, for without them there would be no house of cards.

In many versions of the Tree of Life, Malkuth/10 contains a pentagram (see Figure 14) or is divided into four elemental sections by a cross or an *X*. The four arms of the cross or *X* represent the lowest octave of (יהוה) Yod Heh Vav Heh.

The point in the very center of the cross or *X* is the mysterious *Fifth element*—Spirit. It lies like the invisible germ at the heart of every seed, and it's the spark of Spirit that triggers the process of resurrection.

This is why the tarot Princesses (the Earth Court Cards) are special and called the Throne of the Aces. This is why the first goal of every mystic is to achieve a marriage of two levels of their consciousness: that of the microcosmic Fiveness with that of the macrocosmic Sixness. Magicians call this marriage of consciousness Knowledge and Conversation of the Holy Guardian Angel.

The Lightning Flash—Ten Numbers Going Down!

The ten *Numbers* or sephiroth of the Tree of Life represent ten *descending* levels or frequencies of consciousness—from divine consciousness down to your consciousness. From One to Ten, they descend like a lightning flash. In fact, that's exactly how Qabalists describe this descent of consciousness: a "Lightning Flash" from Godhead to yourhead. (See Figure 15.)

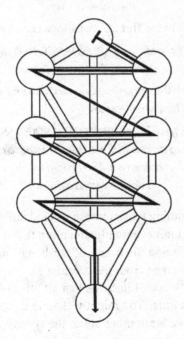

Figure 15.
Lightning Flash

The ten Pips of each tarot suit embody these same ten frequencies of divine consciousness. Think of the Ace as falling asleep and dreaming it is Two. And then *dream-Two* falls asleep and dreams it is Three, and then *dream-Three* falls asleep and dreams it is Four, and so on and so on, until finally *dream-Nine* falls asleep and dreams it is YOU.

> ## Sidebar 8
>
> PLEASE DO THIS NOW!
>
> Take the Ace and nine Small Cards of any suit (e.g., the suit of Cups). Kiss each of them as you lay them out as a Tree of Life.
>
> As you place the Ace at the top, look at it carefully and try to hold its image in your mind as you say to yourself
>
> > *"I am the Ace of Cups, the root idea of all watery things-to-be. I will sleep and dream I am the Two of Cups."*
>
> As you place the Two of Cups, look at it carefully as you say
>
> > *"I am the Two of Cups, LOVE. I will sleep and dream that I am the Three of Cups."*
>
> As you lay down the Three of Cups, look at it carefully as you say
>
> > *"I am the Three of Cups, ABUNDANCE. I will sleep and dream that I am the Four of Cups."*
>
> Continue with the remaining Cup cards down the whole Tree until you reach Ten, when you say
>
> > *"I am the Ten of Cups, PERFECTED SUCCESS. I am living a dream within a dream within a dream within a dream within a dream within a dream within a dream within a dream within a dream within a dream."*

In a real sense, the Lightning Flash represents God falling asleep and dreaming dreams within dreams until eventually dreaming that it is you and your world! The Great Work of building the house of cards will help you to reverse that process and begin to awaken from the dreams.

At the moment, however, I imagine that all this Qabalah talk is starting to make your head spin a little. You might welcome a moment to allow some of this to sink in before we learn more about the twenty-two Letters and Paths. So let's pause here just for a moment for a homework assignment that may seem so mind-numbingly simple you might be tempted to skip over it. But please don't. Mind-numbingly simple is good . . . and devilishly subtle.

Homework Assignment
Exercise 2

Get the Tree of Life Inside Yourself

(Difficulty level: Mind-numbingly simple)

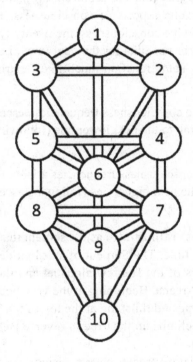

Figure 16.
Simple Tree of Life Pattern

On a full-size sheet of paper, hand-draw a Tree of Life (Figure 16) as you carefully go back and reread the **Tree of Life Qabalah Fairy Tale**. Make sure you properly number the ten sephiroth. Please do this *freehand*. (Don't trace.) That's all! Just do that!

The Serpent of Wisdom—Letters Going Up!

We've just seen how the ten *Numbers* or sephiroth of the Tree of Life represent the Lightning Flash *descent* of light and consciousness down the Tree from the brilliant, fully awake divine consciousness of One to the dark, sleepy dream consciousness of Ten. The ten Pip cards per suit reflect this same degeneration.

Technically the ten sephiroth are the first ten Paths on the Tree of Life. The twenty-two Paths that join the sephiroth are numbered 11 through 32 and also represent unique aspects of consciousness. But instead of being levels or plateaus of divine consciousness, the twenty-two Paths are *dynamic* and serve as channels or conduits for the dual flow of an alternating current of intelligence. These Paths function much like electrical transformers that simultaneously

- *step down* the consciousness frequencies descending from the higher sephirah to the next lower one (following the *Lightning Flash*).

- *step up* the consciousness frequencies arising from the lower sephirah to the next higher one (following ascent of *The Serpent of Wisdom*).

This waking-up process is illustrated as the serpent that ascends up the Tree of Life, one path at a time. The Serpent of Wisdom deals specifically with the twenty-two Letters of the Hebrew alphabet and the twenty-two Trump Cards of the Greater Arcana. Beginning at the very bottom of the Tree with ת Tav and the *Universe* and finishing at the top of the Tree at א Aleph and the *Fool*, the Serpent climbs up the Tree in reverse Hebrew alphabet order. (See Figure 17.)

Your personal initiatory process entails raising or expanding your number Ten consciousness to that of Nine by way of ת Tav and the *Universe* and so on all the way up to One. This rising consciousness slithers up the Tree of Life in a serpentine manner from Ten to One, touching in turn every one of the twenty-two Paths (Hebrew Letters/Trumps of tarot) on its way up.

When the Serpent of Wisdom is projected upon the Tree of Life, its head rests at the top of the Tree on Path 11—Aleph / The Fool—which joins sephirah 1 to sephirah 2. And its tail is at the very bottom and rests on Path 32—Tav / The Universe.

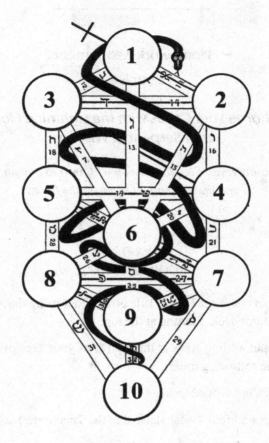

Figure 17.
The Serpent of Wisdom ascends the Tree of Life via the
Twenty-Two Paths/Hebrew Letters/Tarot Trumps.

Homework Assignment
Exercise 3

Charge Your Cards with the Lightning Flash and Serpent of Wisdom

(Difficulty level: Simple, but you will need to pay attention and make plenty of room on the floor.)

PART I
(GOING DOWN!)

Carefully lay out one large Tree of Life on the floor using the *Aces and Small Cards* of your tarot deck. Starting at the top:

Kiss and then put all four Aces at the top (1) of your Tree of Life. Stack the four Aces in the following order:

- Wands/Cups/Sword/Disks

Next kiss and put all four Twos (stacked in the same order) at 2.

Next kiss and put all four Threes (stacked in the same order) at 3.

Next kiss and put all four Fours (stacked in the same order) at 4.

Next kiss and put all four Fives (stacked in the same order) at 5.

Next kiss and put all four Sixes (stacked in the same order) at 6.

Next kiss and put all four Sevens (stacked in the same order) at 7.

Next kiss and put all four Eights (stacked in the same order) at 8.

Next kiss and put all four Nines (stacked in the same order) at 9.

Next kiss and put all four Tens (stacked in the same order) at 10.

Congratulations!

Not only did you simply lay these cards out on the floor or tabletop; you implanted the pattern in your brain and subliminally embedded the *Lightning Flash*.

As above, so below.
In Earth as it is in Heaven.
The path once laid the journey is inevitable.

PART II
(WHAT FLASHES DOWN, MUST SLITHER UP!)

Using the twenty-two **Trump Cards** as Paths, join the ten sephiroth with the appropriate tarot Trumps laying out the path of the Serpent of Wisdom. Kiss each Trump card before you lay it down:

- Between 10 and 9 place Trump 21, The Universe

- Between 10 and 8 place Trump 20, The Aeon (or Judgement)

- Between 9 and 8 place Trump 19, The Sun

- Between 10 and 7 place Trump 18, The Moon

- Between 9 and 7 place Trump 17, The Star

- Between 8 and 7 place Trump 16, The Tower

- Between 8 and 6 place Trump 15, The Devil

- Between 9 and 6 place Trump 14, Art (or Temperance)

- Between 7 and 6 place Trump 13, Death

- Between 8 and 5 place Trump 12, The Hanged Man

- Between 6 and 5 place Trump 11 (*or 8), Justice

- Between 7 and 4 place Trump 10, Fortune

- Between 6 and 4 place Trump 9, The Hermit

- Between 5 and 4 place Trump 8 (*or 11), Lust (or Strength)

- Between 5 and 3 place Trump 7, The Chariot

- Between 6 and 3 place Trump 6, The Lovers.

- Between 4 and 2 place Trump 5, The Hierophant.

- Between 6 and 2 place Trump 4, The Emperor.

- Between 3 and 2 place Trump 3, The Empress.

- Between 6 and 1 place Trump 2, The High Priestess.

- Between 3 and 1 place Trump 1, The Magus (Magician).

- Between 2 and 1 place Trump 0, The Fool.

Congratulations!

You did not simply lay these cards out on the floor or tabletop; you implanted the pattern in your brain and subliminally embedded the Serpent of Wisdom circuitry in your psyche.

As below, so above.
On Earth as it is in Heaven.
The path once laid the Journey is inevitable.

CHAPTER 4

Working Tool 3:
The Cube of Space—Tarot's
Ark of the Covenant

These three mothers, א Aleph, מ Mem, ש Shin, are a great, wonderful,
and unknown mystery, and are sealed by six rings, or elementary circles,
namely: air, water, and fire emanated from them, which gave birth to
progenitors, and these progenitors gave birth again to some offspring.

—Sepher Yetzirah. Chap. III. Section 1

We could call our third working tool tarot's *Ark of the Covenant*, a
magic box out of which emerges existence itself. Its dimensions
create time and space. Its sacred contents are mind, matter, and
energy, and it is populated by a host of gods, angels, spirits, demons, planets,
stars . . . and you and me.

But all these magic powers will remain unaroused and sealed inside until
you first build the Ark within yourself. Once you have successfully down-
loaded the Ark to your operating system, your relationship to the tarot Trumps
will be forever energized and transformed.

Part I
Three Primitive Elemental Trumps
Three Dimensions—Three Mother Letters

ANOTHER FAIRY TALE

The Cube of Space

or

How a Preexistent Point Just Wanted to Have a Little Stretch
and Inadvertently Created Space, Time, and
Absolutely Everything Else

Once upon a *before-there-was-time-and-space* . . . the great **Singularity** brooded blissfully alone as a tiny dimensionless **Point**, without form or position, floating in a nonstate of preexistence. (For the moment, we shall label this primal Point "Saturn" and think of it in much the same way we thought of our fairy tale *Titan King* who ate his children before throwing up the macrocosm and the gods of Olympus.

Figure 18.
The Primal Point

The Point desired to know itself. (Sound familiar?) But instead of reflecting itself as Number One did in our earlier fairy tale, the Point decided to *stretch* itself in order to create cosmic *elbow room* for existence to form. Of course, there weren't any *directions* as yet, so the Point needed to first create them, one at a time, as it stretched.

First, the Point stretched *infinitely upward.*

Wait a minute! What does "infinitely upward" mean? You and I can easily think about the concept of *upward,* but once we are required to think about *infinitely* upward, we run into a problem. It's easy to say, but not easy to think about because our finite meat brains find it impossible to grasp the idea of infinite anything. The ancient qabalists didn't even try. They surrendered to the fact that they were going to need to set conceptual boundaries to all these infinities. So they simply described this eternal upward extension by using the phrase "Sealing the infinite Above."

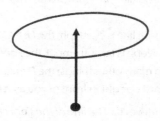

Figure 19.
Then the Point stretched straight downward and sealed the infinite Below.

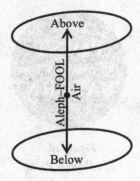

Figure 20.

Sidebar 11

PLEASE DO THIS NOW!

With the **Universe** card still on your lap or in your pocket, take up your **Fool** card. Kiss it, and hold it vertically in front of you.

Imagine yourself as the *Point* stretching up and magically touching the ceiling of your room and visualize the ceiling continuing to rise infinitely upward.

Then imagine yourself as the *Point* stretching downward and magically touching the floor of your room and visualize the floor continuing to drop infinitely downward.

Congratulations! You and the **Fool** card have just created the first dimension: up-down, *height/depth*. It's not much of a cosmos yet, but it's a start.

This impossibly slim line is א, Aleph, the *First Mother Letter* of the Hebrew alphabet. Aleph is tarot Trump 0, the **Fool**, and the Fool represents (among many other things) the *Primitive Element Air*.[1]

Hold the **Fool** card upright in front of you as you say out loud:[2]

*"Aleph. Primitive Air. The line of the **Fool** creates Above and Below."*

Next, the *Point* stretched straight ahead and sealed the infinite *east*; then straight behind and sealed the infinite *west*.

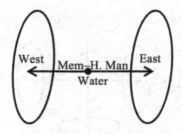

Figure 21.

Sidebar 12

PLEASE DO THIS NOW!

With the **Universe** card still on your lap or in your pocket, take up your **Hanged Man** card. Kiss it, and hold it horizontally pointing straight in front of you.

Imagine yourself as the *Point* stretching straight ahead (east) and magically touching the east wall of your room. Visualize the east wall continuing to extend infinitely before you—eastward.

Then imagine yourself as the Point stretching directly behind you (west) and magically touching the west wall of your room. Visualize the west wall continuing to extend infinitely behind you—westward.

The line that seals the infinite *east* and *west* is מ, Mem, the Second Mother Letter of the Hebrew alphabet. Mem is tarot Trump 12, the **Hanged Man,** and represents (among many other things) the *Primitive Element Water.*

Now, point the **Hanged Man** card directly front of you and say out loud:

*"Mem. Primitive Water. The line of the **Hanged Man** creates East and West."*

Congratulations! The two infinitely extending lines of Aleph (up-down) and Mem (front-back) have created a brand-new second dimension, a *Plane*: a flat surface of two dimensions that keeps endlessly spreading like a square piece of paper that has absolutely no thickness at all.

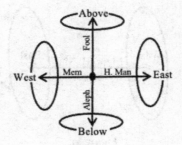

Figure 22.

Sidebar 13

PLEASE DO THIS NOW!

With the **Universe** card still on your lap or in your pocket, take up your **Aeon** (Judgement) card. Kiss it, and hold it horizontally to your left (north) and right (south).

Imagine yourself as the *Point* stretching left and magically touching the north wall of your room. Visualize the wall to your left extending infinitely northward.

Then imagine yourself as the *Point* stretching right (south) and magically touching the south wall of your room. Visualize the wall to your right continuing to extend infinitely southward.

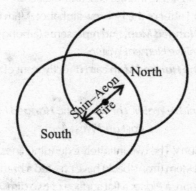

Figure 23.

The third line seals the infinite *north* and *south*. It is 𝒲 Shin, the *Third Mother Letter* of the Hebrew alphabet. Shin is tarot Trump 20, the **Aeon** (or Judgement), and represents (among many other things) the *Primitive Element Fire*. In addition to representing Fire, Shin and the **Aeon** also do double duty by representing the fifth element *Spirit* in the world of Trumps.

Now, hold the **Aeon** card horizontally and say out loud:

> *"Shin. Primitive Fire. The line of the Aeon creates the North and South."*

Congratulations! You (the **Universe**), with the help of the **Fool**, the **Hanged Man**, and the **Aeon**, have just created the third dimension.

This three-part drama is the qabalistic tarot equivalent of the Big Bang. Springing from the *Tav-Universe* card in your pocket, the three Mother Letters (Aleph, Mem, Shin) create an environment of three dimensions whose six sealed extremities (above/below, east/west, north/south) intersect at right angles to create the three-dimensional universe of an infinitely expanding Cube of Space. And, as physicists tell us, relative movements between point-events within three-dimensional space create *time*.

Not bad for a day's work.

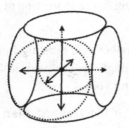   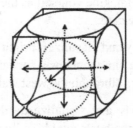

Figure 24   *Figure 25*

Note: You have just created the three dimensions of space, which we can now with confidence identify as *above/below*, *east/west*, and *north/south*.

Ritual 1

The Mother Letter Trumps

With your **Universe** card tucked in your shirt pocket, stand or be seated in the center of your temple room facing *east*.

Clap three times (3-3-3) and clasp your hands upon your breast.

Close your eyes and take two or three deep cleansing breaths.

Imagine yourself as the dancing figure in the ring at the center of the **Universe** card.

Inhale slowly and visualize a bright airy *yellow light* bursting from your heart and shooting simultaneously *upward* through the ceiling above you and *downward* through the floor beneath you.

Exhale slowly, and visualize the image of the **Fool** card superimposed on the vertical yellow line and vibrating within you.

With your eyes still closed, take two or three deep cleansing breaths.

Once again, imagine yourself as the dancing figure in the ring at the center of the **Universe** card.

Inhale slowly and visualize a bright liquid *blue light* bursting from your heart and shooting simultaneously forward (through the east wall in front of you) and backward (through the west wall behind you).

Exhale slowly and visualize the image of the **Hanged Man** card superimposed on the horizontal blue line and vibrating within you.

With your eyes still closed, take two or three deep cleansing breaths.

Once again, imagine yourself as the dancing figure in the ring at the center of the **Universe** card.

Inhale slowly and visualize a bright fiery *red light* bursting from your heart and shooting simultaneously to your left (through the north wall of your room) and to your right (through the south wall).

Exhale slowly and visualize the image of the **Aeon** (Judgement) card superimposed on the red line and vibrating within you.

With your right hand draw a vertical line from the top your head to as low can reach and intone, "Ahhhh."

Point forward toward the east wall in front of you, then backward to the west wall behind you while you intone, "Mmmmm."

Stretch your arms to the sides to form a cross with your body while you intone, "Shhhh."

Clap three times (3-3-3).

Part II
Seven Planetary Trumps—Seven Double Letters

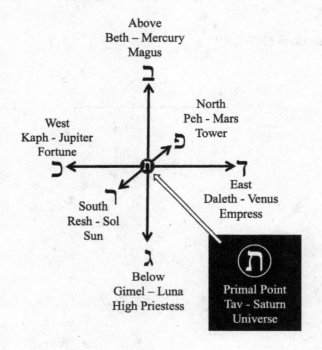

Figure 26.

Figure 26 shows the Primal Point and the infinitely expanding ceiling, floor, and four walls of the Cube of Space. The Three Mother Letters spring from the Primal Point to create three sets of opposite directions. These landmarks are the seven Planetary Trump cards of tarot and the seven Double Letters of the Hebrew alphabet.

Exercise 5

Please do the following:

Using Figure 26 as a guide, place the **Universe** card (ת, Tav) in the center of your table to represent the Primal *Point* (Saturn).

Place the **Fool** card on top and covering the **Universe** to represent the Mother Letter, א, Aleph (Primal Air) extending to infinite *height and depth.*

Place the **Magus** (Magician) card, ב, Beth directly above the **Fool** to represent Mercury and the infinite *above* (the ceiling of the cube).

Place the **High Priestess** card, ג, Gimel directly below the **Fool** to represent Luna and the infinite *below* (the floor of the cube).

Place the **Hanged Man** card horizontally crossing the **Fool** to represent the Mother Letter, מ, Mem (Primal Water) extending to infinite *east and west.*

Place the **Empress** card, ד, Daleth to the right of the **Hanged Man** to represent Venus and the infinite east wall of the cube.

Place the **Fortune** card, כ, Kaph to the left of the **Hanged Man** to represent Jupiter and the infinite west wall of the cube.

Place the **Aeon** (Judgement) card diagonally over the **Hanged Man** and **Fool** to represent the Mother Letter, ש, Shin (Primal Fire) extending to infinite *north and south.*

Place the **Tower** card, פ, Peh near the top of the **Aeon** card to represent Mars and the infinite north wall of the cube.

Place the **Sun** card, ר, Resh near the bottom of the **Aeon** card to represent Sol and the infinite south wall of the cube.

Repeat this exercise until you are able do it without having to read the directions.

But your spiritual house of cards is not built on a flat tabletop. It has to be built inside *you*. So before we move on with more Cube of Space mysteries, let's get proactively mystical and pause for an important meditation.

Meditation 2

Building Your Greater Arcana House of Cards from Within

Universe

Fool – Hanged Man – Aeon

Magus – High Priestess – Empress – Fortune – Tower – Sun

For this meditation you will be seated facing east.

1. With your **Universe** card resting on your lap or in your shirt pocket, be seated comfortably facing east. Clap ten times (1–3-3-3–6-6-6-6-6-6).

2. Close your eyes and take two or three deep cleansing breaths.

3. Imagine yourself as the dancing figure in the ring at the center of the **Universe** card.

4. *Inhale* slowly and visualize a bright airy *yellow light* bursting from your heart and shooting simultaneously *upward* through the ceiling above you and *downward* through the floor beneath you.

5. *Exhale* slowly and visualize the image of the **Fool** card superimposed on the vertical yellow line and vibrating within you.

6. *Inhale* slowly and visualize the image of the **Magus** (Mercury) card looking down at you from the *ceiling*.

7. *Exhale* slowly and visualize the image of the **High Priestess** (Luna) card appearing as the *floor* of beneath you.

8. Repeat this cycle (2–7) two or three times until your breathing and the visualizations become comfortably automatic.

9.   Close your eyes and take two or three deep cleansing breaths.

10. Once again, imagine yourself as the dancing figure in the ring at the center of the **Universe** card.

11. *Inhale* slowly and visualize a bright liquid *blue light* bursting forward from your heart and through the eastern wall in front of you and simultaneously backward through the western wall behind you.

12. *Exhale* slowly and visualize the image of the **Hanged Man** card superimposed on the horizontal blue line and vibrating within you.

13. *Inhale* slowly and visualize the image of the **Empress** (Venus) card forming the wall in front of you.

14. *Exhale* slowly and visualize the image of the **Fortune** (Jupiter) card forming the wall behind you.

15. Repeat this cycle (9–14) two or three times until your breathing and the visualizations become comfortably automatic.

16. Close your eyes and take two or three deep cleansing breaths.

17. Once again, imagine yourself as the dancing figure in the ring at the center of the **Universe** card.

18. *Inhale* slowly and visualize a bright fiery *red light* bursting from your heart and shooting simultaneously to your left (through the north wall) and to your right (through the wall in the south).

19. *Exhale* slowly and visualize the image of the **Aeon** (Judgement) card superimposed on the red line and vibrating within you.

20. *Inhale* slowly and visualize the image of the **Tower** (Mars) card forming the northern wall to your left.

21. *Exhale* slowly and visualize the image of the **Sun** (Sol) card shining from the southern to your right.

22. Repeat this cycle (16–21) two or three times until your breathing and the visualizations become comfortably automatic.

23. Pause and relax. Breathe normally and try to visualize the whole scene: Yourself seated as the **Universe** (Saturn) card with the **Fool** card piercing through you vertically, the **Hanged Man** card piercing through

you front and back, and the **Aeon** card piercing you horizontally left and right.

24. When you have this full image firmly in mind, look up to the ceiling and see the **Magus** gazing intensely down on you. Then look down to the floor and see the **High Priestess** gazing mysteriously up at you.

25. Then look straight ahead and see the **Empress** serenely smiling at you. Then turn around to see the **Fortune** spinning upon wall behind you.

26. Finally, look to you left and see the **Tower** card thunderously shaking the northern wall and to your right and feel the warmth of the **Sun** card brightly shining on the southern wall.

27. When you can comfortably hold this entire image in your mind's eye, open your eyes and clap ten times (1–3-3-3–6-6-6-6-6-6).

Congratulations! Using ten tarot Trumps (representing the three *Mother Letters* and seven *Double Letters* of the Hebrew alphabet) you have just reenacted within yourself the creation of dimensional space and the infinitely expanding cosmos, and in doing so, you have installed tarot's Ark of the Covenant in the Holy of Holies of your soul.

Your house of cards now has an environment in which to exist.

As below, so above.
On Earth as it is in Heaven.
The path once laid the journey is inevitable.

Part III.
War in the Heavens—Twelve Zodiacal Trumps
Twelve Signs of the Zodiac—Twelve Simple Letters

So far, the three *Mother Letters* and seven *Double Letters* (along with their ten tarot Trump representatives) have succeeded in creating the infinitely expanding Cube of Space. The Primitive elements and planetary spheres represent, in a very real sense, unique spiritual personalities with each possessing its own distinct qualities and characteristics.

But there are total of twenty-two letters of the Hebrew alphabet and twenty-two tarot Trumps. The remaining twelve *Simple Letters* are assigned to (among all things twelvish) the twelve Zodiacal Trump cards, and they also have their place on the Cube of Space as the twelve *edges* or oblique angles of the cube (Figure 27).

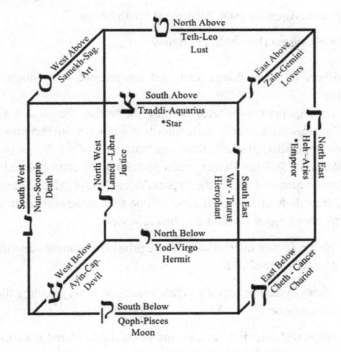

Figure 27.
Twelve Simple Letters, the Signs of the zodiac
and the twelve Zodiacal Trumps arrayed at the edges of the Cube of Space.

ה Heh: Aries (Emperor, *Star) North East

ו Vav: Taurus (Hierophant) South East

ז Zain: Gemini (Lovers) East Above

ח Cheth: Cancer (Chariot) East Below

ט Teth: Leo (Lust) North Above

י Yod: Virgo (Hermit) North Below

ל Lamed: Libra (Justice) North West

נ Nun: Scorpio (Death) South West

ס Samekh: Sagittarius (Art) West Above

ע Ayin: Capricorn (Devil) West Below

צ Tzaddi: Aquarius (Star, *Emperor) South Above

ק Qoph: Pisces (Moon) South Below

And here is where things really get complicated—one might even say combative.

I say things get complicated because the twelve *Simple Letters* and the twelve Zodiacal Trump cards are landlords to a much more complex and often conflicted population of spiritual tenants than those of the *Primitive Elements* or the *Planetary Spheres*. In fact, when describing the character and functions of the twelve *Simple Letters*, the Sepher Yetzirah says, "He made them as a conflict, drew them up like a wall; and set one against the other as in warfare."[3]

Think about that for a moment. Just to review:

- We've got the interaction of three primitive *elemental* qualities (the Mother Letters) . . .

- whose dynamics literally create space and time, injecting their influence on . . .

- seven self-centered, unique, and fickle dual-natured *planetary* qualities (the Double Letters) . . .

- which are now forced to slam against each other to create twelve oblique edges (Simple Letters).

Because each of the three Primitive Elements has *their* fundamental nature that contributes to the complexity of the planetary spheres, and because each planetary sphere has *its* distinctive admixture of elemental and planetary qualities (some of which play well with other and some of which don't), the twelve Simple Letters are in a constant state of war. They war within themselves and among each other—for *conflict* is their nature at this level of dream consciousness.

As in all wars, there is ultimately no *reasonable* motive for conflict. The myopic combatants have fallen deeply asleep within themselves and have poisoned the cast of characters that populate their dreams. They self-identify only as pieces of pieces of pieces the *Primal Point*. They war like children, blindly discharging the elemental and planetary fragments that blindly animate them. In their fevered dreams of separateness, they fight never-ending battles to plant flags of vain victory atop constantly shifting phantom hilltops.

These battlefields are the twelve edges of the expanding cube. They are reflected in the Heavens as the belt of the zodiac. It is the field of battle where the myriad forces of elements, planets, powers, and principles all attract and repel each other and form perpetually shifting alliances, hostilities, truces, marriages, and betrayals. This is the nature of the twelve Zodiacal Trumps.

Sidebar 15

PLEASE DO THIS NOW!
Take your **Emperor, Hierophant, Lovers, Chariot, Lust, Hermit, Justice, Death, Art, Devil, Star,** and **Moon** cards. Kiss each of them, and lay them in counterclockwise order in a circle, starting with the **Emperor** (Aries) on the far left (9 o'clock position).

For the sake of convenience, I've asked you to lay out your twelve Zodiacal Trump cards in a circle (like the wheel of the year). But Figure 27 is a version of the Cube of Space itself that shows precisely how the twelve Simple Letters of the Hebrew alphabet and the twelve Zodiacal Trumps are created as the twelve edges of the cube when the walls, ceiling, and floor of the cube were formed.

(Figure 28 is a Cube of Space pattern you can copy and cut out to form into a three-dimensional cube to study and help you visualize.)

Believe it or not, there is method to the madness of their positions on the cube, and I'm sure you'll enjoy discovering it.

To Summarize

All twenty-two Trumps are represented on the Cube of Space:

- The three Elemental Trumps represent the three Mother Letters.
- They created the seven Planetary Trumps representing the seven Double Letters.
- These formed the twelve Zodiacal Trumps representing the twelve Simple Letters.

Homework Assignment

Exercise 6

Construct a Cube of Space

(Difficulty level: Easy but a little time-consuming)

Print Figure 28 on cardstock. You may wish to enlarge it a little.

Cut out and assemble the three-directional cross of the Mother Letters and the unfolded cube.

Fold the image along with its tabs and assemble. (Use double-sided tape to hold the tabs to the interior of the cube.)

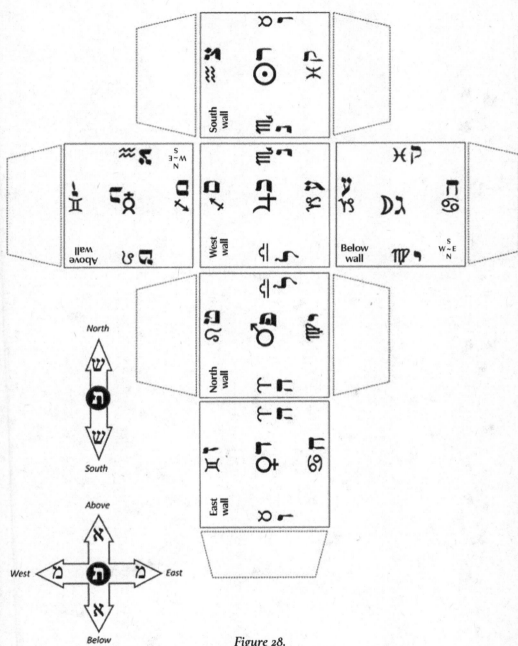

Figure 28.
Your homemade Cube of Space

BOOK II

Creating Your Own Deck

A Little Background
Information

*The rhythm that drives the Music of the Spheres dictates there be
78 tarot cards. No more! No less!*

—Rabbi Lamed Ben Clifford

Where Did Tarot Come From?

I won't spend too much time talking about the empirical history of tarot. It's not that I feel the subject is unimportant, but there are today so many excellent books available that treat quite thoroughly on the subject. Mary Greer, Rachel Pollack, Robert Place, Benebell Wen, M. M. Meline, and T. Susan Chang are just a few modern tarot experts whose works I admire and heartily recommend.

Perhaps the first thing we must realize is there are no records to suggest that tarot cards were used for fortune-telling before the 18th century or that gypsies were known to employ tarot cards for fortune-telling before the 19th century. There is no shortage of wonder stories, romantic conjectures, and qabalistic conspiracy theories concerning the origins of tarot, but one thing seems certain to me: A seventy-eight-card tarot deck did not spring, Minerva-like, fully formed from the split skull of Zeus!

On one hand, we have an assortment of modern spiritual traditions that would have us believe that tarot is the long-lost *Book of Thoth,* penned by the ibis-headed Egyptian god himself or that it was the gift to humanity from the hierophants of ancient Atlantis or Lemuria or that it was presented at a seminar conducted by Hermes Trismegistus or that it was dreamed up by a committee of interdenominational magi attending a world "AdeptaCon" in Fez, Morocco.

Please don't think I'm denigrating those who choose to believe these romantic theories. I love myths and legends as much as the next ceremonial magician. But I'm also grown-up enough to realize that these are, at best, devices that reveal (or conceal) more profound spiritual concepts within the context of allegories or fanciful stories.

On the other hand, tarot's organized internal structure displays what appears to reflect universal mathematical harmonies that are expressions of well-established hermetic, astrological, and qabalistic landmarks. One might even be tempted to speculate that tarot cards were guilefully and meticulously *engineered* by learned astrologers and qabalists in order to graphically illustrate the divine general dynamics of the cosmos.

As much as I'd like to believe this is possible, I can't imagine that our beloved tarot cards were created by a select committee of cloistered alchemist-astrologer-qabalists. (Have you ever tried to get a room full of alchemist-astrologer-qabalists to agree about *anything*? I have! It's not pretty!)

I do believe, however, there is an important spiritual dimension to tarot's genesis, one that I feel it is crucial for us to understand—or at least consider. So I will offer the following thoughts on the matter because I believe that empirical history probably offers us a more reasonable and at the same time an even more amazing wonder story than any of these fables. Truth, after all, *is* stranger than fiction, and I believe the tale of tarot's genesis demonstrates the mysterious power of the most awesome magical force in the cosmos—*human consciousness*.

Let the Games Begin

Every modern seventy-eight-card tarot deck consists of the same two distinct categories of cards; today they are known as the *Greater Arcana* and the *Lesser Arcana*. These terms, however, were not used until the late 19th century.

- The Greater Arcana is comprised of twenty-two Trump (Key) cards numbered 0–21 (often designated by roman numerals), many of which are the remnants of hand-painted game cards originally created for the nobility of 15th- and 16th-century Northern Italy. The game was called tarocchi. The cards themselves were named some variation of *tarot* or *tarok*, *tarock*, or *tarocchi*. The game had rules similar to modern bridge.[1] The decks were referred to as "Il

Trionfos," from the Italian word for "triumph," also "triumphal procession," or "triumphal car or float." The oldest known complete deck is the 15th-century *Sola Busca* deck, which has seventy-eight Trionfos.

- The Lesser Arcana of a modern tarot deck is comprised of fifty-six cards, which are essentially identical[2] in suit and numbering to the common fifty-two-card deck of modern playing cards, which have been popular throughout Europe and the Islamic world since at least 1375.

It is easy for us to jump to the conclusion that tarot's Greater Arcana comes exclusively from the cards of Il Trionfos and the Lesser Arcana comes from decks of Mamluk[3] cards or standard playing cards, but it appears that is not necessarily the case. When I put this issue to Mary Greer (whom I consider perhaps the world's most knowledgeable living tarot expert), this was her response:

There were NOT two separate and popular decks that were merged to become the Tarot we know. The set of twenty-one triumphs plus the Fool (as described in the late fifteenth-century Steele document) were always joined with the four suits and did not exist separately!

Around 1425 CE, stenciling technology made printing and reproduction of cards less expensive. Various game card decks became more common and widely distributed among the European bourgeoisie and general public. Even though many of us would like to believe something more supernaturally exotic or mystical, the actual genesis story of tarot proves to be somewhat lackluster, and its use as divinatory tool a relatively recent phenomenon. As Mary points out:

There is no clear mention of tarot decks being used for predictive fortune-telling before the mid- to late eighteenth century (although I considered it highly probable).

But Things Do Get Spooky

Still, things actually do start to get a little spooky when we realize that the new (seemingly arbitrary) structure of the seventy-eight modern tarot cards just so happens to perfectly mirror the two sublimest mathematical landmarks of the

Hebrew Kabbalah, and the deeper we look into this synchronistic phenomenon of sacred numbers, the spookier and more magical tarot proves to be.

We could debate endlessly about whether it was some brilliant qabalist who was responsible for tinkering with tarot cards or whether it was vaporous spirits of tarot tinkering with some brilliant qabalist. Frankly, I don't believe it was either.

Whatever happened, by the time complete seventy-eight-card packs of tarot cards were being cheaply manufactured and widely distributed to an awakening public hungry for inexpensive portable entertainment (and a bit of *do-it-yourself* prophesying), the effect tarot had upon the human psyche triggered a subtle but significant mutation to the consciousness pool of humanity, especially Western civilization.

The Wand of Human Consciousness

I don't believe I am overstating the situation. We need look no further than the effects radio had upon the world's consciousness in the 1920s, television and rock 'n' roll in 1950s, the computer in the 1970s, cell phones in the 1980s, and today's social networking to see examples of mutation of consciousness in action.

When universal influences such as these touch human consciousness, human consciousness eventually touches back and intuitively demands ever more perfect evolutionary adjustments to the initial influence.

In the case of tarot bursting onto the consciousness pool of Western civilization, our instinctual resonances with the very real natural laws that govern our three-dimensional "reality" demanded order for us to unconsciously feel comfortable with the perfection of this new medium.

- *Human consciousness* demanded that the Greater Arcana have twenty-two cards—no more, no less.

- *Human consciousness* demanded that of those twenty-two cards there must be

  - *three cards* that embody qualities of a primitive *elemental* nature

  - *seven cards* that embody qualities of a *planetary* nature

  - *twelve cards* that embody qualities of a *zodiacal* nature

- *Human consciousness* demanded that the Lesser Arcana have fifty-six cards—no more, no less.

- *Human consciousness* demanded that those fifty-six cards should be divided into *four suits* of an elemental nature:

  - (*Wands* = Fire, *Cups* = Water, *Swords* = Air, *Disks* = Earth)[4]

  - Each suit should contain *four Court Cards*[5] that represent subqualities the same four elemental natures (i.e., *King*[6] *of Wands* = Fire of Fire; *Queen of Wands* = Water of Fire; *Knight*[7] *of Wands* = Air of Fire; *Page*[8] *of Wands* = Earth of Fire) and ten Pip Cards—no more, no less.

- *Human consciousness* demanded that each of the four suits contain one Ace and nine Small Cards (2–10).

But before we continue, let's pause here to make sure you have a good grasp of the things we've discussed so far. To do that, I'm going to give you your first homework assignment of Book II. You may think these homework assignments are a bit silly, but I'm serious. Please don't skip over them. As Miss Schumacher (my disturbingly attractive fifth-grade teacher) repeatedly reminded me, "You'll only be cheating yourself."

Sidebar 16

I hope you have (or can obtain) a tarot deck! Until your personal deck is completed, you will need one to practice with.

You will soon be given the opportunity to create your own personalized deck of tarot cards. But in order for you to immediately perform the various exercises and meditations in Book II, you should already have in your possession a full seventy-eight-card deck of tarot cards.

Any seventy-eight-card deck will do, as long as it is a standard formatted deck comprised of
- twenty-two Trump cards
- four suits that generally represent Wands, Cups, Swords, and Disks (or Coins)
- each suit containing four Court Cards (i.e., a Knight or King, Queen, a Prince or Knight, and a Princess or Page) and Ten Pip Cards (Ace through Ten)

Homework
Assignment 1

Put Your Universe in Order

(Difficulty level: Mind-numbingly simple)
(You will need a deck of seventy-eight tarot cards and a notebook.)
(Do this exercise at least once a week for the rest of your life.
It may be the only perfect thing you will do that day.)

Note: From here forward we will be using the Court Card titles of Knight, Queen, Prince, and Princess (rather than King, Queen, Knight, and Page). Please readjust your mind to accept this designation.

Shuffle the cards by whatever method you prefer and then *reorder* your deck in the following manner:

First separate the twenty-two cards of the Greater Arcana (Trumps) from the fifty-six cards of the Lesser Arcana. Then stack your Trumps face up in the following order and set them aside:

- 0 through 21 (The Fool through the Universe)

From the fifty-six cards of the Lesser Arcana separate the sixteen Court Cards from the Small Cards, and stack the Court Cards in the following order:

- **Wands**: Knight, Queen, Prince, Princess

- **Cups**: Knight, Queen, Prince, Princess

- **Swords**: Knight, Queen, Prince, Princess

- **Disks**: Knight, Queen, Prince, Princess

Set aside your ordered stack of Court Cards and stack the remaining Aces and Small Cards the following order:

- **Wands**: Ace through 10
- **Cups**: Ace through 10
- **Swords**: Ace through 10
- **Disks**: Ace through 10

Recombine the stacks of Court Cards and Small Cards in the following order:

- **Wands**: Ace, followed by Knight, Queen, Prince, Princess, followed by Small Cards 2–10
- **Cups**: Ace, followed by Knight, Queen, Prince, Princess, followed by Small Cards 2–10
- **Swords**: Ace, followed by Knight, Queen, Prince, Princess, followed by Small Cards 2–10
- **Disks**: Ace, followed by Knight, Queen, Prince, Princess, followed by Small Cards 2–10

Place your Greater Arcana stack on top your Lesser Arcana stack and admire.

Congratulations! You've just put a universe in perfect order and lubricated your own consciousness.

As above, so below.
In Earth as it is in Heaven.
The path once laid the journey is inevitable.

Log this exercise in your notebook, along with any thoughts, observations, or impressions you may have. Especially note changes in dreams.

———————————

The Cards

The more you play around with the cards,
the more the cards will play around with you.

—RABBI LAMED BEN CLIFFORD

Hopefully, you now feel comfortably equipped with your three qaba-listic working tools. The lessons, assignments, meditations, and fairy tales in Book I, while being disarmingly simple and repetitive, were designed to implant the blueprint[1] of the house of cards in the fertile soil of your psyche.[2] Now it's time for you to give those seeds a chance to sprout into full manifestation on the material plane.[3]

Do you feel ready to start work on your own tarot deck?

Of course you don't! But don't let that stop you! You'll never feel ready! Nobody who has created a tarot deck ever felt ready to start! Just keep reading, and take things one page at a time. Do the little exercises and meditations even if they seem childish and silly, even if you don't feel like doing them. The more you play around with the cards, the more they will play around with you, and before you know it, you'll be beyond the point of no return and up to your *Assiah* in a project that will change your life forever.

Seventy-Eight Shells

Throughout the pages that follow are seventy-eight full-size tarot card images in draft form. Think of them as shells. Each card is individually titled and displays its relevant astrological and magical attributes. They are the unfin-ished, uncolored designs of the *Tarot of Ceremonial Magick* deck.[4] Obvious, they are really going to need *your* help to get them looking nice.

I apologize if the design images aren't as recognizably iconic as the popular Waite-Smith or the Crowley-Harris *Thoth Tarot*. They are simply the crude illustrations I handed over to Constance many years ago when I asked her to color and flesh out our *TCM* deck.

They do, however, display what I consider to be the most essential archetypal elements, and should give you a basic starting point to begin your work. In fact, I'm expecting you to modify, customize, and (if you feel it necessary) completely paint over my images and draw your own designs informed by your own taste, inspiration, and understanding within the shells of the card forms.

Colors Are Important

Tarot is a visual instrument. The magical soul of each card is an admixture of elements, planets, and multiple qabalistic features, all of which vibrate at their own particular frequencies of light and color. These colors are important, and I strongly encourage you to be aware of them as you customize your cards. I've provided the same color tables I gave to Constance. They outline the qabalistic color scales appropriate to each of the cards.

Other Magical Features

Each *TCM* card form is numbered and displays various pertinent astrological and magical information (e.g., Enochian magick squares, Goetic spirit names and sigils, and qabalistic angel names) associated with it. If any of these esoteric magical items do not interest you, please feel free to ignore them completely. Color over them if you wish.

However, if you *are* interested in this important aspect of tarot, I've provided more information about them in the appendices, along with general divinatory meanings for each card.

Are you ready to begin? If so, we will start with the Greater Arcana. For this you'll need to get out your Cube of Space working tool—or should I say, *Cube of Trumps*?

CHAPTER 1

Introduction to the Trumps

If you wish to make an apple pie from scratch,
you must first invent the universe.

—CARL SAGAN

Why Create the Trumps in This Particular Order?

It might seem logical to begin working on your twenty-two Trumps in a straightforward sequence, beginning with 0—the Fool and working through to 21—the Universe. Of course, you are free to do that. However, this is *not* the sequence in which I would like you to proceed.

I believe that in order for you to most effectively activate your cards, it is best to bring them to life the way the Sepher Yetzirah describes the steps of creation—the same developmental sequence by which existence comes[1] into existence, the way time and space become time and space, how matter and energy become matter and energy, the way you and I become you and I. *This* is the way I believe your tarot cards can most naturally and effectively come alive within you.

Don't panic. I'm *not* suggesting you change the order or the Key numbers of the Trumps. I only want you to bring your deck into material manifestation, one card at a time, in a particular order. By doing so, you will hop aboard the momentum train of life and become synchronized with the most fundamental dynamics of creation. You will be calibrating the tuning fork of your *personal* consciousness to the great tuning fork of *universal* consciousness. I hope you will see the method to the madness.

A Twenty-Two-Hour Meditation?

Let's assume that it will take you, at the very least, *one hour* to color and customize each Trump card. This means a minimum of twenty-two hours to just to complete the Greater Arcana. Consider these hours an extended meditation—a laser-focused dharana[2] upon these twenty-two archetypal images. As you carefully apply the specific colors and as you add your own artistic flourishes, your breathing will automatically slow—and occasionally even stop. In these moments you'll free yourself, as every artist is freed, from external distractions and monkey-chattering thoughts. You'll be doing real yoga, real meditation, real magic. You will be performing true invocations: extended consecration ceremonies with the intent of transforming twenty-two immaterial *ideas* into twenty-two magically charged *material talismans*.

Creation Began with Nothing—So Will You!

As you begin work, I urge you to regularly refer back to the material in Book I, especially chapter 4 and the fairy tale and meditations that deal with the development of the *Tree of Life* and the *Cube of Space*.

Recall how the Fool and the Universe Trumps represent the two very special kinds of Zero?

- The Fool's Zero from which existence first *emerges* at the birth of a creation cycle

- The Universe's Zero through which existence *returns* upon absolute completion of the manifestation cycle

Remember the meditation exercise? When you put the Universe in your shirt pocket or on your lap to help you identify as the central *Primal Point* of precreation?

Do you recall how the three Mother Letter Trumps (three Primitive Elements)—the Fool, Hanged Man, and Aeon—burst from the point in your pocket and extended *up and down*, and then *forward and backward*, , and then *right* and *left* to create *above* and *below*, *east* and *west*, *north* and *south*?

Do you recall how the six sealed extremities of the three Mother Letter lines created the floor, ceiling, and four walls of an infinitely expanding cube and how together with the center source, the Universe, created the seven Double Letter (Planetary) Trumps—Magus, High Priestess, Empress, Fortune, Tower, and Sun?

Do you recall how the walls, ceiling, and floor by their very existences instantly formed the twelve *edges* of the cube represented by the twelve Simple Letters (Zodiacal) Trumps—Emperor, Hierophant, Lovers, Chariot, Lust, Hermit, Justice, Death, Art, Devil, Star, Moon?

If you don't recall these lessons from Book I, please take a few moments right now and go back to review and practice them because this is precisely the order in which I would like you to awaken the Trumps within yourself.

By these same steps you will magically *charge* your cards and synchronize yourself with the universal stages of creation. This is how you will transform your deck (and how your deck will transform *you*) into a *miniature working model of the cosmos*—a living, breathing Ark of the Covenant.

Are you ready to begin?

Not sure?

Turn the page anyway.

Features of the Trumps

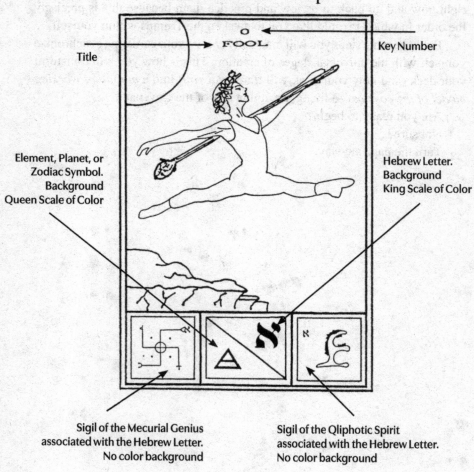

Title

Key Number

Element, Planet, or
Zodiac Symbol.
Background
Queen Scale of Color

Hebrew Letter.
Background
King Scale of Color

Sigil of the Mecurial Genius
associated with the Hebrew Letter.
No color background

Sigil of the Qliphotic Spirit
associated with the Hebrew Letter.
No color background

Figure 29.
Format features of the Twenty-Two Trumps.

CHAPTER 2

The Mother Letter Trumps

This chapter is titled "The Mother Letter Trumps," and that is indeed where we will start . . . *eventually*.

The Fool is the first Mother Letter Trump and represents the Primitive Element[1] Air. The Hanged Man is the second Mother Letter Trump. The Aeon is the third Mother Letter Trump.

The Mother Letter Trumps:

0 Fool—Air—א

XII Hanged Man—Water—מ

XX Aeon—Fire (and Spirit)— ש

(Please see Appendix 2, Table 1 on page 325 for a chart of the correspondences for the Mother Letter Trumps.)

But first, I want us to begin even *before* the beginning, with the two Trump cards that represent the two mysterious Zeros of creation: the Universe and the Fool. The Universe, while not a Mother Letter Trump, plays a double role in the Greater Arcana:

- As Saturn, a Planetary Trump

- As the representative of the Primitive Element Earth

As a Planetary Trump, Saturn is the mystical central point from which spring the three Mother Letters. Therefore, the Universe is where I would like us to start building our house of cards.

• • •

To start, let's take a look at the formatting of all the cards of the Greater Arcana, shown in Figure 29.

Key XXI—The Universe

Great One of the Night of Time

SATURN & PRIMAL EARTH

Traditional Image **A demonstration of the** **Quadrature of the Circle**	*On the Tree of Life* **Path 32 Joins Sephiroth 10 and 9** **Administrative Intelligence**
Hebrew Letter **Double Letter: Tav** *Meaning:* **Cross, Mark, Seal**	*Color Scales* **See Table 2** **(King & Queen Predominate)**
On the Cube of Space **The Central Point**	*Musical Note:* **A** *Vowel Sound:* **"Thah"**

The *TCM* Card: Has a dark indigo background flecked with yellow stars.

Central Figure: Dancer is flesh-colored (note the cloven hooves) and encircled by a **Green** snake. Behind the dancer's head a **Golden** Sun is cradled by a **Silver** crescent Moon. Zodiac signs are colored: *Aries*—**Scarlet**, *Taurus*—**Red-Orange**, *Gemini*—**Orange**, *Cancer*—**Amber**, *Leo*—**Greenish-Yellow**, *Virgo*—**Yellowish-Green**, *Libra*—**Emerald**, *Scorpio*—**Green-Blue**, *Sagittarius*—**Blue**, *Capricorn*—**Indigo**, *Aquarius*—**Violet**, *Pisces*—**Crimson**. The Key on the right of the zodiac ring is **Gold**; the Key to the left is **Silver**.

Additions or Changes: Add the head of the **Green** snake atop the **Golden** Sun. Perhaps clouds around the four Kerubic beasts.[2]

Lower Panel, Left Horizontal Rectangles: Two long spirit sigils leave uncolored, or use Prince and Princess color scales.

Lower Panel, Right Square: Bottom section: **Light Green** behind a small **Dark Green** triangle of Earth. Left section: **Indigo** behind **Saturn** symbol. Upper right section: **Blue-Black** behind Hebrew letter **Tav**.

Key 0—The Fool
Spirit of the Aether

PRIMAL AIR

Traditional Image **A bearded ancient seen in profile**	*On the Tree of Life* **Path 11 Joins Sephiroth 1 and 2** **Scintillating Intelligence**
Hebrew Letter **Mother Letter: Aleph** *Meaning:* **Ox**	*Color Scales:* **See Table 1** **King & Queen Predominate**
On the Cube of Space **Creates and joins Above & Below**	*Musical Note:* **E** *Vowel Sound:* **"Aah"**

The *TCM* Card: Has a bright **Pale Yellow** background, a **White** Sun, **Green** grass, and **earth-dark** cliffs.

Central Figure: The Motley Fool can wear checked or brightly colored tights like those of a court jester; **Red** and **Green** are suggested. The Fool is crowned with a **Green** wreath. A **Red** feather can be added. His wand is the pine cone–tipped Thyrsus of Dionysus.

Additions or Changes: You may wish to draw a small dog nipping at the Fool's heels or a crocodile menacing from below, snow-peaked mountains in the background, a bag or knapsack hanging from the staff.

Lower Panel, Right and Left Squares: Two spirit sigils leave uncolored, or use Prince and Princess color scales.

Lower Panel, Center Square: Lower section: **Sky Blue** behind the small **Yellow** triangle of Air. Upper section: bright **Pale Yellow** behind Hebrew letter **Aleph**.

Key XII—The Hanged Man
Spirit of the Mighty Waters

PRIMAL WATER

Traditional Image	On the Tree of Life
The figure of a hanged or crucified man	**Path 23 Joins Sephiroth 5 and 8 Stable Intelligence**
Hebrew Letter	*Color Scales:* **See Table 1**
Mother Letter: Mem	**King & Queen Predominate**
Meaning: **Water, Sea**	
	Musical Note: **G Sharp**
On the Cube of Space:	*Vowel Sound:* **"Mah"**
Creates and joins East & West	

The *TCM* Card: Has a background of **Deep Blue** (top half) and **Sea Green** (lower half). The arms of the cross are **Golden Yellow** and the 49 petals of the rose **Scarlet**. The barbs of the rose are **Bright Green.**

Central Figure: The Hanged Man is dressed in a **Blue** top and **Grey** or **Sea Green** shorts.

Additions or Changes: You may wish to add a bright **Golden** glory around his head, **Red** leggings, and **Yellow** socks.

Lower Panel, Right and Left Squares: Two spirit sigils leave uncolored, or use Prince and Princess color scales.

Lower Panel, Center Square: Lower section: **Sea Green** field behind the small **Deep Blue** triangle of **Water**. Upper section: **Deep Blue** behind Hebrew letter **Mem**.

Key XX—The Aeon

Spirit of the Primal Fire

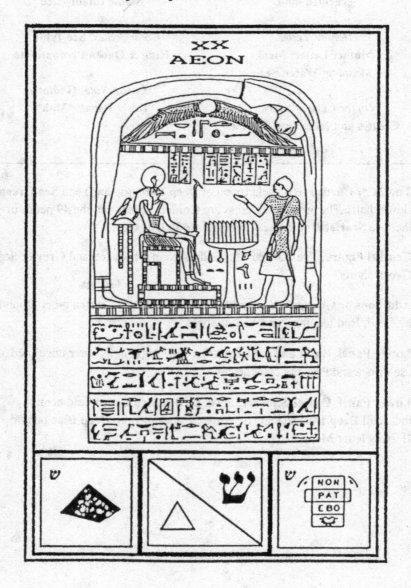

PRIMAL FIRE / SPIRIT

Traditional Image	*On the Tree of Life*
Angel Israfel blowing the last trumpet. The dead rising from their tombs.	**Path 31 Joins Sephiroth 10 and 8 Perpetual Intelligence**
	Color Scales: **See Table 1**
Hebrew Letter	**King & Queen Predominate**
Mother Letter: Shin	
Meaning: **Tooth**	*Musical Note:* **C**
	Vowel Sound: **"Shah"**
On the Cube of Space	
Creates and joins North & South	

The *TCM* Card: Has a background of **Orange Scarlet** and displays a reproduction of the Egyptian stele known as "The Stele of Revealing" or the "Stele of Ankh af-na Khonsu." Color images of the stele are easily found.

Central Figures on the Stele: Goddess Nuit is **Blue**; the skin of the seated God Horus is **Green**; the Sun on his head is **Red** and wrapped with a **Green** snake. The Sun of the Winged Solar Disk is **Red**. Priest wears a leopard skin. Offerings on the table are alternately **Red** and **Green**.

Additions or Changes: I do not suggest you add any other images to the stele itself. But feel free to add Fire-related images or symbols to the sides of the stele.

Lower Panel, Right and Left Squares: Two spirit sigils leave uncolored, or use Prince and Princess color scales.

Lower Panel, Center Square: Lower section: **Vermilion** behind the small **Orange Scarlet** triangle of Fire. Upper section: **Orange Scarlet** behind Hebrew letter **Shin**.

Special Note: Because the Aeon also represents the element *Spirit*, please add the symbol of Spirit (a small **White** circle with eight spokes) near the Hebrew letter **Shin**.

Meditation 3

Attunement Meditation upon Completion of the Mother Letter Trumps

Universe
Fool—Hanged Man—Aeon

You will need a pitch pipe or another means of determining various musical notes.

MUSIC?

In addition to four scales of light and color, each Hebrew letter and each tarot Trump vibrates at a frequency of *sound* and is assigned a particular musical note. In order for you to chant the various vowel sounds in this meditation, you will want to have a pitch pipe or electronic keyboard or other means of determining the appropriate pitches.

Be aware that this chanting will likely have an immediate and overtly powerful effect upon your consciousness and should not be omitted. (Once you actually do it, you will know exactly what I mean.)

I recommend you include this simple chant as part of your regular meditation warm-up routine.

1. Seated comfortably facing east, with your **Universe** card resting on your lap or in your shirt pocket, take three deep cleansing breaths and clap four times (1-3-3-3).

2. Blow an **A** on your pitch pipe, close your eyes, and try to hold the image of **Universe** card in your mind's eye.

3. Holding the image in your mind, take a deep breath and forcefully intone "THAH" (on A) until your breath is exhausted. Repeat three times.

4. You should feel a certain lightheaded "glow" around your head and body. This glow—this aura—is *you* radiating as the primal singularity.

5. Open your eyes, blow an **E** on your pitch pipe, and visualize the **Fool** card extending vertically through your body and piercing the ceiling and floor.

6. Holding the image in your mind, take a deep breath and forcefully intone "AAH" (on E) until your breath is exhausted. Repeat three times.

7. Again, you should feel a certain lightheaded glow around your head and body. This glow—this aura—is *you* as the **Fool**. Use your lightheaded glow as an energy to give life to your vertical **Fool** self.

8. Open your eyes, blow a **G sharp** on your pitch pipe, and visualize your **Hanged Man** card running horizontally from back to front through your body and piercing the walls in front (east) and back (west) of you.

9. Holding the image in your mind, take a deep breath and forcefully intone "MAH" (on G sharp) until your breath is exhausted. Repeat three times.

10. Again, you should feel a certain lightheaded glow around your head and body. This glow—this aura—is *you* as the **Hanged Man**. Use your lightheaded glow as an energy to give life to your horizontal **Hanged Man** self.

11. Open your eyes, blow a **C** on your pitch pipe, and visualize your **Aeon** card running horizontally left to right through your body and piercing the walls to your left (north) and right (south).

12. Holding the image in your mind, take a deep breath and forcefully intone "SHAH" (on C) until your breath is exhausted. Repeat three times.

13. Again, you should feel a certain lightheaded glow around your head and body. This glow—this aura—is *you* as the **Aeon**. Use your lightheaded glow as an energy to give life to your horizontal **Aeon** self.

14. Take three deep cleansing breaths. Intone the following:

    - Thah (A)

    - Aah (E)

- Mah (G sharp)

- Shah (C)

15. Continue this four-note mantra for as long as you wish, as you visualize yourself as the centered **Universe**, with the **Fool**, **Hanged Man**, and **Aeon** bursting from you to create dimensional space.

16. Clap four times (1-3-3-3).

CHAPTER 3

The Double Letter Trumps

The Double Letter Trumps are as follows:

I Magus—Mercury—ב

II High Priestess—Luna—ג

III Empress—Venus—ד

X Fortune—Jupiter—כ

XVI Tower—Mars—פ

XIX Sun—Sun—ר

XXI Universe—Saturn (and Earth)—ת

(Please see Appendix 2, Table 2, page 326 for a full list of correspondences beyond those discussed in this chapter.)

Key I—The Magus

Magus of Power

<table>
<tr><td>Traditional Image</td><td>On the Tree of Life</td></tr>
</table>

Traditional Image	*On the Tree of Life*
A fair youth with winged helmet &	**Path 12 Joins Sephiroth 1 and 3**
heels, equipped as a Magician,	**Intelligence of Transparency**
displays his art.	
	Color Scales: **See Table 2**
Hebrew Letter	**King & Queen Predominate**
Double Letter: Beth	
Meaning: **House**	*Musical Note:* **E**
	Vowel Sound: **"Bah"**
On the Cube of Space	
Above (ceiling)	

The *TCM* Card: Has a background of **Yellow**. On the table rests **Silver** Cup, a Sword, and reproduction of "The Stele of Revealing" (see the Aeon card).

The Central Figure: The Magus's robe is **Purple**, as is the rim of the pantacle behind his head. His wand is **Wood Brown** and surrounded with a glowing glory.

Additions or Changes: You may wish to add your own personal magical symbols or devices to the back wall. You may also wish to color his outer robe **Red** and the collar and interior sleeves **White**. You may also wish to add your own personal lamen or crest to the magician's robe.

Lower Panel, Right and Left Squares: Two spirit sigils leave uncolored, or use Prince and Princess color scales.

Lower Panel, Center Square: **Yellow** field behind Hebrew letter **Beth**; **Purple** field behind the symbol of **Mercury**.

Key II—The High Priestess
Priestess of the Silver Star

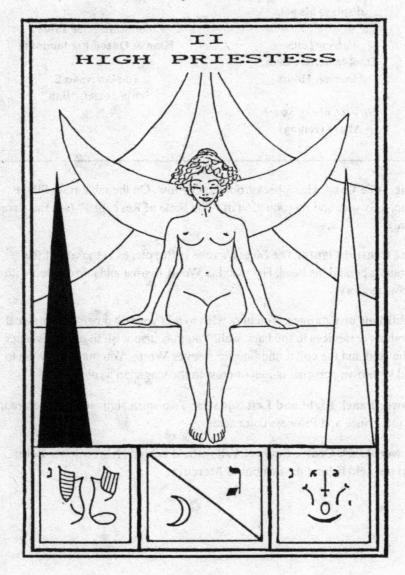

THE MOON

The *TCM* **Card:** Has a background of **Blue**. The altar veil is **Deep Blue** with **Silver** stars with **Pale Blue** lining.

The Central Figure: The High Priestess is unrobed and sits before a large **Silver** crescent Moon.

Additions or Changes: The High Priestess is "bare and rejoicing," but you may wish give her a **Blue** robe trimmed in **Silver**, a silver crown, pearls, or other lunar adornments. The **Black** pillar can show a **White** letter B (or Hebrew Beth), and the **White** pillar can show a **Black** letter J (or Hebrew Yod).

Lower Panel, Right and Left Squares: Two spirit sigils leave uncolored, or use Prince and Princess color scales.

Lower Panel, Center Square: Blue field behind Hebrew letter **Gimel**; **Silver** behind the symbol of the **Moon**.

Key III—The Empress
Daughter of the Mighty One

VENUS

Traditional Image	On the Tree of Life
Crowned with stars, a winged god-dess stands upon the Moon.	**Path 14 Joins Sephiroth 2 and 3 Illuminating Intelligence**
Hebrew Letter **Double Letter: Daleth** *Meaning:* **Door**	*Color Scales:* **See Table 2 King & Queen Predominate**
On the Cube of Space **East Wall**	*Musical Note:* **F#** *Vowel Sound:* **"Dah"**

The *TCM* Card: Has a **Sky Blue** sky and a **Brownish** garden temple.

The Central Figure: The Empress's dress is **Emerald Green** with a **Red** girdle and **Red** heart-shaped epaulets at her shoulders. The crescent Moon at her feet is **Silver**. The roses in her garden are **Red.**

Additions or Changes: The temple garden in the background can be adorned to your liking.

Lower Panel, Right and Left Squares: Two spirit sigils leave uncolored, or use Prince and Princess color scales.

Lower Panel, Center Square: Emerald Green behind Hebrew letter **Daleth**; **Sky Blue** behind the symbol of **Venus**.

Key X—Fortune

Lord of the Forces of Life

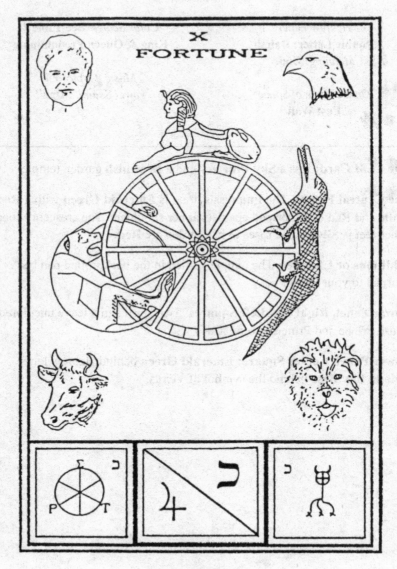

JUPITER

Traditional Image **A wheel of six shafts whereon** **revolve the triad of Hermanubis,** **Sphinx, and Typhon**	*On the Tree of Life* **Path 21 Joins Sephiroth 4 and 7** **Intelligence of Conciliation**
	Color Scales: **See Table 2** **King & Queen Predominate**
Hebrew Letter **Double Letter: Kaph** *Meaning:* **Closed wand (palm)**	*Musical Note:* **B Flat** *Vowel Sound:* **"Kah"**
On the Cube of Space **West Wall**	

The *TCM* Card: Has a background of **Sky Blue** with **Purplish** clouds. The elemental emblems of the Kerubic (Fixed) Signs of the zodiac appear at the corners: Leo (Fixed Fire) at the lower right, Scorpio (Fixed Water) at the upper right, Aquarius (Fixed Air) at the upper left, and Taurus (Fixed Earth) at the lower left.

The Central Figures: The wheel is divided by twelve spokes, and each section is subdivided in three to represent the thirty-six decans of the zodiac and the thirty-six Small cards of the tarot. The Alchemical Ape (Mercury), Crocodile (Sulfur), and Sphinx (Salt) perpetually turn the wheel in their effort to reach the top.

Additions or Changes: Clouds surrounding the corner Kerubic beasts.

Lower Panel, Right and Left Squares: Two spirit sigils leave uncolored, or use Prince and Princess color scales.

Lower Panel, Center Square: **Violet** behind Hebrew letter **Kaph**; **Blue** behind the symbol of **Jupiter**.

Key XVI—The Tower (House of God)

Lord of the Hosts of the Mighty

MARS

Traditional Image	On the Tree of Life
A tower struck by forked lightning	**Path 27 Joins Sephiroth 7 and 8**
	Exciting Intelligence
Hebrew Letter	
Double Letter: Peh	*Color Scales:* **See Table 2**
Meaning: **Mouth**	**King & Queen Predominate**
On the Cube of Space	*Musical Note:* **C**
North Wall	*Vowel Sound:* **"Pah"**

The *TCM* Card: Shows a **Black** sky and a **Scarlet** pyramid, before which is a red-crowned Tower blasted by a lightning bolt of **Scarlet** from an orb of flashing **Reds** and **Yellows**.

The Central Figure: A **Reddish** image of Shiva Nataraja Lord of the Dance.

Additions or Changes: You may wish to add storm clouds and a number (3, 7, 12) of small Yod-shaped flames falling from the sky. You also could add small images of two individuals falling from the Tower.

Lower Panel, Right and Left Squares: Two spirit sigils leave uncolored, or use Prince and Princess color scales.

Lower Panel, Center Square: **Scarlet** behind Hebrew letter **Peh**; **Red** behind the symbol of **Mars**.

Key XIX—The Sun

Lord of the Fire of the World

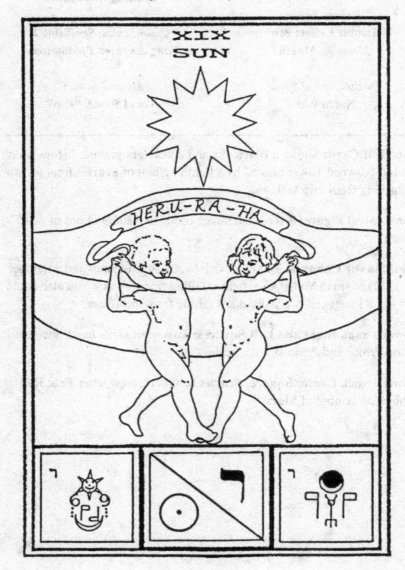

THE SUN

Traditional Image	On the Tree of Life
The Sun.	**Path 30 Joins Sephiroth 8 and 9**
Two children dance before	**Collecting Intelligence**
a red wall.	
	Color Scales: **See Table 2**
Hebrew Letter	**King & Queen Predominate**
Double Letter: Resh	
Meaning: **Face, Head**	*Musical Note:* **D**
	Vowel Sound: **"Rah"**
On the Cube of Space	
South Wall	

The *TCM* Card: Has a bright **Golden-Yellow** Sun against a clear **Sky Blue** sky directly above a grassy hill of **Bright Green** ringed by a **Red** brick wall.

The Central Figures: Two children in their innocence dance before the wall. They hold a **Golden Yellow** banner that clearly says "Heru-ra-ha" (the Horus twins of Egyptian mythology: the *passive* Hoor-paar-kraat and the *active* Ra-Hoor-Khuit).

Additions or Changes: Additional rays from the Sun, sunflowers, mortar lines to the brick wall.

Lower Panel, Right and Left Squares: Two spirit sigils leave uncolored, or use Prince and Princess color scales.

Lower Panel, Center Square: Orange behind Hebrew Letter **Resh**; **Golden Yellow** behind the symbol of the **Sun**.

Meditation 4

Attunement Meditation upon Completion of the Double Letter Trumps

Magus—High Priestess—Empress—Fortune

Tower—Sun

(Have a pitch pipe at hand.)

1. Seated comfortably, facing east, with your **Universe** card resting on your lap or in your shirt pocket, take three deep cleansing breaths and clap seven times (3-3-3–1–3-3-3).

2. Blow an **E** on your pitch pipe, close your eyes, and visualize your **Magus** card on the ceiling above you.

3. Holding the image in your mind, take a deep breath and forcefully intone "BAH" (on E) until your breath is exhausted. Repeat three times.

4. Once again, you should feel the lightheaded glow around your head and body. This glow—this aura—is you as the **Magus**. Use your glow as an energy to give life to the **Magus** you on the ceiling.

5. Blow an **E**—yes, E again[1]—on your pitch pipe, close your eyes, and visualize your **High Priestess** card on the floor beneath you.

6. Holding the image in your mind, take a deep breath, and forcefully intone "GAH" (on G sharp) until your breath is exhausted. Repeat three times.

7. The lightheaded glow around your head and body is *you* as the **High Priestess**. Use your glow as an energy to give life to the **High Priestess** you on the floor.

8. Blow an **F sharp** on your pitch pipe, close your eyes, and visualize your **Empress** card on the wall directly in front of you (east).

9. Holding the image in your mind, take a deep breath and forcefully intone "DAH" (on F sharp) until your breath is exhausted. Repeat three times.

10. Once again, use the glow of your aura to give life to the **Empress** *you* on the wall in front of you.

11. Blow a **B flat** on your pitch pipe, close your eyes, and visualize your **Fortune** card on the wall directly behind you (west).

12. Holding the image in your mind, take a deep breath and forcefully intone "KAH" (on B flat) until your breath is exhausted. Repeat three times.

13. Again, use the glow of your aura as energy to spin the wheel of the **Fortune** you on the wall behind you.

14. Blow a **C** on your pitch pipe, close your eyes, and visualize your **Tower** card on wall to your left (north).

15. Holding the image in your mind, take a deep breath and forcefully intone "PAH" (on C) until your breath is exhausted. Repeat three times.

16. Once again, use this aura as an energy to give life to the **Tower** you on the wall to your left.

17. Blow a **D** on your pitch pipe, close your eyes, and visualize your **Sun** card on the wall to your right (south).

18. Holding the image in your mind, take a deep breath, and forcefully intone "RAH" (on D) until your breath is exhausted. Repeat three times.

19. Once again, you should feel a certain lightheaded glow around your head and body. This glow—this aura—is *you* shining as the **Sun** on the wall to your right.

20. With your pitch pipe in hand, take three deep cleansing breaths. If possible, intone the following:

    - Bah (E)

    - Gah (G sharp)

    - Dah (F sharp)

    - Kah (B flat)

- Pah (C)
- Rah (D)

21. Continue this six-note mantra for as long as you wish, as you visualize yourself as the centered **Universe** surrounded by the **Magus** above, the **High Priestess** below, the **Empress** before you, **Fortune** behind you, the **Tower** on your left, and the **Sun** on your right.

22. Clap seven times (3-3-3–1–3-3-3).

23. Make special note of your dreams or other subtle changes in your consciousness.

———————————————

CHAPTER 4

The Simple Letter Trumps

The Simple Letter Trumps are as follows:

IV Emperor—Aries—צ (ה*)

V Hierophant—Taurus—ו

VI Lovers—Gemini—ז

VII Chariot—Cancer—ח

XI Lust—Leo—ט

IX Hermit—Virgo—י

VIII Justice—Libra—ל

XIII Death—Scorpio—נ

XIV Art—Sagittarius—ם

XV Devil—Capricorn—ע

XVII Star—Aquarius—ה (צ*)

XVIII Moon—Pisces—ק

(Please see Appendix 2, Table 3, page 327 for a full list of correspondences beyond those discussed in this chapter.)

Key IV—The Emperor
Sun of the Morning, Chief Among the Mighty

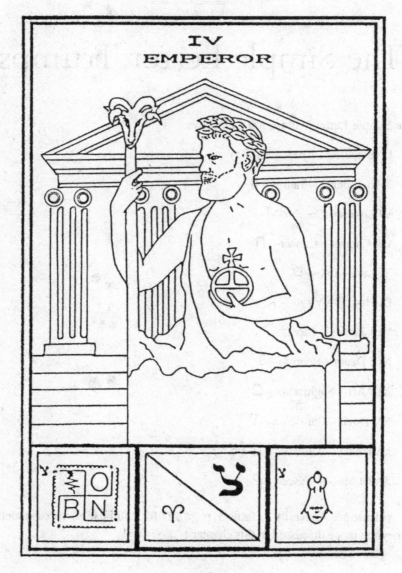

ARIES

Traditional Image	On the Tree of Life
A flame-clad god bearing equivalent symbols	**Path 15 Joins Sephiroth 2 and 6 Natural Intelligence**

Hebrew Letter	*Color Scales:* **See Table 3**
Simple Letter: *Tzaddi (or Heh)	**King & Queen Predominate**
Meaning: ***Fishhook** (or **Window**)	

On the Cube of Space
North-East Edge

Musical Note for Path 15: **C**
Vowel Sound for Path 15: **"Hah"**

The *TCM* Card: Has a background of **Scarlet**. The Emperor sits before five steps leading up to a Romanesque civic building with four columns with Ionic capitals.

The Central Figure: The Emperor emerges as a statue from a stone cube. He holds a **Green** and **Gold** orb and a baton capped with a ram's head.

Additions or Changes: If you wish, you can add imperial vestments to the body and head of the Emperor.

Lower Panel, Right and Left Squares: Two spirit sigils leave uncolored, or use Prince and Princess color scales.

Lower Panel, Center Square: Scarlet behind Hebrew letter **Tzaddi;**[1] **Red** behind the symbol of **Aries**.

Key V—The Hierophant
Magus of the Eternal

TAURUS

Traditional Image	On the Tree of Life
Between the pillars sits an Ancient	**Path 16 Joins Sephiroth 2 and 4**
	Triumphal Intelligence
Hebrew Letter	
Simple Letter: Vav	*Color Scales:* **See Table 3**
Meaning: **Nail**	**King & Queen Predominate**
On the Cube of Space	*Musical Note:* **C Sharp**
South-East Edge	*Vowel Sound:* **"Vah"**

The *TCM* Card: Shows **Blue** sky over **Sandy Brown** desert. Palm trees are **Green** and **Brown**. Tent its **Blue** with **White** trim and opening.

The Central Figures: The Hierophant is robed in **Red-Orange** trimmed in **Gold**. His turban is **Golden Yellow**. The two acolytes are robed in **Black** with **White** turbans.

Additions or Changes: You may wish to embellish the Hierophant's robe with symbols suggesting Taurus and the element **Earth**.

Lower Panel, Right and Left Squares: Two spirit sigils leave uncolored, or use Prince and Princess color scales.

Lower Panel, Center Square: Red Orange behind Hebrew letter **Vav**; **Deep Indigo** behind the symbol of **Taurus**.

Key VI—The Lovers
Children of the Voice / Oracle of the Mighty Gods

GEMINI

<table>
<tr><td>Traditional Image
A prophet, young, and in the Sign of Osiris Risen</td><td>On the Tree of Life
Path 17 Joins Sephiroth 3 and 6 Disposing One</td></tr>
<tr><td>Hebrew Letter
Simple Letter: Zain
Meaning: **Sword**</td><td>Color Scales: **See Table 3**
King & Queen Predominate</td></tr>
<tr><td>On the Cube of Space
East-Above Edge</td><td>Musical Note: **D**
Vowel Sound: **"Zah"**</td></tr>
</table>

The *TCM* Card: A reproduction (on **Papyrus Beige**) of the classic Egyptian vignette of the god Osiris Risen supported and shielded by the goddesses Isis and Nephthys.

The Central Figures: Osiris is wrapped in **White** mummy cerements and crowned with a **Golden** crown. The headdresses of the goddesses are also **Gold**. The winged scarab beetle hovers above the central figures. The beetle's body is **Red**.

Additions or Changes: I do not suggest you add any other images to the vignette itself. But you may feel free to richly color the feathers of the goddesses' wings and those of the scarab.

Lower Panel, Right and Left Squares: Two spirit sigils leave uncolored, or use Prince and Princess color scales.

Lower Panel, Center Square: Orange behind Hebrew letter **Zain**; **Pale Mauve** behind the symbol of **Gemini**.

Key VII—The Chariot

Child of the Powers of the Waters / Lord of the Triumph of the Light

CANCER

Traditional Image	*On the Tree of Life*
A young and holy king under the starry canopy	**Path 18 Joins Sephiroth 3 and 5 House of Influence Intelligence**
Hebrew Letter	*Color Scales:* **See Table 3**
Simple Letter: Cheth	**King & Queen Predominate**
Meaning: **Fence**	
	Musical Note: **D Sharp**
On the Cube of Space	*Vowel Sound:* **"Chah"**
East-Below Edge	

The *TCM* Card: Has a background of **Light Amber.**

The Central Figures: An armored Charioteer bears the Holy Grail. His flowing cape is **Red** lined in pure **White.** He is stands in a crescent Moon-shaped chariot beneath a starry canopy supported by eight **Amber** pillars. The wheels of chariot are **Red.** In front of the Chariot are two Egyptian sphinxes (a **White** one on the right, a **Black** one on the left).

Additions or Changes: The Holy Grail itself can be enhanced to make it more radiant.

Lower Panel, Right and Left Squares: Two spirit sigils leave uncolored, or use Prince and Princess color scales.

Lower Panel, Center Square: Amber behind Hebrew letter **Cheth; Maroon** behind the symbol of **Cancer.**

Key XI[2]—Lust[3]

Daughter of the Flaming Sword

LEO

Traditional Image	On the Tree of Life
A smiling woman holds the open jaws of a fierce and powerful lion.	**Path 19 Joins Sephiroth 5 and 6 Intelligence of all the activities of the Spiritual Being**
Hebrew Letter	
Simple Letter: Teth	*Color Scales:* **See Table 3**
Meaning: **Serpent**	**King & Queen Predominate**
On the Cube of Space	*Musical Note:* **E**
North-Above Edge	*Vowel Sound:* **"Tah"**

The *TCM* Card: Has a background of **Deep Purple**.

The Central Figures: The naked goddess Babalon (with flaming **Red** hair) sits astride a lion-headed serpent. The lion's head is **Tawny Yellow** and its body **Greenish-Yellow**. The scales of the serpent can be colorfully enhanced and shaded with **Grey** and **Purple** overtones.

Additions or Changes: You may wish to add the image of Holy Grail itself filled with blood . . . but *not* spilled blood.

Lower Panel, Right and Left Squares: Two spirit sigils leave uncolored, or use Prince and Princess color scales.

Lower Panel, Center Square: Greenish-Yellow behind Hebrew letter **Teth**; **Deep Purple** behind the symbol of **Leo**.

Key IX—The Hermit

Prophet of the Eternal / Magus of the Voice of Power

VIRGO

<table>
<tr><td>

Traditional Image
Wrapped in a cloak and cowl, an Ancient walketh, bearing a lamp and staff.

Hebrew Letter
Simple Letter: Yod
Meaning: **Hand**

On the Cube of Space
North-Below Edge

</td><td>

On the Tree of Life
Path 20 Joins Sephiroth 4 and 6
Intelligence of Will

Color Scales: **See Table 3**
King & Queen Predominate

Musical Note: **F**
Vowel Sound: **"Yah"**

</td></tr>
</table>

The *TCM* Card: Has a **Black** background.

The Central Figures: The bearded face of the hooded Hermit and a glowing **Yellow** unicursal hexagram as his lamp.

Additions or Changes: You may wish to add (or suggest the presence of) a staff and a mountaintop landscape in the background.

Lower Panel, Right and Left Squares: Two spirit sigils leave uncolored, or use Prince and Princess color scales.

Lower Panel, Center Square: Yellowish Green behind Hebrew letter **Yod**; **Slate Grey** behind the symbol of **Virgo**.

Key VIII⁴—Justice

Daughter of the Lords of Truth / Ruler of the Balance

LIBRA

Traditional Image	On the Tree of Life
A conventional figure of Justice with scales and balances	**Path 22 Joins Sephiroth 5 and 6 Faithful Intelligence**

Hebrew Letter	Color Scales: **See Table 3**
Simple Letter: Lamed *Meaning:* **Oxgoad**	**King & Queen Predominate**

On the Cube of Space
North-West Edge

Musical Note: **F Sharp**
Vowel Sound: **"Lah"**

The *TCM* Card: Has a **Black** and **White** checkerboard background.

The Central Figures: The goddess Thmaist, dancing in an **Emerald Green** dress and balanced on toe point. She holds the scales and balances. She is superimposed upon a large **Yellow** or **Pale Green** vesica piscis and the downward-pointing Sword of Justice.

Additions or Changes: Any additions or alterations to the card should not disturb the fundamental balance of images. The Feather of Maat would be appropriate.

Lower Panel, Right and Left Squares: Two spirit sigils leave uncolored, or use Prince and Princess color scales.

Lower Panel, Center Square: Emerald Green behind Hebrew letter **Lamed**; **Blue** behind the symbol of **Libra**.

Key XIII—Death

Children of the Great Transformers / Lord of the Gates of Death

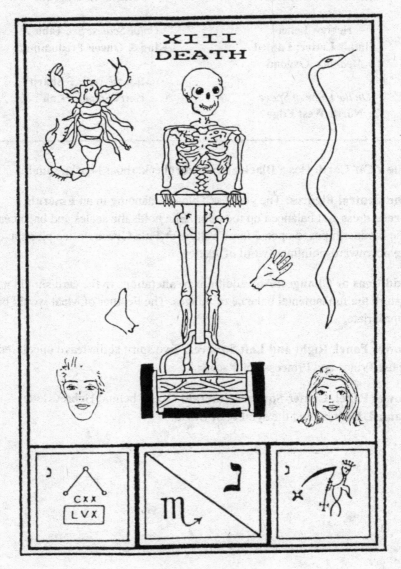

SCORPIO

Traditional Image	On the Tree of Life
A skeleton with a Tau-shaped scythe mowing men	**Path 24 Joins Sephiroth 6 and 7 Imaginative Intelligence**
Hebrew Letter **Simple Letter: Nun** *Meaning:* **Fish**	*Color Scales:* **See Table 3 King & Queen Predominate**
On the Cube of Space **South-East Edge**	*Musical Note:* **G** *Vowel Sound:* **"Nah"**

The *TCM* Card: Background has a **Dark Red** sky above a **Green** lawn or field.

The Central Figures: The skeleton of Death pushes a lawn mower with a Tau handle. Human heads and body parts strew the landscape. In the sky is a scorpion and a serpent (symbols of Scorpio).

Additions or Changes: Put in a bright **Yellow Orange** setting Sun. You will have to carefully draw the bony fingers of the skeleton's hands around the lawn mower's handle. You may also wish to add in the sky an eagle (or eagle's head) as another emblem of Scorpio.

Lower Panel, Right and Left Squares: Two spirit sigils leave uncolored, or use Prince and Princess color scales.

Lower Panel, Center Square: Green Blue behind Hebrew letter **Nun**; **Dull Brown** behind the symbol of **Scorpio**.

Key XIV—Art

Daughter of the Reconcilers / Bringer-Forth of Life

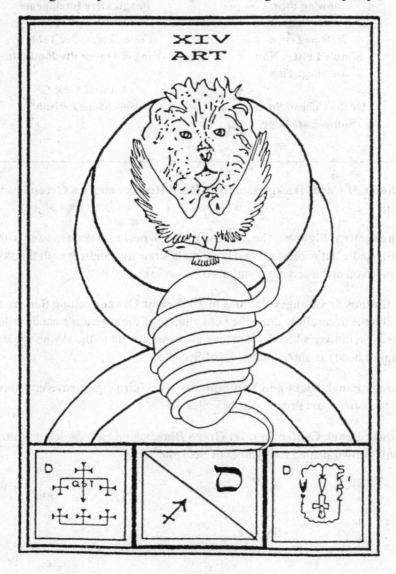

SAGITTARIUS

Traditional Image	On the Tree of Life
The figure of Diana Huntress	**Path 25 Joins Sephiroth 6 and 9**
	Intelligence of Probation
Hebrew Letter	**or Tentative One**
Simple Letter: Samekh	
Meaning: **Prop, Tent Pole**	*Color Scales:* **See Table 3**
	King & Queen Predominate
On the Cube of Space	
West-Above Edge	*Musical Note:* **G Sharp**
	Vowel Sound: **"Sah"**

The *TCM* Card: Has a background of **Blue**, upon which is a large **Yellow** Sun, caressed by a **Silver** Moon, above a **Rainbow**.

The Central Figures: A large egg wrapped by a **Green** serpent. A **White** eagle is perched on the serpent's head. A **Red** lion is embraced by the eagle's wings.

Additions or Changes: All **seven colors of the Rainbow** must be represented.

Lower Panel, Right and Left Squares: Two spirit sigils leave uncolored, or use Prince and Princess color scales.

Lower Panel, Center Square: Blue behind Hebrew letter **Samekh**; **Yellow** behind the symbol of **Sagittarius**.

Key XV—The Devil
Lord of the Gates of Matter / Child of the Forces of Time

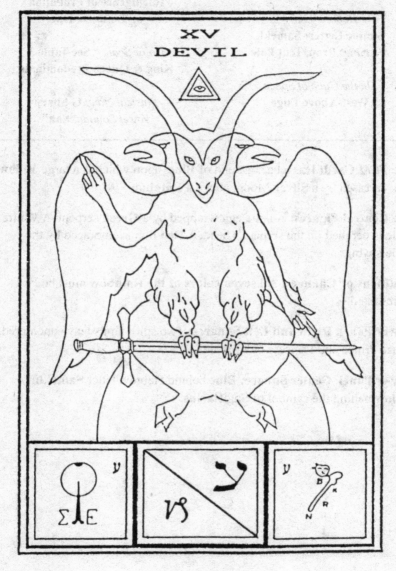

CAPRICORN

Traditional Image	On the Tree of Life
The figure of Pan or Priapus	**Path 26 Joins Sephiroth 6 and 8**
	Renovating Intelligence

Hebrew Letter	
Simple Letter: Ayin	*Color Scales:* **See Table 3**
Meaning: **Eye**	**King & Queen Predominate**

On the Cube of Space	*Musical Note:* **A**
West-Below Edge	*Vowel Sound:* **"Oyoy"**

The *TCM* Card: Has a background of marbled **Indigo** and **Grey**.

The Central Figures: Seated on a terrestrial globe is the classic image of a horned Baphomet projected and superimposed upon the Masonic **Black** double-headed eagle perched on the blade of a **Black** sword. Baphomet's body is **Cold Dark Grey**, and its face is **White**. Above and between the horns of Baphomet and above the heads of the eagle is a **Black** triangle with the all-seeing eye of God.

Additions or Changes: The symbol of Saturn might be applied to Baphomet's belly. Be sure to shade the breasts so one is obviously male and one female.

Lower Panel, Right and Left Squares: Two spirit sigils leave uncolored, or use Prince and Princess color scales.

Lower Panel, Center Square: Indigo behind Hebrew letter **Ayin**; **Black** behind the symbol of **Capricorn**.

Key XVII—The Star

Daughter of the Firmament / Dweller between the Waters

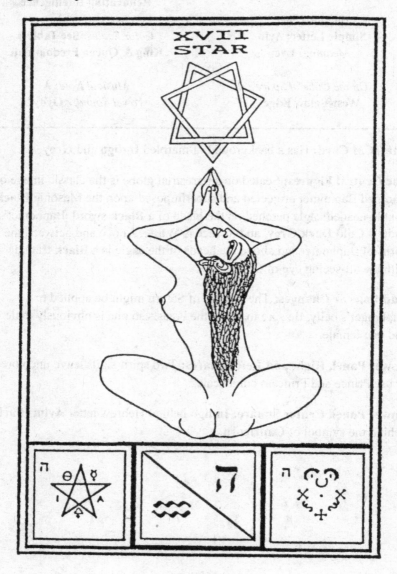

AQUARIUS

Traditional Image	On the Tree of Life
The figure of a water-nymph disporting herself	**Path 28 Joins Sephiroth 7 and 9 Constituting Intelligence**
Hebrew Letter	*Color Scales:* **See Table 3**
Simple Letter: *Heh (or Tzaddi) *Meaning:* ***Window (or Fishhook)**	**King & Queen Predominate**
	Musical Note for Path 28:
On the Cube of Space	**B Flat**
South-Above Edge	*Vowel Sound for Path 28:* **"Tzah"**

The *TCM* Card: Has a background of **Dark Violet.**

The Central Figure: The naked goddess Shakti embracing her invisible lover, Shiva, who is seen here as the seven-pointed Star of Babalon.

Additions or Changes: Add galaxies of **Silver** stars streaming from the nipple of her breast to populate the night sky. Try to make it very apparent that the stars of the universe are streaming from her breast.

Lower Panel, Right and Left Squares: Two spirit sigils leave uncolored, or use Prince and Princess color scales.

Lower Panel, Center Square: Violet behind Hebrew Letter **Heh;**[5] **Sky Blue** behind the symbol of **Aquarius.**

Key XVIII—The Moon

Ruler of the Flux and Reflux / Child of the Sons of the Mighty

PISCES

THE TAROT ARCHITECT

Traditional Image **The waning Moon**	*On the Tree of Life* **Path 15 Joins Sephiroth 7 and 10** **Corporal Intelligence**
Hebrew Letter **Simple Letter: Qoph** *Meaning:* **Back of head**	*Color Scales:* **See Table 3** **King & Queen Predominate**
On the Cube of Space **South-Below Edge**	*Musical Note:* **B** *Vowel Sound:* **"Quah"**

The *TCM* Card: Shows new or eclipsed **Blood Red** Moon. It rises between two **Stone-Colored** pyramids and illuminates a path through the darkness to the water's edge, to where a **Crimson** scarab, the Sun in its claws, climbs out of the water and onto the path.

The Central Figures: Two figures of the jackal-headed god Anubis flank the path.

Additions or Changes: Add Yod-shaped drops of blood falling from the sky.

Lower Panel, Right and Left Squares: Two spirit sigils leave uncolored, or use Prince and Princess color scales.

Lower Panel, Center Square: Crimson behind Hebrew letter **Qoph**; **Buff,** flecked **Silver-White,** behind the symbol of **Pisces**.

Meditation 5

Attunement Meditation upon Completion of the Simple Letter Trumps

Emperor—Hierophant—Lovers—Chariot—Lust—Hermit

Justice—Death—Art—Devil—Star—Moon

(Have a pitch pipe at hand.)

[Note: This meditation is based on the traditional Hebrew assignments outlined in the Sepher Yetzirah. The Emperor will remain as Heh, and the Star will remain as Tzaddi.]

1. Select a room (preferably a square or rectangular room) in your home or temple. Seat yourself comfortably facing **east**.

2. With your **Universe** card resting on your lap or in your shirt pocket, take three deep cleansing breaths and clap twelve times (4-4-4-4—4-4-4-4—4-4-4-4).

3. Look up to the ceiling and imagine the image of the **Magus** card looking down upon you; he holds his wand to heaven with his right hand and points down at you with his left hand as if to bless your meditation.

4. Now look down to the floor and see a pool of deep blue water and the shimmering image of the **High Priestess** serenely looking up at you.

5. Gaze now directly in front of you to the east. Imagine for a moment the image of the **Empress** card. See her green garden as a gateway to the wonders of this magical meditation.

6. Next, in your mind's eye look directly behind you (west) and see the spinning wheel of **Fortune** against a wall of bright violet.

7. Now turn slightly to your left (north). Imagine for a moment the image of the **Tower** card. Feel its thundering power shake the northern wall.

8. Now turn slightly to your right (south). Feel the bright warmth of the **Sun** card. Listen to the laughter of innocent twin children.

9. When you have this whole scene comfortably fixed in your mind, take a deep breath and return your attention to the east.

10. Now imagine yourself looking slightly to your left (to the vertical edge of the room) where the east wall meets the north wall.

11. Blow a **C** on your pitch pipe, close your eyes, and visualize your **Emperor** card standing as the North-East edge of the room.

12. Holding the Emperor's image in your mind, take a deep breath and forcefully intone "HAH" (on **C**) until your breath is exhausted. Repeat three times.

13. You should feel a certain lightheaded glow around your head and body. This glow—this aura—is *you* as the **Emperor**. Use your glow as an energy to give life to the image.

14. Now look slightly to your right (to the vertical edge of the room) where the east wall meets the south wall.

15. Blow **C sharp** on your pitch pipe, close your eyes, and visualize your **Hierophant** card standing as the South-East edge of the room.

16. Holding the image in your mind, take a deep breath, and forcefully intone "VAH" (on **C sharp**) until your breath is exhausted. Repeat three times.

17. You should feel a certain lightheaded glow around your head and body. This glow—this aura—is *you* as the **Hierophant**. Use your glow as an energy to give life to the image.

18. Still facing east, look up and directly in front of you to the horizontal edge of the room where the east wall meets the ceiling.

19. Blow a **D** on your pitch pipe, close your eyes, and visualize your **Lovers** card spanning the East-Ceiling edge of the room.

20. Holding the image in your mind, take a deep breath and forcefully intone "ZAH" (on **D**) until your breath is exhausted. Repeat three times.

21. You should feel a certain lightheaded glow around your head and body. This glow—this aura—is *you* as the **Lovers**. Use your glow as an energy to give life to the image.

22. Still facing east, look down and directly in front of you to the horizontal edge of the floor where the east wall meets the floor.

23. Blow a **D sharp** on your pitch pipe, close your eyes, and visualize your **Chariot** card spanning the East-Floor edge of the room.

24. Holding the image in your mind, take a deep breath and forcefully intone "CHAH" (on **D sharp**) until your breath is exhausted. Repeat three times.

25. You should feel a certain lightheaded glow around your head and body. This glow—this aura—is *you* as the **Chariot**. Use your glow as an energy to give life to the image.

26. Still facing east, look above you and slightly to your left to the horizontal edge of the room where the ceiling meets the north wall.

27. Blow an **E** on your pitch pipe, close your eyes, and visualize your **Lust** card spanning the North-Ceiling edge of the room.

28. Holding the image in your mind, take a deep breath and forcefully intone "TAH" (on **E**) until your breath is exhausted. Repeat three times.

29. You should feel a certain lightheaded glow around your head and body. This glow—this aura—is *you* as the **Lust**. Use your glow as an energy to give life to the image.

30. Still facing east, look down and slightly to your left to the horizontal edge of the room where the floor meets the north wall.

31. Blow an **F** on your pitch pipe, close your eyes, and visualize your **Hermit** card spanning the North-Floor edge of the room.

32. Holding the image in your mind, take a deep breath and forcefully intone "YAH" (on **F**) until your breath is exhausted. Repeat three times.

33. You should feel a certain lightheaded glow around your head and body. This glow—this aura—is *you* as the **Hermit**. Use your glow as an energy to give life to the image.

34. Now, readjust your chair or your seating position so you are facing the *west* wall of your room.

35. Gaze for a moment at the (west) wall in front of you. Imagine for a moment the image of the **Fortune** card. Think for a moment how great wheel is perpetually in motion like the Sun sweeping around the belt of the zodiac.

36. Still facing west, look slightly to your right to the vertical edge of the room where the north wall meets the west wall.

37. Blow **F sharp** on your pitch pipe, close your eyes, and visualize your **Justice** card standing as the North-West edge of the room.

38. Holding the image in your mind, take a deep breath and forcefully intone "LAH" (on **F sharp**) until your breath is exhausted. Repeat three times.

39. You should feel a certain lightheaded glow around your head and body. This glow—this aura—is *you* as **Justice**. Use your glow as an energy to give life to the image.

40. Still facing west, look slightly to your left to the vertical edge of the room where the south wall meets the west wall.

41. Blow a **G** on your pitch pipe, close your eyes, and visualize your **Death** card standing as the South-West edge of the room.

42. Holding the image in your mind, take a deep breath and forcefully intone "NAH" (on **G**) until your breath is exhausted. Repeat three times.

43. You should feel a certain lightheaded glow around your head and body. This glow—this aura—is *you* as the **Death**. Use your glow as an energy to give life to the image.

44. Still facing west, look up directly in front of you to the horizontal edge of the room where the west wall meets the ceiling.

45. Blow **G sharp** on your pitch pipe, close your eyes, and visualize your **Art** card spanning the West-Ceiling edge of the room.

46. Holding the image in your mind, take a deep breath and forcefully intone "SAH" (on **G sharp**) until your breath is exhausted. Repeat three times.

47. You should feel a certain lightheaded glow around your head and body. This glow—this aura—is *you* as **Art**. Use your glow as an energy to give life to the image.

48. Still facing west, look down directly in front of you to the horizontal edge of the room where the west wall meets the floor.

49. Blow an **A** on your pitch pipe, close your eyes, and visualize your **Devil** card spanning the West-Ceiling edge of the room.

50. Holding the image in your mind, take a deep breath and forcefully intone "AYAH" (on **A**) until your breath is exhausted. Repeat three times.

51. You should feel a certain lightheaded glow around your head and body. This glow—this aura—is *you* as the **Devil**. Use your glow as an energy to give life to the image.

52. Still facing west, look above you and slightly to your left to the horizontal edge of the room where the ceiling meets the south wall.

53. Blow **B flat** on your pitch pipe, close your eyes, and visualize your **Star** card spanning the South-Ceiling edge of the room.

54. Holding the image in your mind, take a deep breath and forcefully intone "TZAH" (on **B flat**) until your breath is exhausted. Repeat three times.

55. You should feel a certain lightheaded glow around your head and body. This glow—this aura—is *you* as the **Star**. Use your glow as an energy to give life to the image.

56. Still facing west, look down and slightly to your left to the horizontal edge of the room where the floor meets the south wall.

57. Blow **B** on your pitch pipe, close your eyes, and visualize your **Moon** card spanning the South-Floor edge of the room.

58. Holding the image in your mind, take a deep breath and forcefully intone "QUAH" (on **B**) until your breath is exhausted. Repeat three times.

59. You should feel a certain lightheaded glow around your head and body. This glow—this aura—is *you* as the **Moon**. Use your glow as an energy to give life to the image.

60. Take three deep cleansing breaths and clearly experience yourself as the primal Universe center of the cube with the twelve edges glowing like neon light all around you. Savor the moment.

61. Pick up your pitch pipe and (if possible) sing the twelve words in order:

   - Hah (C)
   - Vah (C sharp)
   - Zah (D)
   - Chah (D sharp)
   - Tah (E)
   - Yah (F)
   - Lah (F sharp)
   - Nah (G)
   - Sah (G sharp)
   - Ayah (A)
   - Tzah (B flat)
   - Quah (B)

62. Continue this mantra for as long as you wish. (Note: For most people this twelve-note melody will be particularly difficult to replicate. You may wish to simple intone all twelve on a single note or a melody of your liking.)

63. Clap twelve times (4-4-4-4—4-4-4-4—4-4-4-4).

64. Note your dreams or other changes in consciousness.

CHAPTER 5

Introduction to the Lesser Arcana

The cosmic duty of the elements is to mix with each other in infinite combinations and proportions in order to knit manifest creation together.

T he foundation of the Lesser Arcana of tarot is built primarily using our first working tool, יהוה, Yod Heh Vav Heh. As we learned in Book I, each of the four suits epitomizes one letter of the Great Name, and represents

- one of four *Qabalistic Worlds*

- one of four *Parts of the Human Soul*

- one of four primary *elements* (Fire, Water, Air, Earth)

- and one tarot *suit* (Wands, Cups, Swords, Disks)

The four Aces are the superstars and mother ships of their respective suits. They are the primary representatives of יהוה, Yod Heh Vav Heh, in the elemental cosmos. Each Ace contains within itself:

- a full set of four Court Cards[1] (a miniature subset יהוה, Yod Heh Vav Heh)

- and nine Small Cards (Twos–Tens) of the suit

Elements—Four or Five?

In addition to four elements, Qabalistic Worlds, and Parts of the Soul, the Aces represent a fifth super-element, *Spirit*, which vivifies, binds, separates, and permeates the cards of all four elemental suits.

Just as Kether is the primal singularity and supreme emanation out of which develop the remaining nine sephiroth of the Tree of Life, so the entire Lesser Arcana emanates *from* and exist *within* the Aces.

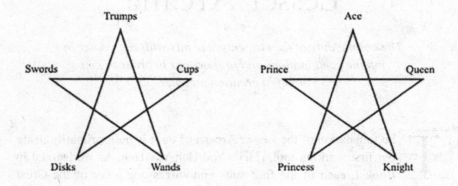

Figure 30.
Spirit is represented as the top point of the pentagram.
The Trumps represent Spirit relative to the four suits.
The Ace represents Spirit relative to the four Court Cards.

The Aces are the purest representatives of their element, but they are not completely pure. Indeed, if each element were not marbled with minute quantities (and qualities) of the other three elements, it would be unable to attract and combine with others to form the matter and energy necessary for a properly functioning phenomenal universe. Simply put, there would be no creation, with its infinite variety, if the individual elements remained completely unalloyed and isolated from one another.

Cosmic Duty

The most important thing to remember when dealing with the elements is that it is their *cosmic duty* to perpetually mix with each other in infinite combinations and proportions in order to knit manifest creation together.

The four Court Cards live inside their respective Ace and embody the elemental mixing process in the guise of four complex and eclectic family members. (Please review chapter 4 of Book I.)

Why Should I Create My Lesser Arcana in This Peculiar Order?

You are now probably anxious to begin work on your own Lesser Arcana cards. Once again, I'm going to suggest you bring them to life in a sequential order that may appear rather peculiar at first. This sequence harmonizes closely with the working-tool dynamics of both the יהוה, Yod Heh Vav Heh, and the Tree of Life qabalistic formulae.

Aces and Princesses—Bookends of Existence

When you created your Trump Cards, I asked you to start with the two Trumps that represented the two inscrutable Zeros: the Universe and the Fool. These two cards are in essence *bookends* of Greater Arcana; indeed, they are the bookends of existence itself. The Lesser Arcana also has its bookends—*elemental* bookends—the Ace and the Princess of each suit.

Serving as the "Throne" of her Ace, the Princess *grounds* the Ace and gives it a bed to lie in. Without the Princess, the Ace would not have place to manifests its pure potentiality, no womb to receive and manifest the elemental DNA of the suit.

All four Court Cards of the suit live inside their Ace, but the Princess has a special status because she is magically wed to the Ace itself. Together, she and her Ace rule 90-degree quadrants of zodiacal *Space*. (The middle 30 degrees of their rulership are anchored by the fixed zodiac sign of their suit's element: Fire—Leo, Water—Scorpio, Air—Aquarius, Earth—Taurus.)

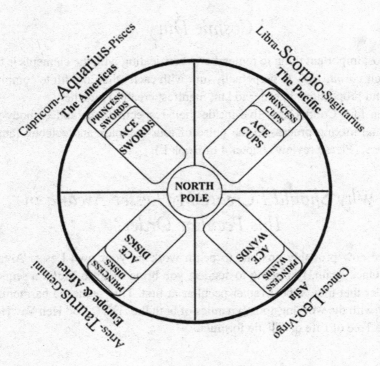

Figure 31.

Sidebar 17

PLEASE DO THIS NOW!

Take your four Aces and your four Princesses. Kiss them, pair them, and lay them before you on the table as you see in Figure 31. Just casually gaze at this layout while you consider the following.

Imagine yourself in a helicopter hovering high above the North Pole of the Earth. Project the wheel of the zodiac encircling the Earth beneath you. Divide the surface of the globe in four quarters, as shown in Figure 31. The initial line runs through the Great Pyramid at Giza. Working our way east in יהוה, Yod Heh Vav Heh (Wands, Cups, Swords, Disks) order, we see . . .

the Ace and Princess of Wands—covering Asia

the Ace and Princess of Cups—the Pacific

the Ace and Princess of Swords—the Americas

the Ace and Princess of Disks—Europe and Africa

For your convenience, this information is clearly printed near the top of each of the Princess card forms of the *Tarot of Ceremonial Magick*. It can be very important information if, for instance, your tarot questions concern travel or anything to do with geographic locations.

Other Symbols Appearing on the Lesser Arcana Cards

As we proceed with our work on the Lesser Arcana, we will notice that the Aces, Court Cards, and Small Cards of the *Tarot of Ceremonial Magick* also display a number of other magical devices and images. These represent fundamental aspects of other magical systems that, while seemingly not associated with tarot, nonetheless have important and direct counterparts to the elemental worlds represented in tarot's Lesser Arcana.

While these particular magical features are a unique to the *Tarot of Ceremonial Magick*, they nonetheless represent universal forces that are invisibly present in all traditionally structured tarot decks.

If any of these more overtly magical features do not interest you, please feel free to ignore or even paint over them as you work on your cards. If, however, you *are* curious as to how they might further enhance these building blocks of your house of cards, I will briefly offer a few words about them.

I Ching Hexagrams on the Court Cards

As you begin work, you will notice that the sixteen Court Cards of the *Tarot of Ceremonial Magick* display a stack of six lines up in the upper left corner of the card. These are images from the *I Ching*, or the *Chinese Book of Changes*. We will soon learn a bit more about how this ancient oracle relates to Court Cards on my "Chinese Digression" in chapter 7.

Hindu Tattwa Symbols on the Aces and Court Cards

You will also notice that the four Aces and the sixteen Court Cards display a composite symbol in the lower right-hand area of the card. These are the twenty Hindu elementary tattwa symbols. *Tattwa* literally means "reality" or "state of being," and these images, when brightly colored, can indeed be the doorway to the specific elemental realities or states of being represented by the Aces and Court Cards.

The five tattwa images are:

Spirit (Akasha) represented by a Black Egg

Fire (Tejas) represented by a Red Triangle

Water (Apas) represented by a Silver Crescent

Air (Vayu) represented by a Blue Circle

Earth (Prithivi) represented by a Yellow Square

When any two of these five symbols are combined, their colors and forms visually create the same elemental realities of consciousness as those represented as the four Aces and the sixteen Court Cards.

For example:

Ace of Wands = *Spirit of Fire* = Black Egg of Spirit inside Red Triangle of Fire

Knight of Cups = *Fire of Water* = Red Triangle of Fire inside Silver Crescent of Water

Queen of Disks = *Water of Earth* = Yellow Square of Earth inside Silver Crescent of Water

Princess of Swords = *Earth of Air* = Yellow Square of Earth inside Blue Circle of Air

The card images you will be working on are uncolored, so you will need to color them in yourself. In doing so, you will be further attuning yourself to the cards. Besides being very cool looking and mystical, the tattwa symbols have another serious and powerful magical potential. They can, under proper circumstances, serve as the focus of meditation by which you can literally *project* into the elemental plane of consciousness associated with the symbol. While in that mildly altered state of consciousness, you may receive visions and insights as to the nature of the card as it relates to you personally.

In other words, with practice and using the tattwa symbols that appear on the cards themselves, you can ceremonially induce magical visions, explore the spiritual landscapes, and contact the angelic residents of the card.

Table 4. Color Scales for Aces and Small Cards

Card	Sephirah	Wands *King Scale*	Cups *Queen Scale*	Swords *Prince Scale*	Disks *Princess Scale*
Ace	1 Kether	Brilliance	White Brilliance	White Brilliance	White-Flecked Gold
Two	2 Chokmah	Pale Soft Blue	Grey	Blue Pearl Grey, like Mother-of-Pearl	White-Flecked Red, Blue, and Yellow
Three	3 Binah	Crimson	Black	Dark Brown	Grey-Flecked Pink
Four	4 Chesed	Deep Violet	Blue	Deep Purple	Deep Azure–Flecked Yellow
Five	5 Geburah	Orange	Scarlet Red	Bright Scarlet	Red-flecked Black
Six	6 Tiphareth	Clear Rose Pink	Yellow (Gold)	Rich Salmon	Golden Amber
Seven	7 Netzach	Amber	Emerald	Bright Yellow Green	Olive-Flecked Gold
Eight	8 Hod	Violet	Orange	Red Russet	Yellowish-Brown-Flecked White
Nine	9 Yesod	Indigo	Violet	Very Dark Purple	Citrine-Flecked Azure
Ten	10 Malkuth	Yellow	*Citrine *Olive *Russet *Black	Same as Disks but Gold-Flecked Black	Black-Rayed Yellow

This may seem rather fanciful and far-fetched, but I will show you a simple technique in the homework assignment and meditation found at the end of chapter 8, and you will be able to judge for yourself.

And while we're on the subject of magic . . .

Lesser Arcana and Enochian Magick and Goetia

Enochian Magick and Solomonic Magick (or Goetia) are two of the most widely practiced systems of magic in use today. Spirits of both these systems have a rich traditional history and have comfortable apartments and condos in the tarot house of cards.

Enochian Magick, created by (through?) John Dee and Edward Kelley in the late 1580s, is perhaps the most complex and initially intimidating magical system imaginable. Fortunately for us, the elemental aspect of Enochian Magick is rather simple and straightforward. It dovetails perfectly with the elemental dynamics of tarot. For example:

> The Enochian **Tablet of Fire** actually *is* one way of viewing the spiritual essence of the **Ace of Wands.**

> The **Water Subangle** of the Enochian **Tablet of Earth** actually *is* the elemental mix that is the **Queen of Disks.**

> The **first decan of Aries** square on the Grand Crosses of all four Enochian Elemental Tablets actually *is* the angelic essence that is the **Two of Wands**.

Don't worry. This book is not intended to be a manual of Enochian Magick, but because all fifty-six cards of the Lesser Arcana do have their homes on the various Enochian tablets and squares, these images appear on the cards of the *TCM* and are designated on the card descriptions that accompany the images you'll be working on.

If you are interested in exploring Enochian Magick further, I shamelessly recommend my own book *Enochian Vision Magick—A Practical Guide to the Magick of Dr. John Dee and Edward Kelley.*[2]

Angels of the Shemhamphorash

The seventy-two qabalistic angels of the Shemhamphorash (the divided name of God) are the traditional qabalistic rulers of the thirty-six Small Cards. Assigned in pairs to each Small Card, they each rule five degrees of their host decan.

Their names were extracted by the qabalistic manipulation of three consecutive verses of Exodus, each of which contains seventy-two Hebrew letters. The three verses, when written one over the other (right to left, then left to right, then right to left) result in seventy-two columns of three letters. These are treated as the seventy-two three-letter names of God: the Shem-hamphorash. Each three-letter name is a particular facet of divine power, and each God Name sends forth an angel to execute its particular power in the cosmos.

The angel's name is formed by simply adding two letters to the three letters of the God Name: "IH" for an angel of Mercy, or "AL" for an angel of Judgement.

The duties of the seventy-two angels of the Shemhamphorash are deter-mined by seventy-two verses of scripture where the name יהוה, Yod Heh Vav Heh, appears.

Aren't you sorry you asked?

The names of the seventy-two Shemhamphorash angels appear above the left and right seals on the lower panel of each Small Card. The angel of the first five degrees of the decan is on the left; the angel of the second five degrees is on the right.

What Are "Demons" Doing in My Small Cards?

Goetic evocation (Solomonic Magick) is one of the most popular and widely practiced techniques of Western ceremonial magick. The technique is classic; The magician stands within a magical circle protected by divine names. After a great deal of serious soul-searching, sincere appeal *to* (and commu-nion *with*) the Supreme deity, the magician, by means of pure will (and duly observed rules of magical etiquette) evokes one of seventy-two spirits into a triangle outside the circle. The magician then charges the spirit to perform tasks which, by tradition, the spirit is known to be capable of performing.

These seventy-two spirits are assigned in pairs (one by day and one by night) to the thirty-six decans of the zodiac and the corresponding thirty-six Small Cards of tarot. Their seals appear on the lower right and lower left of each of the Small Cards of the *Tarot of Ceremonial Magick*.

The seventy-two spirits of the Goetia are taken from the first book of the Lemegaton, commonly called *The Lesser Key of Solomon*. It is a text with which you should be intimately familiar if you seriously wish to pursue the practice of Solomonic Magick.

Let us now, without further digressions, proceed to color and design your own Aces and Princesses.

CHAPTER 6

The Aces and Princesses

tated in chapter 5, but repeated again in order to stress the concept and introduce this chapter, the Ace and the Princess of each suit serve as *elemental* bookends in the Lesser Arcana.

The Princess is the "Throne" of the Ace. The Princess *grounds* the Ace. Without the Princess, the Ace would not have place to manifest its pure potentiality, no womb to receive and manifest the elemental DNA of the suit.

As with all four Court Cards of the suit, the Princess lives *inside* their Ace. However, the Princess has a special status because she is magically wed to the Ace itself. Together, she and her Ace rule 90-degree quadrants of zodiacal *Space*.

Figure 32 shows the format features of the aces. The Princess shares most of her formatted features with her Court Card family—examples of the Princesses appear in chapter 7.

Figure 33 presents the Enochian Elemental Tablet in detail and provides instructions for color.

Features of the Aces

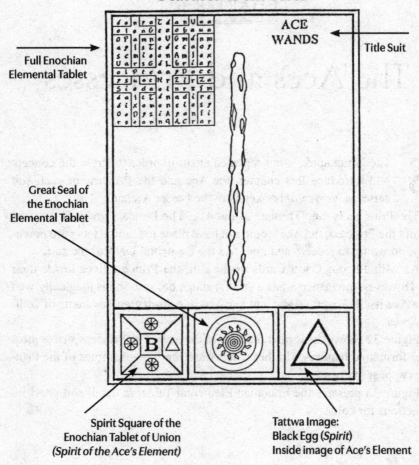

Full Enochian Elemental Tablet

ACE WANDS

Title Suit

Great Seal of the Enochian Elemental Tablet

Spirit Square of the Enochian Tablet of Union *(Spirit of the Ace's Element)*

Tattwa Image: Black Egg (*Spirit*) Inside image of Ace's Element

Figure 32.
Format features of the Aces

Enochian Elemental Tablet in the Aces of All Suits

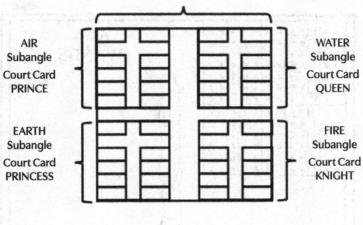

AIR
Subangle

Court Card
PRINCE

WATER
Subangle

Court Card
QUEEN

EARTH
Subangle

Court Card
PRINCESS

FIRE
Subangle

Court Card
KNIGHT

Figure 33.

The large Elemental Tablet square in the upper left corner each of the Aces can be colored as follows:

The *Great Cross* in the center can be left White (for Spirit).

The four smaller Subangle *Crosses* (in the four quadrants) can be colored the elemental color of the suit (Red for the Ace of Wands, Blue for the Ace of Cups, Yellow for Ace of Swords, Green for the Ace of Disks).

The other areas of the four subangles of each tablet are colored: Red for the lower right subangle, Blue for the upper right subangle, Yellow for the upper left subangle, and Green for the lower left subangle.

If possible, color lightly enough for the lettering to be read.

Ace of Wands
Root of the Powers of Fire

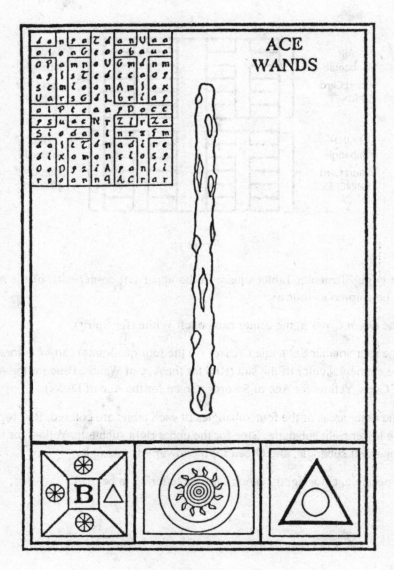

SPIRIT OF FIRE

ן

Yod of **Yod** Heh Vav Heh

With the Princess of Wands as its Throne, the Ace of Wands governs the
Cancer-LEO-Virgo
Quadrant of Space and the geographic area of Asia.

Represents Kether, Sephirah 1
of the Atziluth Tree of Life.

Traditional Image: A radiant right hand appears from clouds on the right holding a Wand with small leaves still attached.

The *TCM* Card: Simply displays a large **Reddish-Brown** wooden Wand surrounded by a bright **White** glory. The background is bright **Yellow**. The Wand itself is the pattern for all the Wands of the suit.

Additions or Changes: You may wish to add flames or buds in the shape of Yods and/or other phallic symbols.

Upper Left Square: The entire Enochian Elemental Tablet of Fire (see note under Figure 32 on page 150).

Lower Panel, Left Square: The B-lettered Square (Spirit of Fire) from the Enochian Tablet of Union (see Appendix 3). The three sections with the Spirit wheels are **White**. The section with the upward-pointing fire triangle (right) is **Red**.

Lower Panel, Center Square: Great Seal of Enochian Elemental Tablet of Fire (**Red** circles over **Green** with rays of **Red** and **Yellow** Yods).

Lower Panel, Right Square: Tattwa symbol Tejas-Akasha, Spirit of Fire (**Black** Egg in a **Red** Triangle).

Princess of Wands

Princess of the Shining Flame / Rose of the Palace of Fire

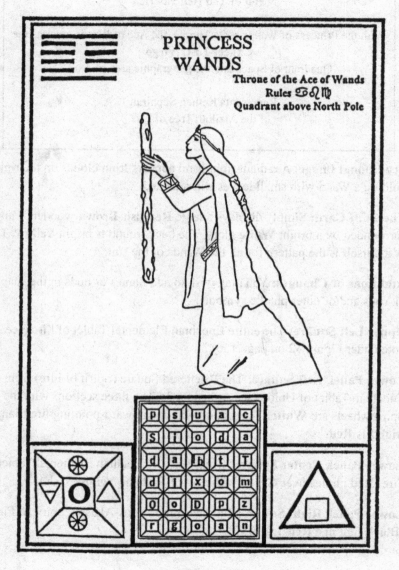

EARTH OF FIRE

> Serving as the Throne of the Ace of Wands,
> the Princess of Wands governs the
> Cancer-LEO-Virgo
> Quadrant of Space and the geographic area of Asia.
>
> The Princess of Wands is the Court Card ruler of
> Malkuth,
> Sephirah 10
> of the
> Atziluth Tree of Life.
>
> As such, she crystallizes and completely manifests
> all that rests in pure potentiality in the Ace of Wands.

The *TCM* Card: Against a background of bright **Yellow** with scattered **Red** flames, the Princess is seen in profile. She holds the Wand. She has long braided **Red** hair, a **Golden** tiara, a **Red** robe with a **Golden** cape, and a **Gold** bracelet and belt.

Additions or Changes: You may wish add a tiger's pelt to her cape, an altar of fire, and flames on the ground and background, or anything that suggests to you Earth of Fire.

Upper Left Area: I Ching Hexagram 27, Nourishment (see Appendix 1, page 320, for meaning).

Lower Panel, Left Square: The O-lettered Square (Earth of Fire) from the Enochian Tablet of Union (see Appendix). The two sections with the Spirit wheels are **White**; the section with the downward-pointing Earth triangle (left) is **Green**; the section with the upward-pointing Fire triangle (right) is **Red**.

Lower Panel, Center Square: Earth Subangle of Enochian Elemental Tablet of Fire. Center column and second row from the top: **Green** for **Earth**; the rest of the square: **Red** for **Fire.**

Lower Panel, Right Square: Tattwa symbol Tejas-Prithivi, Earth of Fire (**Yellow** Square in a **Red** Triangle).

Ace of Cups
Root of the Powers of Water

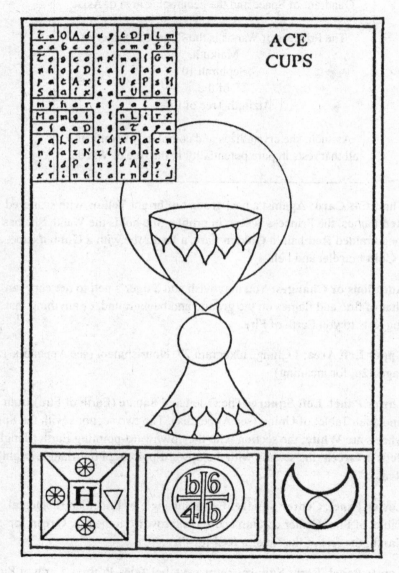

SPIRIT OF WATER

Heh of Yod **Heh** Vav Heh

With the Princess of Cups as its Throne,
the Ace of Cups
governs the
Libra-SCORPIO-Sagittarius
Quadrant of Space and the Geographic area of the Pacific.

Represents Kether, Sephirah 1
of the Briah Tree of Life.

Traditional Image: A radiant left hand appears from clouds on the right holding a fountaining Cup above which a dove descends.

The *TCM* Card: Simply displays a large **Greenish-Blue** Cup adorned with **White** lotus petals, and surrounded by a **Golden** Sun and a bright glory. The background is **Sky Blue**. The Cup itself is the pattern for all the Cups of the suit.

Additions or Changes: You may wish to add gushing water and/or other female/yoni symbols.

Upper Left Square: The entire Enochian Elemental Tablet of Water (see note under Figure 32).

Lower Panel, Left Square: The H-lettered Square (Spirit of Water) from the Enochian Tablet of Union (see Appendix). The three sections with the Spirit wheels are **White**. The section with the downward-pointing Water triangle (right) is **Blue**.

Lower Panel, Center Square: Great Seal of Enochian Elemental Tablet of Water. **Orange** circle within a **Blue** ring, **Blue** cross and letters.

Lower Panel, Right Square: Tattwa symbol Apas-Akasha Spirit of Water (**Black** Egg in a **Silver** Crescent).

Princess of Cups

Princess of the Waters / Lotus of the Palace of the Floods

EARTH OF WATER

> Serving as the Throne of the Ace of Cups,
> the Princess of Cups governs the
> Libra-SCORPIO-Sagittarius
> Quadrant of Space and the geographic area of the Pacific.
>
> The Princess of Cups is the Court Card ruler of
> Malkuth, Sephirah 10
> of the
> Briah Tree of Life.
>
> As such, she crystallizes and completely manifests all that rests
> in pure potentiality in the Ace of Cups.

The *TCM* Card: Against a background awash with **Blues** and **Light Blues**, the Princess is seen in profile. She holds the Cup. She has long braided hair, a **Silver** tiara, a **Greenish-Blue** robe with a **Blue** cape, and a **Silver** bracelet and belt.

Additions or Changes: You may wish drawn an ocean horizon with dolphins playing, and so forth. Traditional images show a turtle in the Princess's Cup. Add anything that suggests to you Earth of Water.

Upper Left Area: I Ching Hexagram 41, Decrease (see Appendix for meaning).

Lower Panel, Left Square: The M-lettered Square (Earth of Water) from the Enochian Tablet of Union (see Appendix). The two sections with the Spirit wheels are **White**; the section with the downward-pointing Earth triangle (left) is **Green**; the section with the downward-pointing Water triangle (right) is **Blue**.

Lower Panel, Center Square: Earth Subangle of Enochian Elemental Tablet of Water. Center column and second row from the top: **Green** for **Earth**; the rest of the square: **Blue** for **Water.**

Lower Panel, Right Square: Tattwa symbol Apas-Prithivi, Earth of Water (**Yellow** Square in a **Silver** Crescent).

Ace of Swords

Root of the Powers of Air

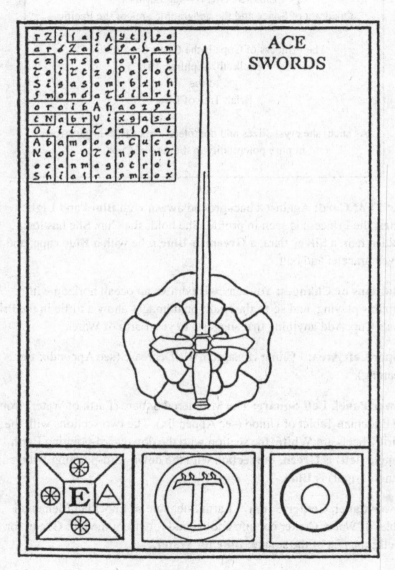

SPIRIT OF AIR

THE TAROT ARCHITECT

ו

Vav of Yod Heh **Vav** Heh

With the Princess of Swords as its Throne,
the Ace of Swords
governs the
Capricorn-AQUARIUS-Pisces
Quadrant of Space and the geographic area of the Americas.

Represents Kether, Sephirah 1
of the Yetzirah Tree of Life.

Traditional Image: A radiant right hand appears from clouds on the left holding a Sword, the point of which penetrates a **Golden** crown.

The *TCM* Card: Simply displays a large upward-pointing **Silver** Sword with a **White** grip, surrounded by a bright glory and placed before a huge **Red** rose blossom. The background is bright **Yellow**. The Sword itself is the pattern for all the Swords of the suit.

Additions or Changes: You may wish to add light wispy clouds to the background and adorn the Sword blade with you own magical motto or other personal words of power.

Upper Left Square: The entire Enochian Elemental Tablet of Air (see note under Figure 32).

Lower Panel, Left Square: The E-lettered Square (Spirit of Air) from the Enochian Tablet of Union (see Appendix). The three sections with the Spirit wheels are **White**; the section with the upward-pointing Air triangle (right) is **Yellow**.

Lower Panel, Center Square: Great Seal of Enochian Elemental Tablet of Air. **Purple** circle within which are a **Yellow** ring and cross with four **Yellow** Yods.

Lower Panel, Right Square: Tattwa symbol Vayu-Akasha, Spirit of Air (**Black** Egg in a **Blue** Circle).

Princess of Swords

Princess of the Rushing Winds / Lotus of the Palace of Air

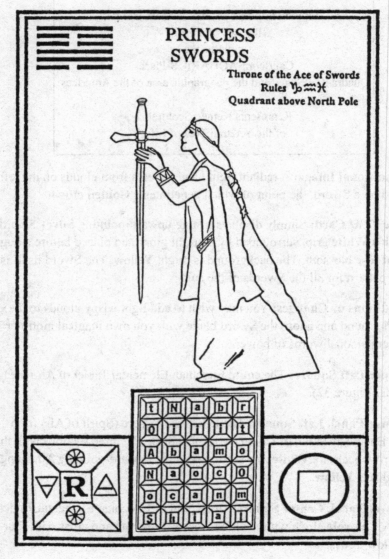

EARTH OF AIR

Serving as the Throne of the Ace of Swords,
the Princess of Swords governs the
Capricorn-AQUARIUS-Pisces
Quadrant of Space and the geographic area of the Americas.

The Princess of Swords is the Court Card ruler of
Malkuth, Sephirah 10
of the
Yetzirah Tree of Life.

As such, she crystallizes and completely manifests all that
rests
in pure potentiality in the Ace of Swords.

The *TCM* Card: Against a background of **Sky Blue**, the Princess is seen in profile. She holds the Sword. She has long braided **Golden** hair, a **Golden** tiara, a **Sky Blue** robe with a **Yellow** cape, and a **Silver** bracelet and belt.

Additions or Changes: You may wish add a smoking fire altar and dusty clouds or a landscape of wind-bent trees. Include anything that suggests to you Earth of Air.

Upper Left Area: I Ching Hexagram 18, Decay or Work on what has been spoiled (see Appendix for meaning).

Lower Panel, Left Square: The R-lettered Square (Earth of Air) from the Enochian Tablet of Union (see Appendix). The two sections with the Spirit wheels are **White**; the downward-pointing Earth triangle (left) is **Green**; the upward-pointing Air triangle (right) is **Yellow**.

Lower Panel, Center Square: Earth Subangle of Enochian Elemental Tablet of Air. Center column and second row from the top: **Green** for **Earth**; the rest of the square: **Yellow** for **Air.**

Lower Panel, Right Square: Tattwa symbol Vayu-Prithivi Earth of Air (**Yellow** Square in a **Blue** Circle).

Ace of Disks

Root of the Powers of Earth

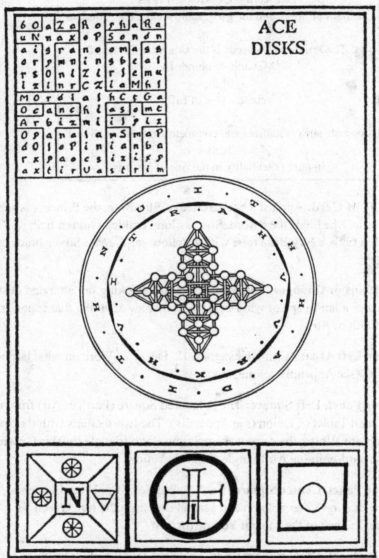

SPIRIT OF EARTH

ה

Heh of Yod Heh Vav **Heh**

With the Princess of Disks as its Throne, the Ace of Disks
governs the
Aries-TAURUS-Gemini
Quadrant of Space
and the geographic area of Europe & Africa.

Represents Kether, Sephirah 1
of the Assiah Tree of Life.

Traditional Image: Radiant right hand appears from clouds on the left holding a Disk.

The *TCM* Card: Simply displays the personal pantacle of LMD against a **White** field flecked **Gold**. The ring of the Disk is **Green** and surrounds an eleven-sided **White** field. This Disk image is the model for all the Small Cards of the suit of Disks.

Additions or Changes: If you have designed your own magical pantacle or have a preferred Disk design, you may wish to paint over this one and replace it with yours.

Upper Left Square: The entire Enochian Elemental Tablet of Earth (see note under Figure 32).

Lower Panel, Left Square: The N-lettered Square (Spirit of Earth) from the Enochian Tablet of Union (see Appendix). The three sections with the Spirit wheels are **White**; the section with the downward-pointing Earth triangle (right) is **Green**.

Lower Panel, Center Square: Great Seal of Enochian Elemental Tablet of Earth. **Black** circle within which is a simple cross. Top arm: **Citrine**; right arm: **Olive Green**; bottom arm: **Black**; left arm: **Russet**.

Lower Panel, Right Square: Tattwa symbol Prithivi-Akasha, Spirit of Earth (**Black** Egg in a **Yellow** Square).

Princess of Disks

Princess of the Echoing Hills / Rose of the Palace of Earth

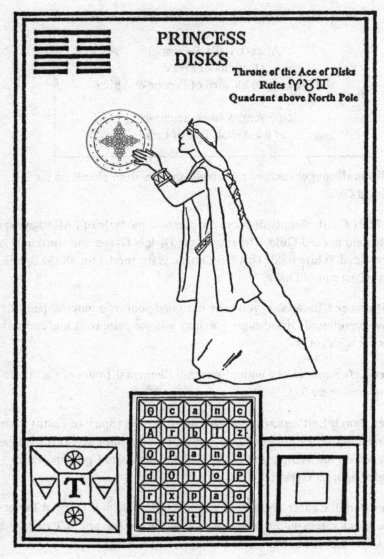

PRINCESS DISKS

Throne of the Ace of Disks
Rules ♈ ♉ ♊
Quadrant above North Pole

EARTH OF EARTH

Note: The Princess of Disks and the Ten of Disks (her Small Card equivalent) represent the "climax of the descent into Matter." Together they hold the key to jump-starting an entirely new cycle of creation.

Serving as the Throne of the Ace of Disks,
the Princess of Disks governs the
Aries-TAURUS-Gemini
Quadrant of Space and the geographic area of Europe and Africa.

The Princess of Disks is the Court Card ruler of
Malkuth, Sephirah 10
of the
Assiah Tree of Life.

As such, she crystallizes and completely manifests all that lays
in pure potentiality in the Ace of Disks.

The *TCM* Card: Against a background of **Green** rolling hills, the Princess is seen in profile. She holds the Disk. She has long braided **Brown** hair, a **Golden** tiara, a **Dark Green** robe with a **Light Brown** cape, and a **Gold** bracelet and belt.

Additions or Changes: You may wish add trees and rocks and cave openings or anything that suggests to you Earth of Earth.

Upper Left Area: I Ching Hexagram 52, Peace or Mountain (see Appendix for meaning).

Lower Panel, Left Square: The T-lettered Square (Earth of Earth) from the Enochian Tablet of Union (see Appendix). The two sections with the Spirit wheels are **White**; the two sections with the downward-pointing triangles (left and right) are **Green**.

Lower Panel, Center Square: Earth Subangle of Enochian Elemental Tablet of Earth. All of the square: **Green** for **Earth**.

Lower Panel, Right Square: Tattwa symbol Prithivi-Prithivi, Earth of Earth (**Yellow** Square in a **Yellow** Square).

Meditation 6

Attunement Meditation upon Completion of the Aces & Princesses

Note: Magical circles represent the particular magical environment in which the magician is working. This meditation is designed to attune you to the world of the four elements and the elemental dynamics of the Lesser Arcana. The four-quarter landmarks of an Elemental Circle are the Fixed Signs of the Zodiac: Leo for Fire, Scorpio for Water, Aquarius for Air, and Taurus for Earth.

Cards needed for this meditation:

From the Greater Arcana:

> Lust (Leo—Fixed Fire)
>
> Death (Scorpio—Fixed Water)
>
> Star (Aquarius—Fixed Air)
>
> Hierophant (Taurus—Fixed Earth)

From the Lesser Arcana:

> Ace and Princess of Wands
>
> Ace and Princess of Cups
>
> Ace and Princess of Swords
>
> Ace and Princess of Disks

1. If you are able, seat yourself comfortably on the floor facing **south**.

2. Clap 5 times (2-2–1–2-2).

3. Take your **Lust** card (representing **Leo**), kiss it, and place it at a comfortable distance in front of you to mark the **south**.

4. Take your **Death** card (representing **Scorpio**), kiss it, and place it at a comfortable distance to your left to mark the **east**.

5. Take your **Star** card (representing **Aquarius**), kiss it, and place it at a comfortable distance behind you to mark the **north**.

6. Take your **Hierophant** card (representing **Taurus**), kiss it, and place it at a comfortable distance to your right to represent **west**.

7. As you complete the circle and return your attention to the south, take a moment to look around and get comfortable with your position: Fiery Leo straight ahead in the **south;** Watery Scorpio to your left in the **east**; behind you in the **north** Airy **Aquarius**; and to your right, in the **west,** Earthy **Taurus**.

8. Still facing **south**, close your eyes, and take two or three deep cleansing breaths.

9. In your mind's eye, try to picture an overhead view of yourself seated on the floor, facing **south** surrounded by those four cards. Think of the cards as forming a protective magical circle around you—a circle that you have cast specifically to orient yourself to the elemental *Fixed Signs* of the Zodiac.

10. When you feel comfortably centered, open your eyes, and take your **Ace** and **Princess of Wands** and lay them side by side near the **Lust** card in front of you (**south**).

11. Then take your **Ace** and **Princess of Cups** and lay them side by side near the **Death** card to your left (**east**).

12. Then take your **Ace** and **Princess** of **Swords** and lay them side by side near the **Star** card behind you (**north**).

13. Then take your **Ace** and **Princess** of **Disks** and lay them side by side near the **Hierophant** card to your right (**west**).

14. Look around at the circle of cards surrounding you to reaffirm your position in this elemental universe. Close your eyes and say:

My four magick weapons turn the Wheel of Life.
Before me, the Ace and Princess of Wands.
With the Wand I create my universe.[1]

To my left, the Ace and Princess of Cups.
With the Cup I preserve my universe.

Behind me, the Ace and Princess of Swords,
With the Sword I destroy my universe.

To my right, the Ace and Princess of Disks.
With the Disk I shall redeem my universe.

15. Clap 5 times 2-2–1–2-2.

CHAPTER 7

Introduction to the Astrological Court Cards

W hen I read tarot cards for others, I'm usually relieved when cards of the Lesser Arcana appear in the spread. Unlike great cosmic concepts and karmic profundities the Trumps often suggest, these fifty-six cards of the Lesser Arcana frequently offer candid objective insights pertinent to everyday questions or issues. The thirty-six Small Cards bear unambiguous titles like Love, Happiness, Disappointment, Cruelty; and the sixteen Court Cards, in many instances, indicate the querent or actual living-breathing individuals involved in the querent's life.

Twelve of the Court Cards—the Knights, Queens, and Princes[1] (because they each rule 30 degrees of the solar year)—make perfect candidates to serve as birthday cards (*Significators*) to represent either the client or other individuals in a reading. All sixteen Court Cards, because of their elemental makeup, have characteristics that can carry great significance in a reading.

The Lesser Arcana of all tarot decks by virtue of their general qabalistic structure embody the same elemental and subelemental significance, but the *Tarot of Ceremonial Magick* also incorporates features of elemental landmarks of other and more ancient oracular traditions—the *I Ching* and the Hindu *tattwa images*.

The tattwa symbols, in particular, can be used in an overtly magical manner, which we will learn in an upcoming homework/meditation assignment. But first, let's talk for moment about the I Ching.

Chinese Digression

While all sixteen Court Cards are rich in traditional meanings, they can often be difficult to interpret within the context of an actual tarot reading. About thirty-five years ago (after years of being frustrated by my incompetence to easily interpret Court Cards in readings) I stumbled upon something quite amazing and helpful, something that gave my tarot skills a little boost from perhaps the oldest surviving oracle on earth, the *I Ching* or *Chinese Book of Changes*. I briefly mentioned the I Ching earlier, but now I'd like to expand on it just a little bit more.

I view the I Ching as *Chinese Qabalah*. But instead of being based on the mathematical dynamics of 4 and 10 and 22 like the Qabalah, the I Ching comes at things from a simpler and more elegant direction by dissecting the mechanics of *duality* itself: by observing simply that something either *is* or *isn't*—on or off—positive or negative—light or dark—male or female. Furthermore, anything we can call a "something" is in a constant process of *changing* into *something else*.

This heads-or-tails reality is graphically expressed in the I Ching with breathtaking elegance as simply being either an *unbroken* line ———— or a broken line —— —— .

Just as Qabalah venerates the Supernal Triad as its mysterious foundation, the I Ching groups these two lines into stacks of three whose various combinations produce eight unique trigrams whose images represent eight fundamental principles of existence. Their titles in English can be translated: Sun, Moon, Male, Female, Fire, Water, Air, and Earth.[2]

Obviously, where the cards of the Lesser Arcana are concerned, we are most interested in the four elemental trigrams of Fire, Water, Air, and Earth.

To consult the I Ching, one simply asks a question and randomly generates two of the eight trigrams, which are stacked one on top the other to form one of sixty-four *hexagrams*. The text of the I Ching is a treasure house of profound and inspired philosophical commentaries, and there are many other complexities that make a full I Ching reading quite an elaborate (and detailed) operation.

Only *sixteen* of the I Ching's sixty-four hexagrams are comprised of the same elemental combinations (Fire of Air; Water of Earth, Fire of Fire, etc.) as the sixteen Court Cards of tarot. I've found that the traditional commentaries on these sixteen hexagrams can offer profound wisdom, often delivered with breathtaking wit and fortune-cookie brevity. I've provided brief divinatory meanings of the sixteen tarot-related hexagrams in the appendix.

Court Card Hexagrams

One of these sixteen hexagrams appears in the upper left corner of each of the Court Cards of the *Tarot of Ceremonial Magick*, and their titles and brief meanings can be found in the accompanying text. If you have one of the many fine translations of the I Ching in your library, your Court Card readings can be further enhanced.

Please remember: If this or any other magical or astrological features of the *TCM* Court Cards do not interest you, you are free to ignore or paint over them when you begin work on your deck.

An Astrological Digression

I'll remind you once again that all four Court Cards live inside their respective Aces, but that the *Princesses* play a unique role within their family unit because they are magically wed to their Aces. The Princesses, together with their Aces, rule 90-degree quadrants of *zodiacal space,* while the Knights, Queens, and Princes each rule 30-degree periods of *time*. For convenience we'll call these other twelve family members *Astrological Court Cards*.

You might be wondering why tarot would need two sets of 30-degree astrological cards. After all, don't we already have twelve perfectly well-behaved Trump cards that represent the Zodiac, cards that enjoy elite status as the twelve Simple Letters of the Hebrew alphabet, cards that live in the Greater Arcana's high-rent district on the edges of the Cube of Space?

Yes, we do! But this chapter is about the fifty-six cards of the *Lesser* Arcana, and these cards illustrate how things play out on the *elemental* side of the manifest universe. And furthermore, as we all know: "It is the duty of the elements to mix!"

Unlike the Zodiacal Trumps, the twelve Astrological Court Cards do *not* represent the 30 degrees of a single Zodiac Sign. Instead, the Knights, Queens, and Princes each represent 30-degree periods that start at 20 degrees of one Sign and rule to 20 degrees of the next Sign. That means that every Astrological Court Card is an elemental mix of two-thirds of its native element and one-third of a foreign element.

But wait! There's even more mixing up happening! (Please forgive a brief remedial astrology digression.)

The twelve Signs of the Zodiac are made up of:

Three *Fire* Signs (Aries, Leo, Sagittarius)

Three *Water* Signs (Cancer, Scorpio, Pisces)

Three *Air* Signs (Libra, Aquarius, Gemini)

Three *Earth* Signs (Capricorn, Taurus, Virgo)

Each of the twelve Signs of the Zodiac functions as one of *three* characteristic categories:

Four *Cardinal* Signs (Aries, Cancer, Libra, Capricorn), which on the wheel of the year represent the initial impulse at the start of the four seasons

Four *Fixed* Signs (Leo, Scorpio, Aquarius, Taurus), which firmly define and embody the elemental character of the heart of the season

Four *Mutable* Signs (Sagittarius, Pisces, Gemini, Virgo), which express the flexibility and willingness to transition into the next season

How does this all play out within the family roles of the twelve Astrological Court Cards?

One might jump to the old *male-chauvinist* conclusion that the patriarchal Knights would naturally lay macho claim to the Cardinal Signs, the domestic and matronly Queens to the Fixed Signs, and the brash and immature Princes (in their fast cars) to the Mutable Signs—but you'd be wrong!

It's the duty of the elements to mix things up, and the twelve Astrological Court Cards kick off their elemental juggling by evolving out of those tired old traditional family roles.

In the house of cards, it's the *Queens* who rule two-thirds of the *Cardinal* Signs:

The Queen of Wands rules two-thirds of Cardinal Fire *Aries*.

The Queen of Cups rules two-thirds of Cardinal Water *Cancer*.

The Queen of Swords rules two-thirds of Cardinal Air *Libra*.

The Queen of Disks rules two-thirds of Cardinal Earth *Capricorn*.

The *Princes* rule two-thirds of the *Fixed* Signs:

The Prince of Wands rules two-thirds of Fixed Fire *Leo*.

The Prince of Cups rules two-thirds of Fixed Water *Scorpio*.

The Prince of Swords rules two-thirds of Fixed Air *Aquarius*.

The Prince of Disks rules two-thirds of Fixed Earth *Taurus*.

The *Knights* rule two-thirds of the *Mutable* Signs:

The Knight of Wands rules two-thirds of Mutable Fire *Sagittarius*.

The Knight of Cups rules two-thirds of Mutable Water *Pisces*.

The Knight of Swords rules two-thirds of Mutable Fire *Gemini*.

The Knight of Disks rules two-thirds of Mutable Earth *Virgo*.

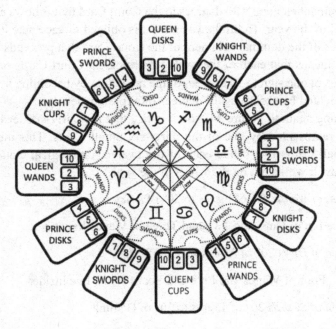

Figure 34.

PLEASE DO THIS NOW!

Take your twelve Astrological Court Cards (the Knights, Queens, and Princes). Kiss them and, using Figure 34 as your pattern, lay out the twelve cards in counterclockwise order (starting with the Queen of Wands at the far left) to form the wheel of the year.

Casually gaze at the wheel as you read the following.

What's with This Two-Thirds of a Sign Thing?

All this elemental mixing results in what I call the "Adopt-a-Decan Program," as illustrated in Figure 34.

In order to qualify for *Platinum Elite Court Card* status, each of the twelve Astrological Court Cards is required to *give up* the final 10 degrees (one decan) of its dominant element's 30 degrees to the Court Card that follows after it on the wheel of the year. To fill the vacancy, it is obliged to vaccinate itself with 10 degrees of the dominant element of the Court Card that proceeds it.

This means that each of the twelve Astrological Court Cards rules from 20 degrees of one sign to 20 degrees of the next, thereby becoming hybridized and augmented by absorbing 10 degrees of a foreign element.

Turning again to Figure 34, you'll notice that the thirty-six decans in the year are represented by one of the thirty-six Small Cards. This means that three Small Cards live inside each of the twelve Astrological Court Cards. Here's how it works out on the wheel of the year:[3]

Queen of Wands 20° of Pisces to 20° of Aries

- Ten of Cups and Two and Three of Wands live inside.

Prince of Disks 20° of Aries to 20° of Taurus

- Four of Wands and Five and Six of Disks live inside.

Knight of Swords 20° of Taurus to 20° of Gemini

- Seven of Disks and Eight and Nine of Swords live inside.

Queen of Cups 20° of Gemini to 20° of Cancer

- Ten of Swords and Two and Three of Cups live inside.

Prince of Wands 20° of Cancer to 20° of Leo

- Four of Cups and Five and Six of Wands live inside.

Knight of Disks 20° of Leo to 20° of Virgo

- Seven of Wands and Eight and Nine of Disks live inside.

Queen of Swords 20° of Virgo to 20° of Libra

- Ten of Disks and Two and Three of Swords live inside.

Prince of Cups 20° of Libra to 20° of Scorpio

- Four of Swords and Five and Six of Cups live inside.

Knight of Wands 20° of Scorpio to 20° of Sagittarius

- Seven of Cups and Eight and Nine of Wands live inside.

Queen of Disks 20° of Sagittarius to 20° of Capricorn

- Ten of Wands and Two and Three of Disks live inside.

Prince of Swords 20° Capricorn to 20° of Aquarius

- Four of Disks and Five and Six of Swords live inside.

Knight of Cups 20° of Aquarius to 20° of Pisces

- Seven of Swords and Eight and Nine of Cups live inside.

Let's use the *Queen of Swords* as an example: If you look to the far right of the wheel (Figure 34 on page 175) you'll find her. Even though she rules the first two decans of her dominant element of Cardinal Air with Libra (represented by the Two and Three of Swords), she is forced by the *Adopt-a-Decan* law to back up a bit on the zodiacal belt and *adopt* the last decan of Virgo (the Ten of Disks). She is forced to donate one-third of her precious *Air*iness to the Court Card of an alien element—an alien suit. At the same time, she is forced to play gracious hostess *to* and allow herself to be influenced *by* the Earthiness of the last decan of *Mutable* Earth with Virgo, in the person of the Ten of Disks.

I know we haven't yet discussed the Small Cards, but as you might imagine, the Ten of Disks is as *Earthy* as you get. It's the lowest of the Small Cards in the suit associated with Earth. This card certainly does not possess the breezy diaphanous qualities the Queen of the Thrones of Air might be looking for in a permanent houseguest.

But incongruent roommates are part of the elemental soap opera that is the Adopt-a-Decan program. It's what gives each Astrological Court Card its complexity and rich-textured character. In the case of the Queen of Swords, this might be what occasionally makes her a bit of a stick-in-the-mud.

But she's not alone. All the Knights, Queens, and Princes must cooperate with the Adopt-a-Decan program. This is what makes these twelve Court Cards stick to each other to form the zodiacal year. One might even say, "This is what make the Court Cards *human*." This is how the elements blend in infinite variations to literally knit a diverse creation and the zodiacal year together.

So I will now suggest you magically attune yourself and bring your Astrological Court Cards to life in the same order the twelve cards function in the elementary cosmos. It is the sequence in which the cards progress through the year. We will start near the beginning of the solar year with the Queen of Wands, who rules the last decan of Pisces and the first two decans of Cardinal Fire Aries.

CHAPTER 8

The Knights, Queens, and Princes

This example is the Prince (Air) of Disks (Earth).

Features of the Astrological Court Cards

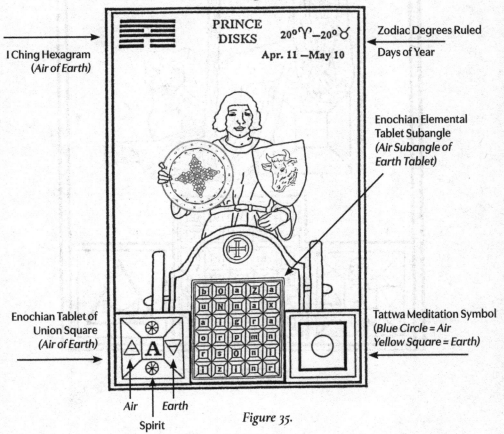

I Ching Hexagram
(*Air of Earth*)

PRINCE
DISKS 20°♈—20°♉

Apr. 11 —May 10

Zodiac Degrees Ruled

Days of Year

Enochian Elemental
Tablet Subangle
(*Air Subangle of
Earth Tablet*)

Enochian Tablet of
Union Square
(*Air of Earth*)

Tattwa Meditation Symbol
(*Blue Circle = Air
Yellow Square = Earth*)

Air   Earth

Spirit

Figure 35.

Queen of Wands

Queen of the Throne of Flame

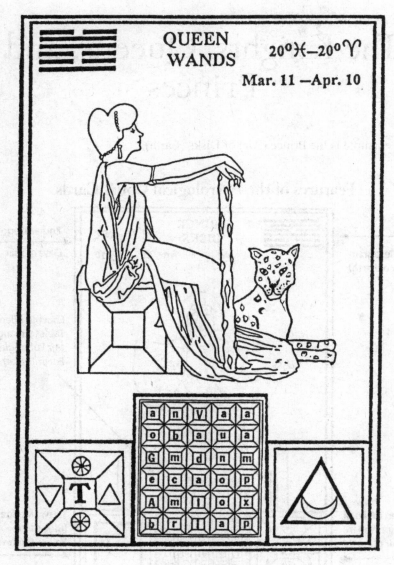

QUEEN
WANDS

20° ♓ – 20° ♈

Mar. 11 – Apr. 10

WATER OF FIRE

Ruling
20° Pisces to 20° Aries
March 11—April 10

The Queen of Wands contains the Ten of Cups &
the Two & Three of Wands.

She is Court Card Ruler of
Binah
Sephirah 3
of the Supernal Triad
of the
Atziluth Tree of Life.

The *TCM* Card: Against a background of **Bright Yellow** with scattered **Red** flames, the Queen is seen in profile, a leopard at her feet. She holds the Wand. She has **Red** hair, jeweled comb and earrings, a **Red** robe, and **Gold** arm bracelets. She is enthroned upon the Water of Fire Enochian Magick square bearing the angelic letter T (colored the same as the Enochian Tablet of Union square that appears in the lower-left of the card).

Additions or Changes: You may wish add a **Golden** crown emanating **Red** and **Gold** rays.

Upper Left Area: I Ching Hexagram 17, Following (see Appendix).

Lower Panel, Left Square: The T-lettered Square (Water of Fire) from the Enochian Tablet of Union (see Appendix 4). The two sections with the Spirit wheels are **White**; the section with the downward-pointing Water triangle (left) is **Blue**; the section with the upward-pointing Fire triangle (right) is **Red**.

Lower Panel, Center Square: Water Subangle of Enochian Elemental Tablet of Fire. (Center column and second row from the top: **Red** for **Fire**; the rest of the square: **Blue** for **Water**.)

Lower Panel, Right Square: Tattwa symbol Tejas-Apas, Water of Fire (**Silver** Crescent in a **Red** Triangle).

Prince of Disks

Prince of the Chariot of Earth

PRINCE DISKS

20° ♈ – 20° ♉

Apr. 11 – May 10

AIR OF EARTH

```
Ruling
20° Aries to 20° Taurus
April 11—May 10

The Prince of Disks contains the Four of Wands &
the Five & Six of Disks.

He is the Court Card Ruler of
Chesed, Geburah, Tiphareth, Netzach, Hod, Yesod,
Sephiroth 4-5-6-7-8-9
of the
Assiah Tree of Life.
```

The *TCM* Card: Against a background of **Green** rolling hills and **Light Brown** sky, the Prince stands face-forward in a **Light-Brown** chariot emblazoned with the Great Enochian Seal of Earth. He has **Brown** hair and wears a **Green** tunic with a **Brown** belt and trim. He holds a large Disk in his right hand. A shield displaying the head of bull is slung over his left shoulder.

Additions or Changes: You may wish add a bull and field of ripe wheat.

Upper Left Area: I Ching Hexagram 53, Gradual Progress (see Appendix).

Lower Panel, Left Square: The A-lettered Square (Air of Earth) from the Enochian Tablet of Union (see Appendix). The two sections with the Spirit wheels are **White**; the section with the upward-pointing Air triangle (left) is **Yellow**; the section with the downward-pointing Earth triangle (right) is **Green**.

Lower Panel, Center Square: Air Subangle of Enochian Elemental Tablet of Earth. Center column and second row from the top: **Green** for **Earth**; the rest of the square: **Yellow** for **Air.**

Lower Panel, Right Square: Tattwa symbol Prithivi-Vayu, Air of Earth (**Blue** Circle in a **Yellow** Square).

Knight of Swords

Lord of the Winds and Breezes / King of the Spirits of Air

KNIGHT SWORDS

20° ♉ – 20° ♊

May 11 – June 10

FIRE OF AIR

```
Ruling
20° Taurus to 20° Gemini
May 11—June 10

The Knight of Swords contains the Seven of Disks and
the Eight and Nine of Swords.

He is the Court Card Ruler of
Chokmah,
Sephirah 2
of the Supernal Triad
of the
Yetzirah Tree of Life.
```

The *TCM* Card: Against a background of airy **Light Blue**, a crowned Knight bearing a large Sword is seen in profile astride a **Brown** horse wearing a **Blue** and **Yellow** poitrel. The Knight wears a **Blue** tunic and boots and **Yellow** leggings. The Sword is also displayed on the shield at the lower right.

Additions or Changes: You might adorn the horse with **Blacks** and **Browns**. You may wish add wind-blown clouds and swift-darting birds.

Upper Left Area: I Ching Hexagram 32, Duration (see Appendix).

Lower Panel, Left Square: The P-lettered Square (Fire of Air) from the Enochian Tablet of Union (see Appendix). The two sections with the Spirit wheels are **White**; the section with the upward-pointing Fire triangle (left) is **Red**; the section with the upward-pointing Air triangle (right) is **Yellow**.

Lower Panel, Center Square: Fire Subangle of Enochian Elemental Tablet of Air. Center column and second row from the top: **Yellow** for **Air**; the rest of the square: **Red** for **Fire.**

Lower Panel, Right Square: Tattwa symbol Vayu-Tejas, Fire of Air (**Red** Triangle in a **Blue** Circle).

Queen of Cups

Queen of the Thrones of Water

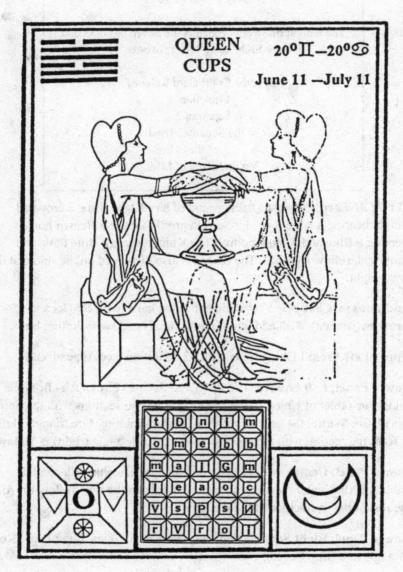

WATER OF WATER

Ruling
20° Gemini to 20° Cancer
June 11—July 11

The Queen of Cups contains the Ten of Swords &
the Two & Three of Cups.

She is the Court Card Ruler of
Binah
Sephirah 3
of the Supernal Triad on the
Briah Tree of Life.

The *TCM* Card: Against a background flooded with **Blue** running water, the Queen is seen in profile facing her own vaporous reflection; the two images rest their arms upon the Cup. She has **Blond** hair, jeweled comb and earrings, a **Greenish-Blue** robe, and **Blue** arm bracelets. She is enthroned upon the Water of Water Enochian Magick square bearing the angelic letter *O* (It is colored the same as the Enochian Tablet of Union square that appears in the lower left of the card).

Additions or Changes: A crayfish traditionally issues from the Cup. You may wish add water lilies and wading birds. Anything you add should be reflected.

Upper Left Area: I Ching Hexagram 58, The Joyous Lake (see Appendix).

Lower Panel, Left Square: The O-lettered Square (Water of Water) from the Enochian Tablet of Union (see Appendix). The two sections with the Spirit wheels are **White**; the two sections with the downward-pointing Water triangle (left and right) are **Blue**.

Lower Panel, Center Square: Water Subangle of Enochian Elemental Tablet of Water. All of the square: **Blue** for **Water**.

Lower Panel, Right Square: Tattwa symbol Apas-Apas, Water of Water (**Silver** Crescent in a **Silver** Crescent).

Prince of Wands

Prince of the Chariot of Wands

PRINCE WANDS

$20°\mathcal{S}-20°\mathcal{N}$

July 12 —Aug. 11

AIR OF FIRE

Ruling
20° Cancer to 20° Leo
July 12– August 11

The Prince of Wands contains the
Four of Cups and
the Five and Six of Wands.

He is the Court Card Ruler of
Chesed, Geburah, Tiphareth, Netzach, Hod, Yesod,
Sephiroth 4-5-6-7-8-9
of the
Atziluth Tree of Life.

The *TCM* Card: Against a background of **Bright Yellow** with scattered **Red** flames, the Prince stands face-forward in a **Yellow** chariot emblazoned with the Great Enochian Seal of Fire. He has **Blond** hair and wears a **Red** tunic with **Yellow** belt and trim. He holds a large Wand in his right hand. A shield displaying the head of lion is slung over his left shoulder.

Additions or Changes: You may wish add flames, a lion, and **Red** rays around his head.

Upper Left Area: I Ching Hexagram 42, Increase (see Appendix).

Lower Panel, Left Square: The I-lettered Square (Air of Fire) from the Enochian Tablet of Union (see Appendix). The two sections with the Spirit wheels are **White**; the section with the upward-pointing Air triangle (left) is **Yellow**; the section with the upward-pointing Fire triangle (right) is **Red**.

Lower Panel, Center Square: Air Subangle of Enochian Elemental Tablet of Fire. Center column and second row from the top: **Red** for **Fire**; the rest of the square: **Yellow** for **Air.**

Lower Panel, Right Square: Tattwa symbol Tejas-Vayu, Air of Fire (**Blue** Circle in a **Red** Triangle).

Knight of Disks

Lord of the Wild and Fertile Land / King of the Spirits of Earth

KNIGHT
DISKS

20° ♌ – 20° ♍

Aug. 12 – Sept. 11

FIRE OF EARTH

```
                    Ruling
            20° Leo to 20° Virgo
          August 12—September 11

        The Knight of Disks contains the
              Seven of Wands and
           the Eight and Nine of Disks.

          He is the Court Card Ruler of
                    Chokmah
                   Sephirah 2
                    of the
             Assiah Tree of Life.
```

The *TCM* Card: Against a background of **Green** rolling hills and **Light-Brown** sky, a crowned Knight is seen in profile astride a **Brown** horse wearing a **Green** and **Brown** poitrel. The Knight wears a **Green** tunic and boots and **Leather Brown** leggings. The Disk is displayed on the **Green** shield at the lower right.

Additions or Changes: You might adorn the horse with **Browns** and **Greens**, and add **Green** corn stalks and deer to the background.

Upper Left Area: I Ching Hexagram 62, Preponderance of the Small (see Appendix).

Lower Panel, Left Square: The A-lettered Square (Fire of Earth) from the Enochian Tablet of Union (see Appendix). The two sections with the Spirit wheels are **White**; the section with the upward-pointing Fire triangle (left) is **Red**; the section with the downward-pointing Earth triangle (right) is **Green**.

Lower Panel, Center Square: Earth Subangle of Enochian Elemental Tablet of Fire. Center column and second row from the top: **Green** for **Earth**; the rest of the square: **Red** for **Fire.**

Lower Panel, Right Square: Tattwa symbol Prithivi-Tejas, Fire of Earth (**Red** Triangle in a **Yellow** Square).

Queen of Swords

Queen of the Thrones of Air

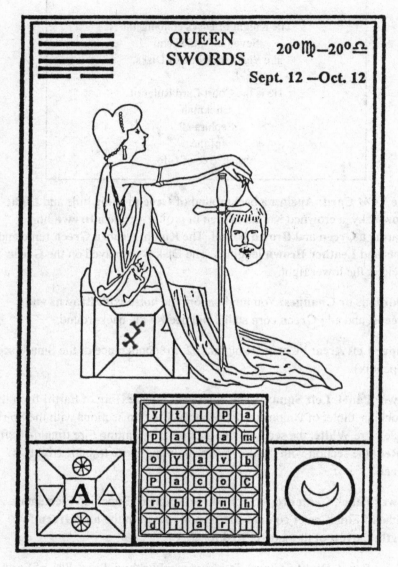

QUEEN
SWORDS

20° ♍ – 20° ♎

Sept. 12 — Oct. 12

WATER OF AIR

The *TCM* Card: Against a background of **Sky Blue**, the Queen is seen in profile. Her hands rest on a downward-pointing Sword, and she holds the severed head of a bearded man. She has **Light-Brown** hair, jeweled comb and earrings, a **Blue** robe, and **Gold** arm bracelets. She is enthroned upon the Water of Air Enochian Magick square bearing the angelic letter *A* (colored the same as the Enochian Tablet of Union square that appears in the lower left of the card).

Additions or Changes: You may wish to add clouds surrounding her throne and crown her with a radiant helmet crested with the face of a child.

Upper Left Area: I Ching Hexagram 28, Preponderance of the Great (see Appendix).

Lower Panel, Left Square: The A-lettered Square (Water of Air) from the Enochian Tablet of Union (see Appendix). The two sections with the Spirit wheels are **White**; the section with the downward-pointing Water triangle (left) is **Blue**; the section with the upward-pointing Air triangle (right) is **Yellow**.

Lower Panel, Center Square: Water Subangle of Enochian Elemental Tablet of Air. Center column and second row from the top: **Yellow** for **Air**; the rest of the square: **Blue** for **Water.**

Lower Panel, Right Square: Tattwa symbol Vayu-Apas, Water of Air (**Silver** Crescent in a **Blue** Circle).

Prince of Cups

Prince of the Chariot of the Waters

PRINCE
CUPS

20° ♎ – 20° ♏

Oct. 13 — Nov. 12

AIR OF WATER

```
Rules
20° Libra to 20° Scorpio
October 13– November 12

The Prince of Cups contains the
Four of Swords and
the Five and Six of Cups.

He is the Court Card Ruler of
Chesed, Geburah, Tiphareth, Netzach, Hod, Yesod,
Sephiroth 4-5-6-7-8-9
of the
Briah Tree of Life.
```

The *TCM* Card: Against a background flooded with **Blue** running water, the Prince stands face-forward in a **Blue** chariot emblazoned with the Great Enochian Seal of Water. He has **Blond** hair and wears a **Greenish-Blue** tunic with a **Blue** belt and trim. He holds a large Cup in his right hand. A shield displaying the head of an eagle is slung over his left shoulder.

Additions or Changes: You may wish add an eagle drawing the chariot. Traditional images show a snake issuing from the Cup.

Upper Left Area: I Ching Hexagram 61, Inner Truth (see Appendix).

Lower Panel, Left Square: The C-lettered Square (Air of Water) from the Enochian Tablet of Union (see Appendix). The two sections with the Spirit wheels are **White**; the section with the upward-pointing Air triangle (left) is **Yellow**; the section with the downward-pointing Water triangle (right) is **Blue**.

Lower Panel, Center Square: Air Subangle of Enochian Elemental Tablet of Water. Center column and second row from the top: **Blue** for **Water**; the rest of the square: **Yellow** for **Air.**

Lower Panel, Right Square: Tattwa symbol Apas-Vayu, Air of Water (**Blue** Circle in a **Silver** Crescent).

Knight of Wands

Lord of the Flame and the Lightning / King of the Spirits of Fire

KNIGHT
WANDS

20° ♏ – 20° ♐

Nov. 13 – Dec. 12

FIRE OF FIRE

```
Rules
20° Scorpio to 20° Sagittarius
November 13—December 12

The Knight of Wands contains the
Seven of Cups and
the Eight and Nine of Wands.

He is the Court Card Ruler of
Chokmah,
Sephirah 2
of the
Atziluth Tree of Life.
```

The *TCM* Card: Against a background of **Bright Yellow** with scattered **Red** flames, a crowned Knight is seen in profile astride a **Black** horse wearing a **Red** and **Yellow** poitrel. The Knight wears a **Red** tunic, **Grey** boots, and **Yellow** leggings. The Wand is displayed on the shield at the lower right.

Additions or Changes: You may wish to show him thrusting a large Wand up and forward. Perhaps include flames bursting from the horse's nostrils, sparks from its hooves.

Upper Left Area: I Ching Hexagram 51, The Arousing, Shock, Thunder (see Appendix).

Lower Panel, Left Square: The M-lettered Square (Fire of Fire) from the Enochian Tablet of Union (see Appendix). The two sections with the Spirit wheels are **White**; the two sections with the upward-pointing Fire triangle (left and right) are **Red**.

Lower Panel, Center Square: Fire Subangle of Enochian Elemental Tablet of Fire. All of the square: **Red** for **Fire**.

Lower Panel, Right Square: Tattwa symbol Tejas-Tejas, Fire of Fire (**Red** Triangle in a **Red** Triangle).

Queen of Disks

Queen of the Thrones of Earth

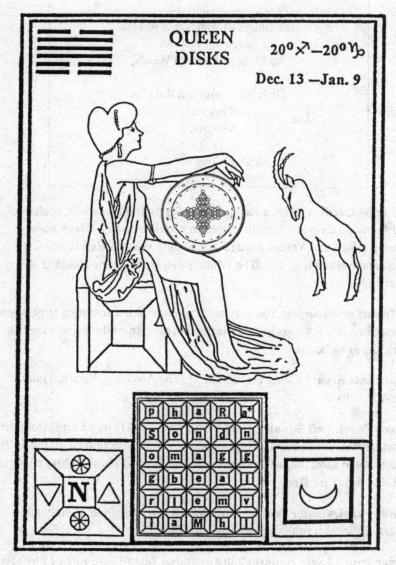

QUEEN
DISKS

20° ♐ —20° ♑

Dec. 13 —Jan. 9

p h a r a
s o n d n
o m a g g
ḡ b e a l
r i e m v
l i a m h

N

WATER OF EARTH

```
Rules
20° Sagittarius to 20° Capricorn
December 13–January 9

The Queen of Disks contains the Ten of Wands and
the Two and Three of Disks.

She is the Court Card Ruler of
Binah,
Sephirah 3
of the
Assiah Tree of Life.
```

The *TCM* Card: Against a background of **Green** rolling hills and **Light-Brown** sky, the Queen is seen in profile; a **Brown** mountain goat in the background. She holds the Disk. She has **Dark-Brown** hair, jeweled comb and earrings, a **Green** robe and **Gold** arm bracelets. She is enthroned upon the Water of Earth Enochian Magick square bearing the angelic letter *N* (colored the same as the Enochian Tablet of Union square that appears in the lower left of the card).

Additions or Changes: You may wish add a winding river flowing from the hills.

Upper Left Area: I Ching Hexagram 31, Wooing (see Appendix).

Lower Panel, Left Square: The N-lettered Square (Water of Earth) from the Enochian Tablet of Union (see Appendix). The two sections with the Spirit wheels are **White**; the section with the downward-pointing Water triangle (left) is **Blue**; the section with the downward-pointing Earth triangle (right) is **Green**.

Lower Panel, Center Square: Water Subangle of Enochian Elemental Tablet of Earth. Center column and second row from the top: **Green** for **Earth**; the rest of the square: **Blue** for **Water.**

Lower Panel, Right Square: Tattwa symbol Apas-Prithivi, Water of Earth (**Silver** Crescent in a **Yellow** Square).

Prince of Swords

Prince of the Chariot of the Winds

AIR OF AIR

THE TAROT ARCHITECT

```
         Rules
20° Capricorn to 20° Aquarius
    January 10–February 8

   The Prince of Swords contains the
         Four of Disks and
     the Five and Six of Swords.

     He is the Court Card Ruler of
Chesed, Geburah, Tiphareth, Netzach, Hod, Yesod,
         Sephiroth 4-5-6-7-8-9
              of the
        Yetzirah Tree of Life.
```

The *TCM* Card: Against a background of **Sky Blue**, the Prince stands face-forward in a **Yellow** chariot trimmed in **Blue** and emblazoned with the Great Enochian Seal of Air. He has **Brown** hair and wears a **Blue** tunic with a **Yellow** belt and trim. He holds a large Sword in his right hand. A shield displaying the head of an angel is slung over his left shoulder.

Additions or Changes: You may wish add a flowing **White** and **Yellow** cape or bubbles in the air.

Upper Left Area: I Ching Hexagram 57, The Gentle Penetrating Wind (see Appendix).

Lower Panel, Right Square: The X-lettered Square (Air of Air) from the Enochian Tablet of Union (see Appendix). The two sections with the Spirit wheels are **White**; the two sections with the upward-pointing Air triangle (left and right) are **Yellow**.

Lower Panel, Center Square: Air Subangle of Enochian Elemental Tablet of Air. Center column and second row from the top: **Yellow** for **Air**; the rest of the square: **Yellow** for **Air.**

Lower Panel, Left Square: Tattwa symbol Vayu-Vayu, Air of Air (**Blue** Circle in a **Blue** Circle).

Knight of Cups

Lord of the Waves and the Waters / King of the Hosts of the Seas

KNIGHT
CUPS

20° ♒ —20° ♓

Feb. 9 —March 11

FIRE OF WATER

The *TCM* Card: Against a background flooded with **Blue** running water, a crowned Knight is seen in profile astride a **White** horse wearing a **Blue** and **Red** poitrel. The Knight wears a **Greenish-Blue** tunic, **Grey** boots, and **Dark-Blue** leggings. The Cup is displayed on the shield at the lower right.

Additions or Changes: You might add a large Cup in his right hand (a crayfish issuing from it). You may wish to adorn the horse with **Blues**, **Reds**, and **Silvers**.

Upper Left Area: I Ching Hexagram 54, The Marrying Maiden (see Appendix).

Lower Panel, Right Square: The A-lettered Square (Fire of Water) from the Enochian Tablet of Union (see Appendix). The two sections with the Spirit wheels are **White**; the section with the upward-pointing Fire triangle (left) is **Red**; the section with the downward-pointing Water triangle (right) is **Blue**.

Lower Panel, Center Square: Fire Subangle of Enochian Elemental Tablet of Water. Center column and second row from the top: **Blue** for **Water**; the rest of the square: **Red** for **Fire.**

Lower Panel, Left Square: Tattwa symbol Tejas-Apas, Fire of Water (**Red** Triangle in a **Silver** Crescent).

Homework Assignment
Introduction

Now that you've installed the Aces and Court Cards in your house of cards, you might be asking, "What do these elements and subelements mean to me personally? How am I personally affected by their influence? What wisdom, what questions, what message do they hold for me?"

Don't you wish you could just close your eyes and jump into the magical world of the cards themselves and have a look around? Perhaps you'd actually like to communicate directly with the facet of divine consciousness that is the Queen of Cups or the Prince of Wands and ask them, "How do you influence my life? How do I see you manifesting in my personality, talents, virtues, or vices? What part of my world is your world? How can I recognize you at work in the circumstances around me?"

Actually . . . you can.

For this exercise and meditation, I will share a simple technique to explore the elemental worlds of the Aces and Court Cards. The doorways to these specific frequencies of consciousness are those little tattwa symbols found on the bottom left panel of the *TCM* cards. They are easy to use. The method is simplicity itself. It works marvelously even if none of us fully understand or appreciate the mechanics behind the phenomena.

It does take a bit of practice to get good at it. But it's a magical skill that will literally open up for you new worlds of wonder.

AN OPTICS DIGRESSION

Have you ever gazed at a colored object or image under a bright light for a minute or two and then suddenly turned your eyes away from it, only to see a cloudy ghost image floating in the air? You can even close your eyes and the image remains there, floating on the inside of your eyelids for a few seconds.

In the quantum world of magical metaphor, that ghost image is the spirit (the true form and color) of the physical object. It's as if you are seeing the soul of the object with the eyes of your soul.

In Qabalah terms, the physical object is only a shell, the lowest vibratory expression of the actual object. It manifests as matter in Assiah, the lowest of the Qabalistic Worlds. The floating ghost image exists just on the other side of the dimensional mirror, in the next higher world, Yetzirah, the Formative World, the world of patterns, the nonmaterial world of ideas, the world of angels. (Do you recall the Four Worlds in a Chair Meditation in Book I, chapter 2? If not please take a moment to review it.)

As we go about our lives, we are comfortable believing our brain when it tells us that the color *red* we see with our physical eyes is actually red. Most of our neighbors (those with brains) also generally agree they see red. In reality what we are seeing with our eyes is not red at all. It is everything *but* red. It's the *absence of red* in the light that is reflected off a totally *unred* object.

Just as the Qabalistic World of Yetzirah floats invisibly behind the material world of Assiah, the *spirit* of red . . . the *soul* of real red . . . the *angel* of red . . . is hidden in the ghost image that exists just behind the red light collected by the cones and rods of our physical eyes. If we could see the actual red, it would instead be the color called cyan, a beautiful greenish-blue (almost turquoise-blue). All the other colors, especially the primary colors, also have their soul color:

Red is seen as cyan in an afterimage.

Blue is seen as yellow in an afterimage.

Yellow is seen as purple in an afterimage.

Silver is seen as deep grey in an afterimage.

Black is seen as white in an afterimage.

But the five tattwa images are more than just the properties of color. The *forms* of the figures are of equal importance. The combination of form and color makes a tattwa symbol a veritable doorway to the world of Yetzirah.

If we could penetrate the ghost-color image with our conscious attention, it would be like passing through a looking glass and into the nonmaterial elemental world behind the physical world. The combined forms and colors of the ancient Hindu tattwas are, on the surface, the visual (Assiah) shells of the elements of Spirit, Fire, Water, Air, and Earth.

When two tattwas are combined, the composite symbols embody the same elemental combinations as the tarot Aces and Court Cards. The ghost images of the tattwas can be used as astral gateways to the elemental worlds of the cards.

This technique takes a bit of practice, and not everyone will succeed in triggering a clear and lucid *out-of-body* projection through a tattwa image into a Court Card. But even practicing these exercises often triggers profound and dramatic visions and dream adventures.

Our Destination

For this exercise we will be experimenting with one Court Card, the *Prince of Wands*, whose tattwa symbol is Tejas-Vayu (Air of Fire), a *Blue Circle* inside an upright *Red Triangle*. You will see the uncolored image in the lower right of your *TCM* Prince of Wands.

> *Wands* (Fire) = Tejas (Red Triangle)
>
> *Prince* (Air) = Vayu (Blue Circle)

MAKE YOUR TATTWA SYMBOL

If you've completed painting your Aces and Court Cards, you already have a complete set of tattwa symbols on the cards themselves. (The Tejas-Vayu appears in the right-hand area of the lower panel of your *TCM* Prince of Wands.) And once you've colored a card, it can be used for this exercise. But for your first experiment it will perhaps be better to create a slightly larger, brighter version of the Tejas-Vayu. I have a couple suggestions that might help.

PAINT YOUR OWN

If you are skilled, you can paint your own Tejas-Vayu using oils, watercolors, or acrylics. Or it might be easier for you to simply make one out of paper or cardstock. All you need is a black sheet of paper or cardstock (to serve as the background), a bright red sheet of paper or cardstock (from which to cut the triangle), a bright blue sheet of paper or cardstock (from which to cut the circle), a plain white sheet of paper or cardstock (to serve as the backdrop for the ghost image to float on), scissors, and some glue.

1. From your red paper cut out a red equilateral triangle (about three inches per side).

2. Paste the triangle (upward-pointing) to the center of the black paper.

3. From your blue paper cut out a blue circle, just big enough to fit within the triangle without touching the sides.

4. Paste the circle to the center of the triangle.

5. Keep your white paper near at hand for the exercise.

USE YOUR COMPUTER

Actually, this is the most dramatically effective way to get a good ghost image:

1. Create a two-page PowerPoint presentation.

2. Create a large (nearly a page wide) upright equilateral triangle with no border. Fill it with bright red.

3. Create a medium-size circle with no border. Fill it with bright blue.

4. Drag the circle into the triangle and center.

5. Finally, choose a pure black background.

6. The second page of your PowerPoint presentation leave pure white.

Exercise 4

Using a Tattwa Symbol to Travel in Spirit Vision the Elemental World of the Prince of Wands

---

PART ONE: PRELIMINARY PRACTICE

(Using a Paper or Cardstock Tattwa Image)

1. Seat yourself comfortably at a well-lit desk or table.

2. Position your black sheet displaying the Tejas-Vayu about eighteen inches from your eyes. (Make sure it is brightly lit.)

3. Hold the white sheet in your hands.

4. Relax and stare at the brightly lit Tejas-Vayu for at least thirty seconds.

5. Quickly raise the white sheet in front of your eyes and observe the ghost image.

6. Repeat this exercise two or three times until the ghost images become clear.

PRELIMINARY PRACTICE (USING YOUR COMPUTER)

1. Seat yourself comfortably before your computer screen. Turn the brightness level high. Bring up your two-page PowerPoint presentation and set view setting to "Slide Show." (This will completely fill your screen with the Tejas-Vayu image.)

2. Pull up the first page of your PowerPoint Tejas-Vayu (Red Triangle with a Blue Circle inside) against a black full background.

3. Relax and stare at the brightly lit Tejas-Vayu for at least thirty seconds.

4. Quickly advance to the next bright white slide and observe the ghost image.

5. Repeat this exercise two or three times until the ghost images become clear.

PART TWO: ADVANCED PRACTICE

Repeat the steps in part one, but once you see the ghost image, *close your eyes* until you can clearly perceive the image floating on the inside of your closed eyelids. When you get good at seeing and holding the image with your eyes closed, continue to Meditation 7.

Meditation 7

Projecting into the World of the Prince of Wands

1. Arrange everything as in your practice exercises, only also have your Prince of Wands tarot card at hand.

2. Gaze upon the Prince of Wands until you feel a living presence in the card. (It is important that you make this subtle connection, even if at first it is only in your imagination.)

3. Say out loud, "It is my will to understand your world."

4. Put the Prince of Wands down and start gazing at the brightly lit Tejas-Vayu for at least thirty seconds, and proceed until you clearly see the ghost image with your closed eyes.

5. As you see it floating, use your imagination and project your consciousness through the image. (Don't be afraid to pretend.)

6. Relax for a moment. Don't *try* to see anything. In fact, just completely relax and let your mind wander where it wants to go. Don't dismiss anything as just being your imagination. Just observe. Daydream, if that's what you want to call it.

7. In a few minutes, open your eyes, and write down any visions, thoughts, or observations.

8. Keep your diary by your bedside, and, upon waking, try to remember and record your dreams.

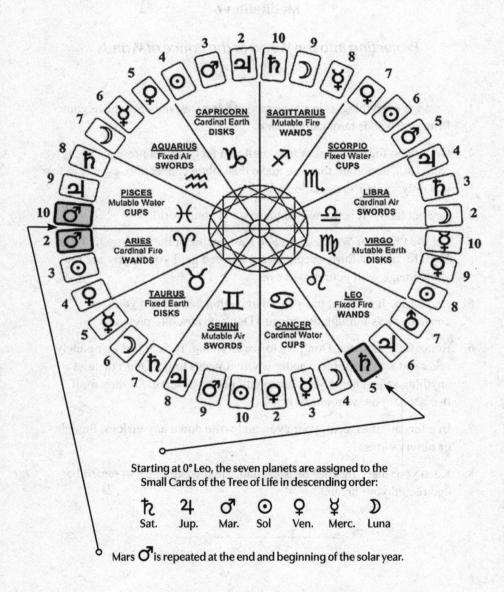

Starting at 0° Leo, the seven planets are assigned to the Small Cards of the Tree of Life in descending order:

♄	♃	♂	☉	♀	☿	☽
Sat.	Jup.	Mar.	Sol	Ven.	Merc.	Luna

Mars ♂ is repeated at the end and beginning of the solar year.

Figure 36. The Thiry-Six Decons.

CHAPTER 9

The Complex World
of the Small Cards:
Spirits and Angels of the
Thirty-Six Decans

Sidebar 19

PLEASE DO THIS NOW!

Take up the thirty-six Small Cards (the 2–10 of each suit). Kiss each of them, and separate them by suits: Wands, Cups, Swords, Disks. Then put them in order Two to Ten. Place the four stacks nearby as you read the following.

What Makes Small Cards Tick?

In the previous chapter we learned how three Small Cards live inside each of the twelve Astrological Court Cards and how all thirty-six Small Cards are cozily nestled together with cards of foreign elements within their host Court Cards. Now we are going to look a little deeper into the qabalistic and astrological wonders of the Small Cards and observe what spiritual forces makes them tick. This time we're going to invite the seven planets to the party.

Figure 36 deals exclusively with the Small Cards. Their numbers appear just outside the ring of cards, and their suit is identified near the large Zodiac Sign toward the center of the wheel.

Take a moment and observe how three Small Cards are assigned to each Zodiac Sign. You will notice the following:

All the **Twos, Threes, Fours** represent the three decans of the *Cardinal* Signs (Aries, Cancer, Libra, Capricorn).

All the **Fives, Sixes, Sevens** represent the three decans of the *Fixed* Signs (Leo, Scorpio, Aquarius, Taurus).

All the **Eights, Nines, Tens** represent the three decans of the *Mutable* Signs (Sagittarius, Pisces, Gemini, Virgo).

Starting with the Five of Wands at 0° Leo (the traditional Chaldean start of the astrological year), and moving counterclockwise, the seven planets are assigned in five repeating sequences throughout the wheel of the year. The sequence they appear is the same order the planetary spheres descend (the Lightning Flash) down the Tree of Life: Saturn. Jupiter, Mars, Sol, Venus, Mercury, and Luna.

Let's use the cards of Leo as an illustration:

Near the center of the wheel locate the Sign of Leo ♌.

The pie-shaped Leo ♌ section of the wheel is identified as "**Leo—Fixed Fire—Wands**."

The three Small Cards that inhabit the three decans of Leo are the Five, Six, and Seven of Wands.

As 0° Leo is the *start* of the planetary sequences, the **Five of Wands** is assigned **Saturn**, the **Six of Wands Jupiter**, and the **Seven of Wands Mars**.

The Saturn-Jupiter-Mars-Sol-Venus-Mercury-Luna sequence repeats five time as it circles counterclockwise around the zodiacal year.

Wait a Minute! Somethin' Ain't Right!

You might be scratching your head because this arrangement doesn't exactly work out. There are seven planets and thirty-six decans. One planet somewhere . . . sometime . . . somehow will have to repeat itself for everything to come out.

That's exactly what happens, and *Mars* is the lucky planet that gets two consecutive decans on the zodiacal calendar. Look to the far left of the wheel (Figure 36) where the last decan of Pisces (Ten of Cups) meets the first decan of Aries (Two of Wands). Mars is assigned to *both decans* and both cards.

To boost the decaying momentum of winter, the flywheel of the year is overweighted with an explosive double shot of the energy of Mars—sort of like a spark to keep the engine of the year running through the critical transition from weakest point of tired winter to the burst anew at the beginning of spring.

What Does Enochian Magick Have to Do with Small Cards?

We've already seen how the four Aces and sixteen Court Cards represent the same cosmic facts of life as those represented by four Elemental Tablets of Enochian Magick and their sixteen subsections (subangles). Each Enochian Elemental Tablet (see the Aces) is divided into four quadrants (the Court Cards) by two vertical columns (running down the center of the tablet) and one horizontal row. There are thirty-six squares in each Grand Cross, and—you guessed it—these are represented in tarot by the thirty-six Small Cards. And, like tarot's thirty-six Small Cards, these Enochian squares are assigned exactly the same planet/Zodiac combinations that we see in Figure 36.

The same three-card sets of Small Cards (arranged in different suit order depending which Elemental Tablet they reside in) serve the same purpose on the Grand Crosses all four Elemental Tablets.

Why am I burdening you with all this Enochian Magick information? First, it is to impress upon you how important the Small Cards are to the machinery of existence, and second, it is to help you understand why we will color the sections of the little Enochian squares that appear in the upper left corner of each of each Small Card the way we do.

Colors of the Zodiac Signs

Looking to the top left section of every Small Card, you will find the image of a truncated pyramid that is the Enochian square the card represents.

The uppermost section of the pyramid contains a small wheel representing Spirit. This should be painted White.

The lowest section of the pyramid we will leave *uncolored* because its color varies depending upon which of the four Elemental Tablets this square occupies.

The *left* section of the pyramid represents its Zodiac assignment and is colored accordingly:

Red for the Fire Signs: Aries, Leo, Sagittarius

Blue for the Water Signs: Cancer, Scorpio, Pisces

Yellow for the Air Signs: Libra, Aquarius, Gemini

Green for the Earth Signs: Capricorn, Taurus, Virgo

The *Right* section of the pyramid represents Planetary assignment and is colored accordingly. The colors assigned to the planets might seem a bit confusing and counterintuitive, so I'm going to take us on another short digression.

The Weird Elemental Color Assignments of the Planets

We must keep in mind that we are dealing with the elemental worlds of the Lesser Arcana and the *astrological* and *elemental* pedigrees of the planets, and not the familiar colors of the *planetary spheres* of the Greater Arcana's Tree of Life.

The right section of the Small Card's Enochian square represents its planet, and it is colored according to the *elemental assignment of the Zodiac Sign* that the planet rules or where it is in exaltation:

Saturn—Exalted in Libra—Air—so Saturn's color is Yellow.

Jupiter—Rules Sagittarius—Fire—so Jupiter's color is Red.

Mars—Rules Scorpio—Water—so Mars's color is Blue.

Sun—Rules Leo—Fire—so the Sun's color is Red.

Venus—Rules Taurus—Earth—so Venus's color is Green.

Mercury—Rules Gemini—Air—so Mercury's color is Yellow.

Moon—Exalted in Taurus—Earth—so the Moon's color is Green.

Even if you don't use the *Tarot of Ceremonial Magick*, *Thoth Tarot*, or *Golden Dawn* decks, these same qabalistic *planet-in-Zodiac* assignments *color* the personalities of the Small Cards of whatever deck you have in front of you.

Small Cards Have a Lot of Stuff Going On.[1]

יהוה SUIT STUFF

Each Small Card carries the overall elemental qualities and characteristics of its suit.

TREE OF LIFE STUFF

Each Small Card has the character and qualities of the numbered sephirah it represents and the corresponding Qabalistic World and Part of the Soul its suit represents.

ZODIAC SIGN STUFF

Each Small Card resides in and represents one decan of a Zodiac Sign.

PLANET STUFF

Each Small Card embodies a specific planetary influence within its home Zodiac Sign and relative to its position on the Tree of Life.

These four factors alone are enough to give each Small Card its unique character and divinatory meaning. Here are some examples:

The Six of Cups—"Pleasure"

Sephirah 6, Tiphareth, "Beauty" the Sun

Cups; Briah, the Creative World; Neshamah, the Soul Intuition

Sun in Scorpio!

The combination of these three factors certainly sounds like Pleasure to me! But for those of us who are interested in magic, there is even more stuff going on in each Small Card.

ANGEL STUFF

This is where we get to meet the wild and wonderful permanent residents of the house of cards.

Each Small Card decan is the home of two of the seventy-two traditional qabalistic angels of the Shemhamphorash or the *Divided Name of God*. (See Table 5.) These angels are living inside the Small Cards of every standard tarot deck whether you choose to recognize them or not, so I think you should at least be aware of them.

Their names are drawn from three consecutive verses from Exodus. Each verse is comprised of seventy-two Hebrew letters. Each angel rules a five-degree period (quinary) of the year. The specific powers and abilities of the Shemhamphorash angels are hinted at in the text of seventy-two different verses of Psalms and Genesis where the Name יהוה, **Yod Heh Vav Heh,** was discovered by qabalists (who obviously had far too much time on their hands).

Each angel of the Shemhamphorash is a specialized executor of very specific facet of Yod Heh Vav Heh's will and can be magically activated and employed, especially during the periods of its assigned quinary.

The names of the Shemhamphorash angels appear near the *bottom* of each Small Card of the *Tarot of Ceremonial Magick*: the angel of the decan's first quinary on the left; the second quinary on the right.

DEMON STUFF

Now don't freak out. I should probably refer to them simply as "spirits of the Goetia." There are seventy-two of them, and they also live in pairs in each of the thirty-six Small Cards. But unlike the quinary-dwelling angels of the Shemhamphorash, the Goetic spirits get an entire decan, one spirit for the *day* and one for the *night*. (See Table 5.)

Table 5. Spirits and Angels of the Small Cards

Days of the year	Zodiac Sign	Decan	72 Angels of the Shem ha-Mephorash	Quinary ruled by Angel	Tarot Suit	Tarot Small Card	Title of Small Card	Day or Night Demon	72 Demons of the Goetia
Jun 21–July 1	CANCER Cardinal Water	0°–10°	Eiael		CUPS	2	LOVE	DAY	BUER
			Habuiah					NIGHT	BIFRONS
July 2–11			Rochel			3	ABUNDANCE	DAY	GUSION
		10°–20°	Iibamiah					NIGHT	VUAL
July 12–21		20°–30°	Haiaiel			4	BLENDED PLEASURE	DAY	SITRI
			Mumiah					NIGHT	HAAGENTI
July 22–Aug 1	LEO Fixed Fire	0°–10°	Vehuiah		WANDS	5	STRIFE	DAY	BELETH
			Ieliel					NIGHT	CROCELL
Aug 2–11			Sitael			6	VICTORY	DAY	LERAIE
		10°–20°	Elemiah					NIGHT	FURCAS
Aug 12–22		20°–30°	Mahashiah			7	VALOUR	DAY	ELIGOS
			Lelahel					NIGHT	BALAM
Aug 23–Sep 1	VIRGO Mutable Earth	0°–10°	Aehaiah		DISKS	8	PRUDENCE	DAY	ZEPAR
			Cahethel					NIGHT	ALLOCES
Sep 2–12			Haziel			9	MATERIAL GAIN	DAY	BOTIS
		10°–20°	Aladiah					NIGHT	CAMIO
Sep 13–22		20°–30°	Lauiah			10	WEALTH	DAY	BATHIN
			Hahiah					NIGHT	MURMUR
Sep 23–Oct 2	LIBRA Cardinal Air	0°–10°	Ieiazel		SWORDS	2	PEACE RESTORED	DAY	SALLOS
			Mebahel					NIGHT	OROBAS
Oct 3–12			Hariel			3	SORROW	DAY	PURSON
		10°–20°	Hakamiah					NIGHT	GREMORY
Oct 13–22		20°–30°	Leviah			4	REST FROM STRIFE	DAY	MARAX
			Caliel					NIGHT	OSÉ
Oct 23–Nov 1	SCORPIO Fixed Water	0°–10°	Leuuiah		CUPS	5	LOSS IN PLEASURE	DAY	IPOS
			Pahliah					NIGHT	AMY
Nov 2–11			Nelchael			6	PLEASURE	DAY	AIM
		10°–20°	Ieiaiel					NIGHT	ORIAS
Nov 12–21		20°–30°	Melahel			7	ILLUSIONARY SUCCESS	DAY	NABERIUS
			Hahuiah					NIGHT	VAPULA
Nov 23–Dec 2	SAGITTARIUS Mutable Fire	0°–10°	Nithhaiah		WANDS	8	SWIFTNESS	DAY	GLASYA-LABOLAS
			Haaiah					NIGHT	ZAGAN
Dec 3–12			Ieathel			9	GREAT STRENGTH	DAY	BUNÉ
		10°–20°	Sahiiah					NIGHT	VALAC
Dec 13–21		20°–30°	Reiiel			10	OPPRESSION	DAY	RONOVÉ
			Amael					NIGHT	ANDRAS
Dec 22–30	CAPRICORN Cardinal Earth	0°–10°	Lecabel		DISKS	2	HARMONIOUS CHANGE	DAY	BERITH
			Vasariah					NIGHT	HAURES
Dec 31–Jan 9			Iehuiah			3	MATERIAL WORKS	DAY	ASTAROTH
		10°–20°	Lehahiah					NIGHT	ANDREALPHUS
Jan 10–19		20°–30°	Chavakiah			4	EARTHLY POWER	DAY	FORNEUS
			Monadel					NIGHT	CIMEIES
Jan 20–29	AQUARIUS Fixed Air	0°–10°	Aniel		SWORDS	5	DEFEAT	DAY	FORAS
			Haamiah					NIGHT	AMDUSIAS
Jan 30–Feb 8			Rehael			6	EARNED SUCCESS	DAY	ASMODAY
		10°–20°	Ihiazel					NIGHT	BELIAL
Feb 9–18		20°–30°	Hahahel			7	UNSTABLE EFFORT	DAY	GÄAP
			Michael					NIGHT	DECARBIA
Feb 19–28	PISCES Mutable Water	0°–10°	Vevaliah		CUPS	8	ABANDONED SUCCESS	DAY	FURFUR
			Ielahiah					NIGHT	SEERE
Mar 1–10			Saliah			9	MATERIAL HAPPINESS	DAY	MARCHOSIAS
		10°–20°	Ariel					NIGHT	DANTALION
Mar 11–20		20°–30°	Asaliah			10	PERFECTED SUCCESS	DAY	STOLAS
			Mihael					NIGHT	ANDROMALIUS
Mar 21–30	ARIES Cardinal Fire	0°–10°	Vehuel		WANDS	2	DOMINION	DAY	BAEL
			Daniel					NIGHT	PHENEX
Mar 31–Apr 10			Heahaziah			3	ESTABLISHED STRENGTH	DAY	AGARES
		10°–20°	Amamiah					NIGHT	HALPHAS
Apr 11–20		20°–30°	Nanael			4	PERFECTED WORK	DAY	VASSAGO
			Nithael					NIGHT	MALPHAS
Apr 21–30	TAURUS Fixed Earth	0°–10°	Mebahiah		DISKS	5	MATERIAL TROUBLE	DAY	SAMIGINA
			Poiel					NIGHT	RÄUM
May 1–10			Nemamiah			6	MATERIAL SUCCESS	DAY	MARBAS
		10°–20°	Ieilael					NIGHT	FOCALOR
May 11–20		20°–30°	Harahel			7	SUCCESS UNFULFILLED	DAY	VALEFOR
			Mizrael					NIGHT	VEPAR
May 21–31	GEMINI Mutable Air	0°–10°	Umabel		SWORDS	8	SHORTENED FORCE	DAY	AMON
			Iahhel					NIGHT	SABNOCK
Jun 1–10			Annauel			9	DESPAIR & CRUELTY	DAY	BARBATOS
		10°–20°	Mekekiel					NIGHT	SHAX
Jun 11–20		20°–30°	Damabiah			10	RUIN	DAY	PAIMON
			Meniel					NIGHT	VINÉ

The spirits of the Goetia can be perhaps the most practical and potentially helpful spirits a magician can enlist to assist with the *in-your-face* issues of everyday life on the material plane. However, if the magician is not yet equipped with at least modicum of common sense and wisdom to recognize what is or is not in their best spiritual interest, the magical adventure can often trigger uncomfortably character-building experiences. Nevertheless, these angels and spirits form the culture of each Small Card.

If you are seriously interested in these systems of the magical work, I suggest you avail yourself of several of the very fine books currently available on the market before experimenting too casually.

As you color your Small Cards, feel free to color the seals of the Goetic spirits anything you like or leave them uncolored.

CHAPTER 10

The Small Cards

This example is the Three (Binah) of Disks (Earth/Assiah).

Features of the Small Cards

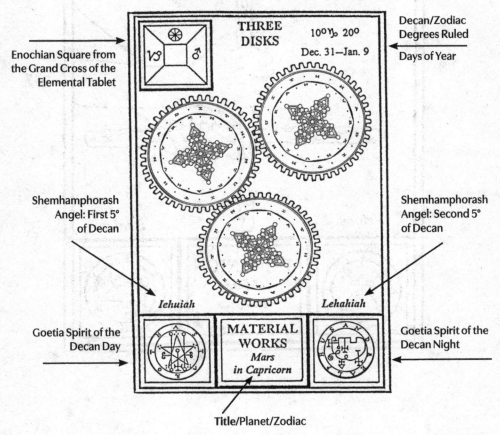

Enochian Square from the Grand Cross of the Elemental Tablet

Decan/Zodiac Degrees Ruled

Days of Year

THREE DISKS

10° ♑ 20°

Dec. 31–Jan. 9

Shemhamphorash Angel: First 5° of Decan

Shemhamphorash Angel: Second 5° of Decan

Iehuiah

Lehahiah

Goetia Spirit of the Decan Day

Goetia Spirit of the Decan Night

MATERIAL WORKS
Mars
in Capricorn

Title/Planet/Zodiac

Two of Wands

Dominion

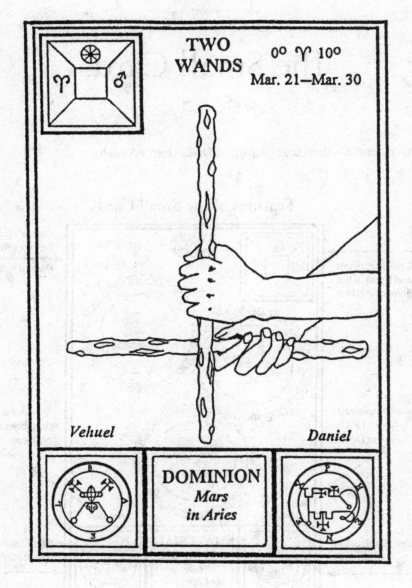

TWO
WANDS

0° ♈ 10°
Mar. 21–Mar. 30

Vehuel

Daniel

DOMINION
*Mars
in Aries*

Mars Rules 0°–10° Aries March 21–March 30	*Shemhamphorash Angels:
	Vehuel: Great and Lofty
Sephirah 2	Daniel: Merciful Judge
Chokmah	
on the Atziluth Tree of Life	*Spirits of the Goetia:
First manifestation of Fire. Ideal will, independent and creative. Control over circumstances.	#1 Bael (day) #37 Phenex (night)

The *TCM* Card: *(See Table 4 for King Scale of Colors.)* Against a background of pure soft **Blue**, two hands appear from the right of the card holding two **Reddish-Brown** Wands in the act of rubbing them together to make fire. **Red** and **Yellow** sparks and flames radiate from where the Wands cross.

Additions or Changes: You may wish to add more **Red** flames in the background, adorn the hands with rings, and clothe the arms in military or regal sleeves and cuffs.

Upper Left Square: Each of the thirty-six decans, together with their planetary ruler, occupies a truncated pyramid square in the Great Central Cross of each of the four Enochian Elemental Tablets. This is the Mars (**Blue**) in Aries (**Red**) square.

Lower Panel, Left Square: The Seal of *Bael*, day Spirit of the Goetia (see Table 5).

Lower Panel, Center Square: Card Title, Planet, and Zodiac Sign.

Lower Panel, Right Square: The Seal of *Phenex*, night Spirit of the Goetia (see Table 5).

Three of Wands

Established Strength

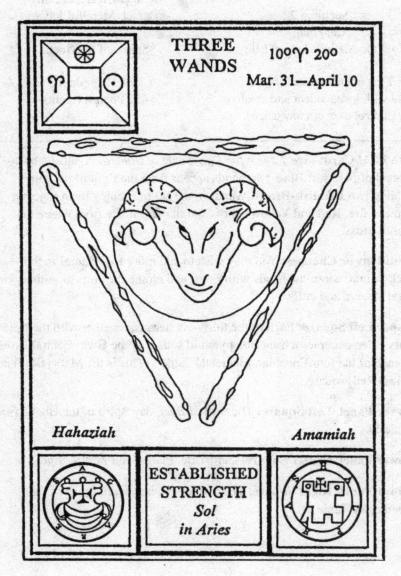

THREE
WANDS

10° ♈ 20°
Mar. 31—April 10

Hahaziah

Amamiah

ESTABLISHED
STRENGTH
*Sol
in Aries*

The *TCM* Card: *(See Table 4 for King Scale of Colors.)* Against a background of **Crimson** three Wands form a downward-pointing triangle enclosing the large ram's head in a **Red** circle.

Additions or Changes: You may wish to color the circle as a **Golden** Sun with **Yellow** and **Red** tongues of flame.

Upper Left Square: Each of the thirty-six decans, together with their planetary ruler, occupies a truncated pyramid square in the Great Central Cross of each of the four Enochian Elemental Tablets. This is the Sol (**Red**) in Aries (**Red**) square.

Lower Panel, Left Square: The Seal of *Agares*, day Spirit of the Goetia (see Table 5).

Lower Panel, Center Square: Card Title, Planet, and Zodiac Sign.

Lower Panel, Right Square: The Seal of *Halphas*, night Spirit of the Goetia (see Table 5).

Four of Wands
Perfected Work

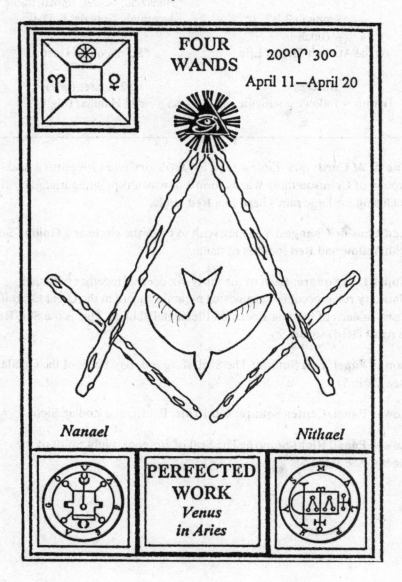

FOUR
WANDS

20° ♈ 30°
April 11–April 20

Nanael

Nithael

PERFECTED
WORK
*Venus
in Aries*

Venus Rules 20°–30° Aries
April 11–April 20

Sephirah 4
Chesed
on the Atziluth Tree of Life

Completion. Order. Limitation.
By tact and gentleness, a strived-for
goal is achieved.

*Shemhamphorash Angels:

Nanael: Caster down of the proud
Nithael: Celestial King

*Spirits of the Goetia:

#3 Vassago (day)
#39 Malphas (night)

The *TCM* Card: *(See Table 4 for King Scale of Colors.)* Against a background of **Deep Violet,** four Wands form the Masonic Square and Compass. They enclose a **White** descending Dove of the Holy Spirit. The head of the compass is the classic Egyptian Eye-in-the-Triangle. It radiates a brilliant **Red** glory.

Additions or Changes: You may wish to add ram's heads and accents of Venusian **Greens** to the background.

Upper Left Square: Each of the thirty-six decans, together with their planetary ruler, occupies a truncated pyramid square in the Great Central Cross of each of the four Enochian Elemental Tablets. This is the Venus (**Green**) in Aries (**Red**) square.

Lower Panel, Left Square: The Seal of *Vassago*, day Spirit of the Goetia (see Table 5).

Lower Panel, Center Square: Card Title, Planet, and Zodiac Sign.

Lower Panel, Right Square: The Seal of *Malphas*, night Spirit of the Goetia (see Table 5).

Five of Wands
Strife

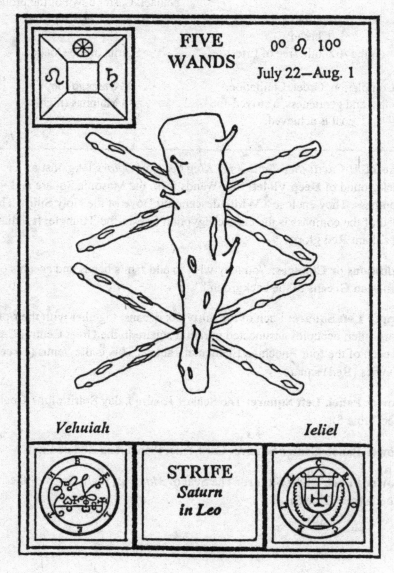

FIVE
WANDS

0° ♌ 10°
July 22—Aug. 1

Vehuiah

Ieliel

STRIFE
*Saturn
in Leo*

```
Saturn Rules 0°–10° Leo          *Shemhamphorash Angels:
   July 22–August 1
                                  Vehuiah: God the exalter
     Sephirah 5                      Jeliel: Strength
      Geburah
on the Atziluth Tree of Life       *Spirits of the Goetia:

Stress. Destruction. Purgation         #13 Beleth (day)
  preceding renewal. Conflict.         #49 Crocell (night)
Vigorous, even violent belligerency.
```

The *TCM* Card: *(See Table 4 for King Scale of Colors.)* Against a background of **Orange** stands a huge rough club. Behind it four smaller Wands cross to form two *X*s.

Additions or Changes: You may wish to add more **Red** flames shot with Saturnian **Greys** and **Blacks**.

Upper Left Square: Each of the thirty-six decans, together with their planetary ruler, occupies a truncated pyramid square in the Great Central Cross of each of the four Enochian Elemental Tablets. This is the Saturn (**Yellow**) in Leo (**Red**) square.

Lower Panel, Left Square: The Seal of *Beleth*, day Spirit of the Goetia (see Table 5).

Lower Panel, Center Square: Card Title, Planet, and Zodiac Sign.

Lower Panel, Right Square: The Seal of *Crocell*, night Spirit of the Goetia (see Table 5).

Six of Wands

Victory

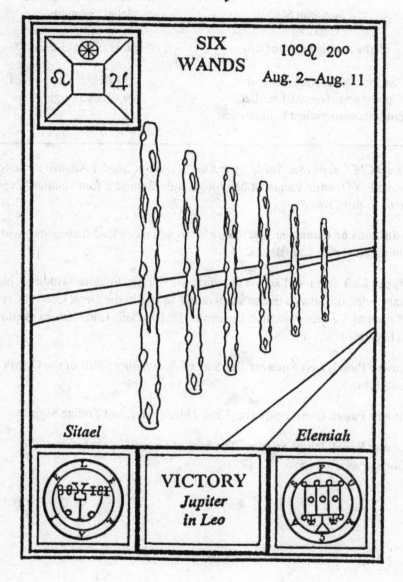

SIX WANDS

10° ♌ 20°

Aug. 2—Aug. 11

Sitael

Elemiah

VICTORY
*Jupiter
in Leo*

Jupiter Rules 10°–20° Leo	*Shemhamphorash Angels:
August 2–August 11	
	Satael: Refuge, Fortress
Sephirah 6	Elemmiah: Concealed, Deliverance
Tiphareth	
on the Atziluth Tree of Life	*Spirits of the Goetia:
Exultation after struggle. Harmony.	#14 Leraie (day)
Beauty. Stability. Perfect balance.	#50 Furcas (night)
Accomplishment. Gain.	

The *TCM* Card: *(See Table 4 for King Scale of Colors.)* Against a background of **Clear Rose Pink,** six Wands appear to march forward on a **White** road.

Additions or Changes: You may wish to add symbols and tokens of victory confidence.

Upper Left Square: Each of the thirty-six decans, together with their planetary ruler, occupies a truncated pyramid square in the Great Central Cross of each of the four Enochian Elemental Tablets. This is the Jupiter (**Red**) in Leo (**Red**) square.

Lower Panel, Left Square: The Seal of *Leraie*, day Spirit of the Goetia (see Table 5).

Lower Panel, Center Square: Card Title, Planet, and Zodiac Sign.

Lower Panel, Right Square: The Seal of *Furcas*, night Spirit of the Goetia (see Table 5).

Seven of Wands

Valour

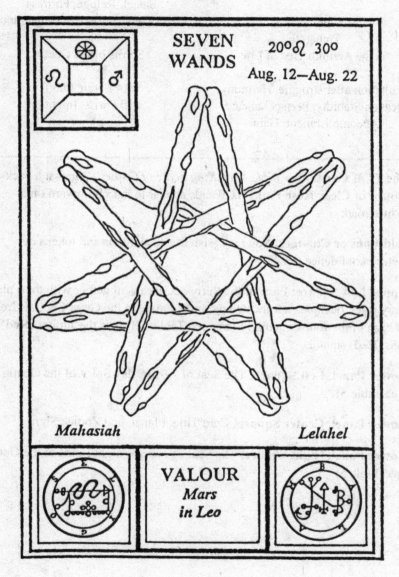

SEVEN WANDS

20° ♌ 30°
Aug. 12—Aug. 22

♌   ♂

Mahasiah

Lelahel

VALOUR
*Mars
in Leo*

Mars Rules 10°–20° Leo August 2–August 11 Sephirah 7 Netzach on the Atziluth Tree of Life Equilibrium disturbed. Loss of confidence. Difficulties requiring courage and tenacity to overcome.	*Shemhamphorash Angels: Mahasiah: Seeking deliverance from fears Daniel: Sing praises *Spirits of the Goetia: #15 Eligos (day) #51 Balam (night)

The *TCM* Card: *(See Table 4 for King Scale of Colors.)* Against an **Amber** background, seven flaming Wands join to form a unicursal heptagram.

Additions or Changes: You may wish to add sparks or flames bursting from the points where the Wands touch.

Upper Left Square: Each of the thirty-six decans, together with their planetary ruler, occupies a truncated pyramid square in the Great Central Cross of each of the four Enochian Elemental Tablets. This is the Mars (**Blue**) in Leo (**Red**) square.

Lower Panel, Left Square: The Seal of *Eligos*, day Spirit of the Goetia (see Table 5).

Lower Panel, Center Square: Card Title, Planet, and Zodiac Sign.

Lower Panel, Right Square: The Seal of *Balam*, night Spirit of the Goetia (see Table 5).

Eight of Wands

Swiftness

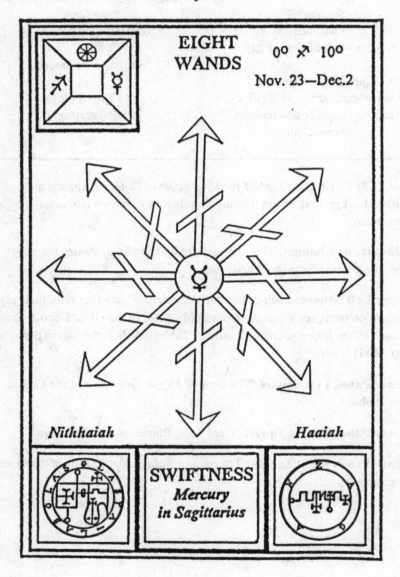

EIGHT
WANDS

0° ♐ 10°

Nov. 23—Dec.2

Nithhaiah

Haaiah

SWIFTNESS
*Mercury
in Sagittarius*

Mercury Rules 0°–10° Sagittarius November 23–December 2	*Shemhamphorash Angels:
	Nithhaiah: Wonderworking
Sephirah 8 Hod on the Atziluth Tree of Life	Haaiah: Heaven in secret
	*Spirits of the Goetia:
Sudden flash of activity; too much too soon. Speech. Electricity. Phone call, letter, electronic message.	#25 Glasya-Labolas (day) #61 Zagan (night)

The *TCM* Card: *(See Table 4 for King Scale of Colors.)* Against a background of **Violet Purple**, eight Sagittarius-arrow-shaped Wands form an eight-pointed star.

Additions or Changes: You may wish to add sparks and electric flames throughout.

Upper Left Square: Each of the thirty-six decans, together with their planetary ruler, occupies a truncated pyramid square in the Great Central Cross of each of the four Enochian Elemental Tablets. This is the Mercury (**Yellow**) in Sagittarius (**Red**) square.

Lower Panel, Left Square: The Seal of *Glasya-Labolas*, day Spirit of the Goetia (see Table 5).

Lower Panel, Center Square: Card Title, Planet, and Zodiac Sign.

Lower Panel, Right Square: The Seal of *Zagan*, night Spirit of the Goetia (see Table 5).

Nine of Wands

Great Strength

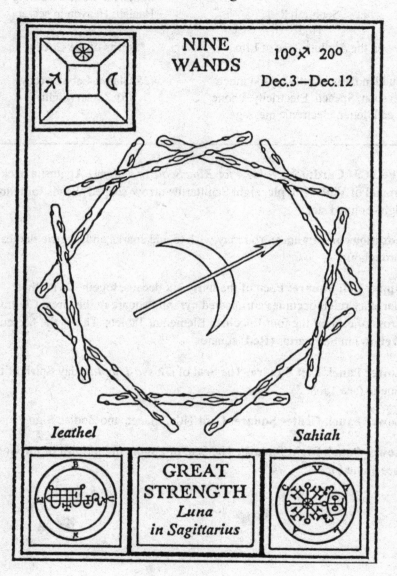

NINE
WANDS

$10° ↗ 20°$

Dec. 3—Dec. 12

Ieathel

Sahiah

**GREAT
STRENGTH**
*Luna
in Sagittarius*

The *TCM* Card: *(See Table 4 for King Scale of Colors.)* Against a background of **Indigo**, nine Wands form a nonagon surrounding the Sign of Sagittarius formed from a **Silver** crescent Moon.

Additions or Changes: You may wish to add a **Yellow** glory behind the Moon.

Upper Left Square: Each of the thirty-six decans, together with their planetary ruler, occupies a truncated pyramid square in the Great Central Cross of each of the four Enochian Elemental Tablets. This is the Moon (**Green**) in Sagittarius (**Red**) square.

Lower Panel, Left Square: The Seal of Buné, day Spirit of the Goetia (see Table 5).

Lower Panel, Center Square: Card Title, Planet, and Zodiac Sign.

Lower Panel, Right Square: The Seal of Valac, night Spirit of the Goetia (see Table 5).

Ten of Wands

Oppression

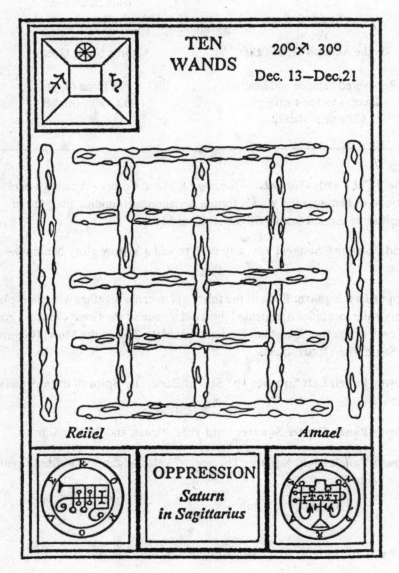

TEN
WANDS

20° ♐ 30°

Dec. 13—Dec. 21

Reiiel

Amael

OPPRESSION

*Saturn
in Sagittarius*

Saturn Rules 20°–30° Sagittarius December 13–December 21	*Shemhamphorash Angels:
	Reiiel: Expectation
Sephirah 10	Amael: Patience
Malkuth	
on the Atziluth Tree of Life	*Spirits of the Goetia:
Blind force. Violent energy. Obstinate cruelty. Self-devouring lust of result.	#27 Ronové (day) #63 Andras (night)

The *TCM* Card: *(See Table 4 for King Scale of Colors.)* Against a background of **Yellow**, ten Wands are arranged to form the window bars of a prison cell. Flames spark where the Wands touch.

Additions or Changes: You may wish to add **Grey** or **Black** highlights to the bars.

Upper Left Square: Each of the thirty-six decans, together with their planetary ruler, occupies a truncated pyramid square in the Great Central Cross of each of the four Enochian Elemental Tablets. This is the Saturn (**Yellow**) in Sagittarius (**Red**) square.

Lower Panel, Left Square: The Seal of Ronové, day Spirit of the Goetia (see Table 5).

Lower Panel, Center Square: Card Title, Planet, and Zodiac Sign.

Lower Panel, Right Square: The Seal of Andras, night Spirit of the Goetia (see Table 5).

Two of Cups

Love

TWO
CUPS

0° ♋ 10°

June 21—July 1

Eiael

Habuiah

LOVE
*Venus
in Cancer*

Venus Rules 0°–10° Cancer
June 21–July 1

Sephirah 2
Chokmah
on the Briah Tree of Life

First manifestation of Water.
Perfect harmony between male and
female. Ecstasy. Joy.

*Shemhamphorash Angels:

Eiael: Delights of the Sons of men
Habuiah: Great benefactor

*Spirits of the Goetia:

#10 Buer (day)
#46 Bifrons (night)

The *TCM* Card: *(See Table 4 for Queen Scale of Colors.)* Against a **Grey** background sit two **Light Blue** bowls overflowing with **Pink** ice cream covered with chocolate and whipped cream and topped with a **Red** cherry.

Additions or Changes: You may wish to add ice-cream shop decor and accoutrements.

Upper Left Square: Each of the thirty-six decans, together with their planetary ruler, occupies a truncated pyramid square in the Great Central Cross of each of the four Enochian Elemental Tablets. This is the Venus (**Green**) in Cancer (**Blue**) square.

Lower Panel, Left Square: The Seal of *Buer*, day Spirit of the Goetia (see Table 5).

Lower Panel, Center Square: Card Title, Planet, and Zodiac Sign.

Lower Panel, Right Square: The Seal of *Bifrons*, night Spirit of the Goetia (see Table 5).

Three of Cups
Abundance

THREE
CUPS

10°♋ 20°
July 2–July 11

Rochel

Iibamiah

ABUNDANCE
*Mercury
in Cancer*

Mercury Rules 10°–20° Cancer July 2–July 11 Sephirah 3 Binah on the Briah Tree of Life Love bears fruit. Bounty. Enjoy but mistrust the good things in life.	*Shemhamphorash Angels: Rochel: All-seeing Iibamiah: Creating by His Word *Spirits of the Goetia: #11 Gusion (day) #47 Vual (night)

The *TCM* Card: *(See Table 4 for Queen Scale of Colors.)* Against a **Black** background, three large **Golden** chalices are arranged in an upward-pointing triangle. They are filled and overflowing with ripe grapes.

Additions or Changes: You may wish to split the background horizontally to suggest a backdrop of a **Light Greenish-Blue** tranquil sea.

Upper Left Square: Each of the thirty-six decans, together with their planetary ruler, occupies a truncated pyramid square in the Great Central Cross of each of the four Enochian Elemental Tablets. This is the Mercury (**Yellow**) in Cancer (**Blue**) square.

Lower Panel, Left Square: The Seal of *Gusion*, day Spirit of the Goetia (see Table 5).

Lower Panel, Center Square: Card Title, Planet, and Zodiac Sign.

Lower Panel, Right Square: The Seal of *Vual*, night Spirit of the Goetia (see Table 5).

Four of Cups

Blended Pleasure

FOUR
CUPS

20°♋30°

July 12—July 21

Haiaiel

Mumiah

**BLENDED
PLEASURE**

*Luna
in Cancer*

Moon Rules 20°–30° Cancer July 12–July 21	*Shemhamphorash Angels:
	Haiah: Lord of the Universe
Sephirah 4	Mumiah: End of the Universe
Chesed	
on the Briah Tree of Life	*Spirits of the Goetia:
Luxury. Seed of the decay of pleasure. Weakness. Surrender to desire.	#12 Sitri (day) #48 Haagenti (night)

The *TCM* Card: *(See Table 4 for Queen Scale of Colors.)* Against a **Blue** background, four **Golden** loving Cups are arranged in a square.

Additions or Changes: You may wish to split the background horizontally to suggest a backdrop of a **Dark Blue** sea with traces of **White**-capped wavelets.

Upper Left Square: Each of the thirty-six decans, together with their planetary ruler, occupies a truncated pyramid square in the Great Central Cross of each of the four Enochian Elemental Tablets. This is the Moon (**Green**) in Cancer (**Blue**) square.

Lower Panel, Left Square: The Seal of *Sitri*, day Spirit of the Goetia (see Table 5).

Lower Panel, Center Square: Card Title, Planet, and Zodiac Sign.

Lower Panel, Right Square: The Seal of *Haagenti*, night Spirit of the Goetia (see Table 5).

Five of Cups

Loss in Pleasure

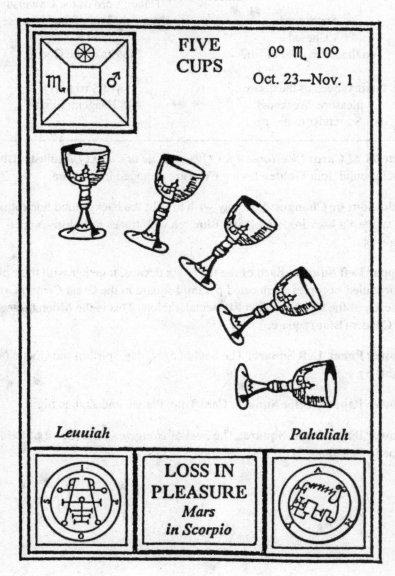

FIVE
CUPS

0° ♏ 10°

Oct. 23—Nov. 1

Leuuiah

Pahaliah

LOSS IN
PLEASURE
*Mars
in Scorpio*

Mars Rules 0°–10° Scorpio October 23–November 1 Sephirah 5 Geburah on the Briah Tree of Life Disappointment in love or pleasure. Expected pleasure thwarted.	*Shemhamphorash Angels: Leuuiah: Hasten to hear Pahliah: Liberator from deceit *Spirits of the Goetia: #22 Ipos (day) #58 Amy (night)

The *TCM* Card: *(See Table 4 for Queen Scale of Colors.)* Against a background of **Scarlet Red,** five Cups appear to be in stop-motion action of spilling their contents.

Additions or Changes: You may wish to split the background horizontally to suggest a backdrop of a dark and troubled sea.

Upper Left Square: Each of the thirty-six decans, together with their planetary ruler, occupies a truncated pyramid square in the Great Central Cross of each of the four Enochian Elemental Tablets. This is the Mars (**Blue**) in Scorpio (**Blue**) square.

Lower Panel, Left Square: The Seal of *Ipos*, day Spirit of the Goetia (see Table 5).

Lower Panel, Center Square: Card Title, Planet, and Zodiac Sign.

Lower Panel, Right Square: The Seal of *Amy*, night Spirit of the Goetia (see Table 5).

Six of Cups

Pleasure

SIX
CUPS

10° ♏ 20°
Nov. 2—Nov. 12

Nelchael

Ieiaiel

PLEASURE
*Sol
in Scorpio*

Sol Rules 10°–20° Scorpio November 2–November 12 Sephirah 6 Tiphareth on the Briah Tree of Life Harmony. Ease. Fertility. Not the gratification of artificial desires, but the fulfillment of the true sexual will.	*Shemhamphorash Angels: Nelchael: Thou alone Ieiaiel: Thy right hand *Spirits of the Goetia: #23 Aim (day) #59 Orias (night)

The *TCM* Card: *(See Table 4 for Queen Scale of Colors.)* Against a background of **Golden Yellow**, six emerald Cups (trimmed in **Gold**) form two triangles. In the center is the symbol of Scorpio surrounded by **White** rays of glory.

Additions or Changes: You may wish to split the background horizontally to suggest a backdrop of a **Rose-Pink** sea reflecting a partially risen Sun.

Upper Left Square: Each of the thirty-six decans, together with their planetary ruler, occupies a truncated pyramid square in the Great Central Cross of each of the four Enochian Elemental Tablets. This is the Sol (**Red**) in Scorpio (**Blue**) square.

Lower Panel, Left Square: The Seal of *Aim*, day Spirit of the Goetia (see Table 5).

Lower Panel, Center Square: Card Title, Planet, and Zodiac Sign.

Lower Panel, Right Square: The Seal of *Orias*, night Spirit of the Goetia (see Table 5).

Seven of Cups

Illusionary Success

SEVEN CUPS

20° ♏ 30°

Nov. 13—Nov. 22

Melahel

Hahuiah

ILLUSIONARY
SUCCESS
*Venus
in Scorpio*

Venus Rules 20°–30° Scorpio November 13–November 22	*Shemhamphorash Angels:
Sephirah 7 Netzach on the Briah Tree of Life	Melahel: Repelling evil Hahuiah: Trusting in Him *Spirits of the Goetia:
Debauchery. Addiction. False pleasure. External pleasure, internal corruption. Guilt. Deception.	#24 Naberius (day) #60 Vapula (night)

The *TCM* Card: *(See Table 4 for Queen Scale of Colors.)* Against a background of clouded **Emerald** are seven martini glasses (one large glass between two stacks of three). Each glass contains an **Olive-Green** olive stuffed with a **Red** pimento and speared with swizzle stick.

Additions or Changes: You may wish to split the background horizontally to suggest a backdrop of a darker and polluted **Green** sea.

Upper Left Square: Each of the thirty-six decans, together with their planetary ruler, occupies a truncated pyramid square in the Great Central Cross of each of the four Enochian Elemental Tablets. This is the Venus (**Green**) in Scorpio (**Blue**) square.

Lower Panel, Left Square: The Seal of *Naberius*, day Spirit of the Goetia (see Table 5).

Lower Panel, Center Square: Card Title, Planet, and Zodiac Sign.

Lower Panel, Right Square: The Seal of *Vapula*, night Spirit of the Goetia (see Table 5).

Eight of Cups
Abandoned Success

EIGHT
CUPS

0° ♓ 10°
Feb. 19—Feb. 28

Vevaliah

Ielahiah

ABANDONED
SUCCESS
*Saturn
in Pisces*

```
Saturn Rules 0°–10° Pisces        *Shemhamphorash Angels:
February 19–February 28
                                  Vevaliah: King and Ruler
          Sephirah 8              Ielahiah: Abiding forever
            Hod
    on the Briah Tree of Life       *Spirits of the Goetia:

Indolence. Unpleasantness.           #34 Furfur (day)
Sorrow plagues pleasure.             #70 Seere (night)
```

The *TCM* Card: *(See Table 4 for Queen Scale of Colors.)* Against an **Orange** background are eight **Lead Grey** Cups arranged in three rows (3-2-3).

Additions or Changes: You may wish to split the background horizontally to suggest a troubled **Black** and **Grey** sea.

Upper Left Square: Each of the thirty-six decans, together with their planetary ruler, occupies a truncated pyramid square in the Great Central Cross of each of the four Enochian Elemental Tablets. This is the Saturn (**Yellow**) in Pisces (**Blue**) in square.

Lower Panel, Left Square: The Seal of *Furfur*, day Spirit of the Goetia (see Table 5).

Lower Panel, Center Square: Card Title, Planet, and Zodiac Sign.

Lower Panel, Right Square: The Seal of *Seere*, night Spirit of the Goetia (see Table 5).

Nine of Cups
Material Happiness

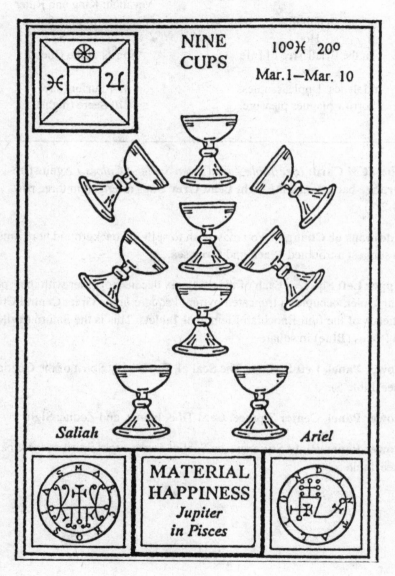

NINE
CUPS

10° ♓ 20°

Mar. 1 – Mar. 10

Saliah

Ariel

MATERIAL
HAPPINESS
*Jupiter
in Pisces*

Jupiter Rules 10°–20° Pisces March 1–March 10 Sephirah 9 Yesod on the Briah Tree of Life Good fortune. Joy. Gladness. Self-fulfillment.	*Shemhamphorash Angels: Saliah: Mover of all things Ariel: Revealer *Spirits of the Goetia: #35 Marchosias (day) #71 Dantalion (night)

The *TCM* Card: *(See Table 4 for Queen Scale of Colors.)* Against a **Violet** background, nine chalices are arranged in Tree of Life order (minus Malkuth at the bottom).

Additions or Changes: You may wish to add pairs of fishes playing in the background. Please add two streams of water burst from the top Cup (Kether) and spill down the tree of Cups like a blue liquid chocolate fountain.

Upper Left Square: Each of the thirty-six decans, together with their planetary ruler, occupies a truncated pyramid square in the Great Central Cross of each of the four Enochian Elemental Tablets. This is the Jupiter (**Red**) in Pisces (**Blue**) in square.

Lower Panel, Left Square: The Seal of *Marchosias*, day Spirit of the Goetia (see Table 5).

Lower Panel, Center Square: Card Title, Planet, and Zodiac Sign.

Lower Panel, Right Square: The Seal of *Dantalion*, night Spirit of the Goetia (see Table 5).

Ten of Cups

Perfected Success

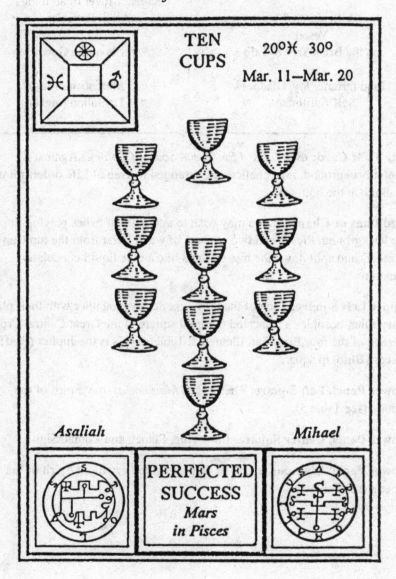

TEN
CUPS

20° ♓ 30°

Mar. 11—Mar. 20

Asaliah

Mihael

PERFECTED
SUCCESS
*Mars
in Pisces*

Mars Rules 20°–30° Pisces March 11–March 20 Sephirah 10 Malkuth on the Briah Tree of Life Satiety. One's cup runneth over and stains the carpet.	*Shemhamphorash Angels: Asaliah: Just judge Mihael: Sending forth as a father *Spirits of the Goetia: #36 Stolas (day) #72 Andromalius (night)

The *TCM* Card: *(See Table 4 for Queen Scale of Colors.)* Against an **Olive** background, ten **Russet** chalices are arranged in Tree of Life. Each Cup is completely full and is spilling **Citrine** wine down the card.

Additions or Changes: The spilled wine might be shown flooding the bottom of the card.

Upper Left Square: Each of the thirty-six decans, together with their planetary ruler, occupies a truncated pyramid square in the Great Central Cross of each of the four Enochian Elemental Tablets. This is the Mars (**Blue**) in Pisces (**Blue**) in square.

Lower Panel, Left Square: The Seal of *Stolas*, day Spirit of the Goetia (see Table 5).

Lower Panel, Center Square: Card Title, Planet, and Zodiac Sign.

Lower Panel, Right Square: The Seal of *Andromalius*, night Spirit of the Goetia (see Table 5).

Two of Swords

Peace Restored

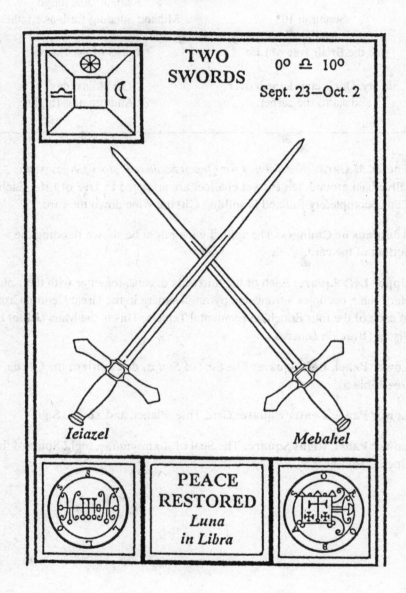

TWO
SWORDS

0° ♎ 10°

Sept. 23—Oct. 2

Ieiazel

Mebahel

PEACE
RESTORED
*Luna
in Libra*

Moon Rules 0°–10° Libra September 23–October 2	*Shemhamphorash Angels:
	Ieiazel: Rejoicing over all
Sephirah 2	Mebahel: Guardian and preserver
Chokmah	
on the Yetzirah Tree of Life	*Spirits of the Goetia:
First manifestation of Air.	#19 Sallos (day)
Equilibrium abiding above	#55 Orobas (night)
disruption. Dormant antagonism.	

The *TCM* Card: *(See Table 4 for Prince Scale of Colors.)* Against a background of **Blue Pearl Grey** two Swords cross to form a simple *X*. The grip on left Sword is **Red;** the grip on the right Sword is **Blue**.

Additions or Changes: You may wish to add symbols of the Moon and scales of Libra.

Upper Left Square: Each of the thirty-six decans, together with their planetary ruler, occupies a truncated pyramid square in the Great Central Cross of each of the four Enochian Elemental Tablets. This is the Moon (**Green**) in Libra (**Yellow**) square.

Lower Panel, Left Square: The Seal of *Sallos*, day Spirit of the Goetia (see Table 5).

Lower Panel, Center Square: Card Title, Planet, and Zodiac Sign.

Lower Panel, Right Square: The Seal of *Orobas*, night Spirit of the Goetia (see Table 5).

Three of Swords

Sorrow

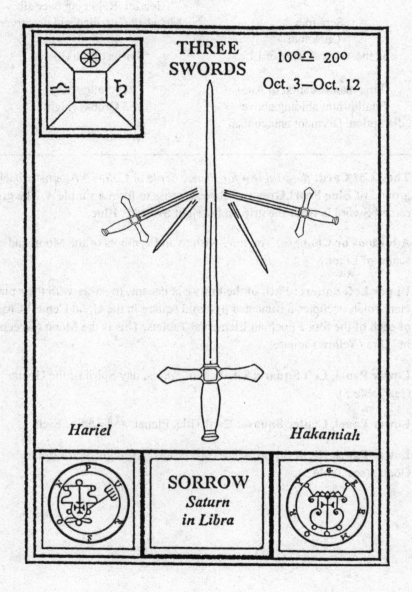

THREE
SWORDS

10° ♎ 20°
Oct. 3—Oct. 12

Hariel

Hakamiah

SORROW
*Saturn
in Libra*

Saturn Rules 10°–20° Libra October 3–October 12 Sephirah 3 Binah on the Yetzirah Tree of Life Profound melancholy engendering either depression or wisdom. Secrecy. Perversion.	* Shemhamphorash Angels: Hariel: Aid Hakamiah: Arise, praying day and night *Spirits of the Goetia: #20 Purson (day) #56 Gremory (night)

The *TCM* Card: *(See Table 4 for Prince Scale of Colors.)* Against a background of **Dark Brown,** two small crossed Swords are broken by the blade of a third much larger Sword.

Additions or Changes: You may wish to add to the background symbols of Libra and Saturn.

Upper Left Square: Each of the thirty-six decans, together with their planetary ruler, occupies a truncated pyramid square in the Great Central Cross of each of the four Enochian Elemental Tablets. This is the Saturn (**Yellow**) in Libra (**Yellow**) square.

Lower Panel, Left Square: The Seal of *Purson*, day Spirit of the Goetia (see Table 5).

Lower Panel, Center Square: Card Title, Planet, and Zodiac Sign.

Lower Panel, Right Square: The Seal of *Gremory*, night Spirit of the Goetia (see Table 5).

Four of Swords

Rest from Strife

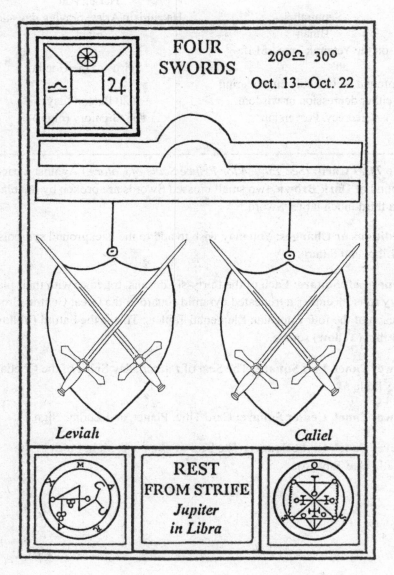

FOUR
SWORDS

20° ♎ 30°

Oct. 13—Oct. 22

Leviah

Caliel

REST
FROM STRIFE

*Jupiter
in Libra*

Jupiter Rules 20°–30° Libra October 13–October 22 Sephirah 4 Chesed on the Yetzirah Tree of Life Truce. Compromise. Tension is relaxed through submission to militaristic discipline and dogma. Refuge from sorrow.	*Shemhamphorash Angels: Leviah: Is wonderful Caliel: Only unto me *Spirits of the Goetia: #21 Marax (day) #55 Osé (night)

The *TCM* Card: *(See Table 4 for Prince Scale of Colors.)* Against a background of deep **Purple** is a large **White** symbol of Libra from which hang two shields bearing two small crossed Swords. The shield on the left is countercharged **Dark Purple** and **White**; the shield to the right, **Yellow** and **White**.

Additions or Changes: You may wish to add symbols of Jupiter and scales of Libra.

Upper Left Square: Each of the thirty-six decans, together with their planetary ruler, occupies a truncated pyramid square in the Great Central Cross of each of the four Enochian Elemental Tablets. This is the Jupiter (**Red**) in Libra (**Yellow**) square.

Lower Panel, Left Square: The Seal of *Marax*, day Spirit of the Goetia (see Table 5).

Lower Panel, Center Square: Card Title, Planet, and Zodiac Sign.

Lower Panel, Right Square: The Seal of *Osé*, night Spirit of the Goetia (see Table 5).

Five of Swords

Defeat

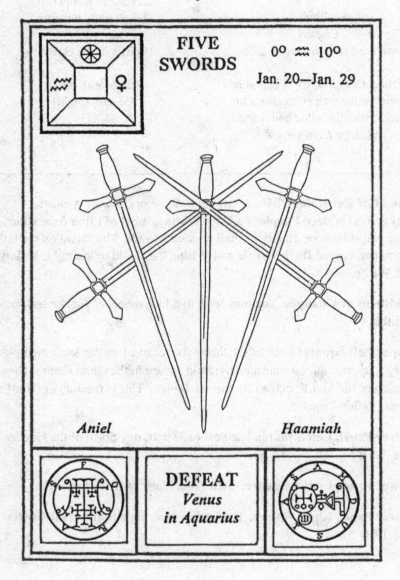

FIVE
SWORDS

0º ♒ 10º

Jan. 20—Jan. 29

Aniel

Haamiah

DEFEAT
*Venus
in Aquarius*

Venus Rules 0°–10° Aquarius January 20–January 29	*Shemhamphorash Angels:
	Aniel: Lord of Virtues
Sephirah 5 Geburah on the Yetzirah Tree of Life	Haamiah: Hope of all the Earth
	*Spirits of the Goetia:
Failure. Inadequate energy to maintain peace. Reason is undone by sentiment.	#31 Foras (day) #67 Amdusias (night)

The *TCM* Card: *(See Table 4 for Prince Scale of Colors.)* Against a background of **Bright Scarlet,** five Swords (two crossed upward-pointing, over three downward-pointing) form an averse pentagram.

Additions or Changes: You may wish to add symbols of Venus and Aquarius.

Upper Left Square: Each of the thirty-six decans, together with their planetary ruler, occupies a truncated pyramid square in the Great Central Cross of each of the four Enochian Elemental Tablets. This is the Venus (**Green**) in Aquarius (**Yellow**) square.

Lower Panel, Left Square: The Seal of *Foras*, day Spirit of the Goetia (see Table 5).

Lower Panel, Center Square: Card Title, Planet, and Zodiac Sign.

Lower Panel, Right Square: The Seal of *Amdusias*, night Spirit of the Goetia (see Table 5).

Six of Swords

Earned Success

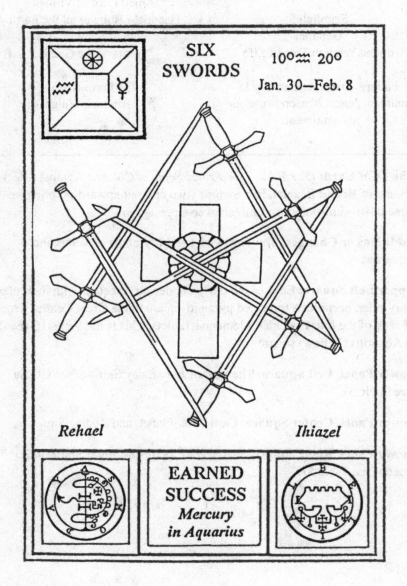

SIX SWORDS

10° ♒ 20°

Jan. 30—Feb. 8

Rehael

Ihiazel

EARNED
SUCCESS
*Mercury
in Aquarius*

Mercury Rules 0°–20° Aquarius January 30–February 8 Sephirah 6 Tiphareth on the Yetzirah Tree of Life Intellectual endeavors rewarded. Equilibrium of mental and moral faculties.	*Shemhamphorash Angels: Rehael: Swift to condone Ihiazel: Makon joyful *Spirits of the Goetia: #32 Asmoday (day) #68 Belial (night)

The *TCM* Card: *(See Table 4 for Prince Scale of Colors.)* Against a background of rich **Salmon**, six Swords form a unicursal hexagram over a small **Golden** cross bearing the twenty-two–petaled qabalistic rose.

Additions or Changes: You may wish to carefully paint each rose petal the Queen scale colors assigned to the Mother, Double, and Simple Hebrew letters.

Upper Left Square: Each of the thirty-six decans, together with their planetary ruler, occupies a truncated pyramid square in the Great Central Cross of each of the four Enochian Elemental Tablets. This is the Mercury (**Yellow**) in Aquarius (**Yellow**) square.

Lower Panel, Left Square: The Seal of *Asmoday*, day Spirit of the Goetia (see Table 5).

Lower Panel, Center Square: Card Title, Planet, and Zodiac Sign.

Lower Panel, Right Square: The Seal of *Belial*, night Spirit of the Goetia (see Table 5).

Seven of Swords

Unstable Effort

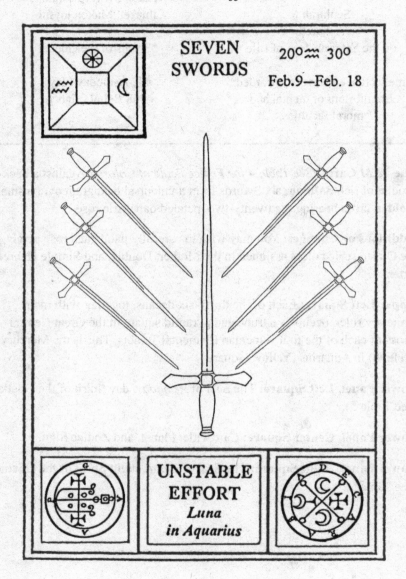

SEVEN
SWORDS

20° ♒ 30°
Feb. 9—Feb. 18

UNSTABLE
EFFORT
*Luna
in Aquarius*

Moon Rules 20°–30° Aquarius
February 9–February 18

Sephirah 7
Netzach
on the Yetzirah Tree of Life

Futility. Indecisiveness.
Appeasement. Swimming against
the tide. Insufficient energy and
will to finish the task.

*Shemhamphorash Angels:

Hahahel: Triune
Michael: Who is like unto Him

*Spirits of the Goetia:

#33 Gaap (day)
#69 Decarabia (night)

The *TCM* Card: *(See Table 4 for Prince Scale of Colors.)* Against a background of **Bright Yellow-Green**, seven Swords are arranged in a balanced pattern; one large Sword upward-pointing in the center, flanked by six smaller Swords pointing diagonally toward the center blade.

Additions or Changes: You may wish to add a symbol of Aquarius or a small crescent Moon as pommels to the Swords.

Upper Left Square: Each of the thirty-six decans, together with their planetary ruler, occupies a truncated pyramid square in the Great Central Cross of each of the four Enochian Elemental Tablets. This is the Moon (**Green**) in Aquarius (**Yellow**) square.

Lower Panel, Left Square: The Seal of *Gaap*, day Spirit of the Goetia (see Table 5).

Lower Panel, Center Square: Card Title, Planet, and Zodiac Sign.

Lower Panel, Right Square: The Seal of *Decarabia*, night Spirit of the Goetia (see Table 5).

Eight of Swords

Shortened Force

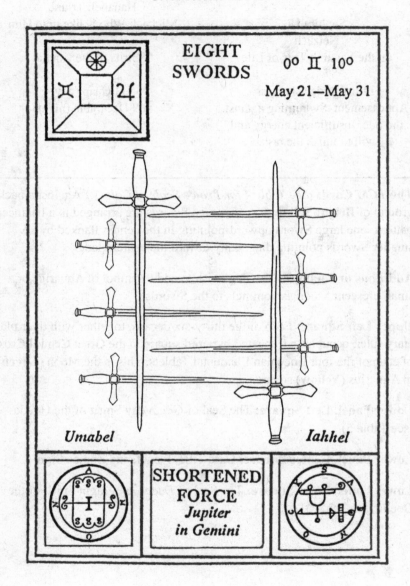

EIGHT SWORDS 0° ♊ 10°
May 21—May 31

Umabel

Iahhel

SHORTENED FORCE
Jupiter in Gemini

Jupiter Rules 0°–10° Gemini May 21–May 31 Sephirah 8 Hod on the Yetzirah Tree of Life Interference. Being good-natured at the wrong time. Unexpected bad luck. Energy wasted on unimportant details.	*Shemhamphorash Angels: Umabel: Everlasting name over all Iahhel: Supreme essence *Spirits of the Goetia: #7 Amon (day) #43 Sabnock (night)

The *TCM* Card: *(See Table 4 for Prince Scale of Colors.)* Against a background of **Red Russet,** eight Swords are arranged in a pattern: three pointing horizontally right; three pointing horizontally left; one1 pointing down; and one pointing up.

Additions or Changes: You may wish to add dull sparks where certain Swords touch.

Upper Left Square: Each of the thirty-six decans, together with their planetary ruler, occupies a truncated pyramid square in the Great Central Cross of each of the four Enochian Elemental Tablets. This is the Jupiter (**Red**) in Gemini (**Yellow**) square.

Lower Panel, Left Square: The Seal of *Amon*, day Spirit of the Goetia (see Table 5).

Lower Panel, Center Square: Card Title, Planet, and Zodiac Sign.

Lower Panel, Right Square: The Seal of *Sabnock*, night Spirit of the Goetia (see Table 5).

Nine of Swords

Despair & Cruelty

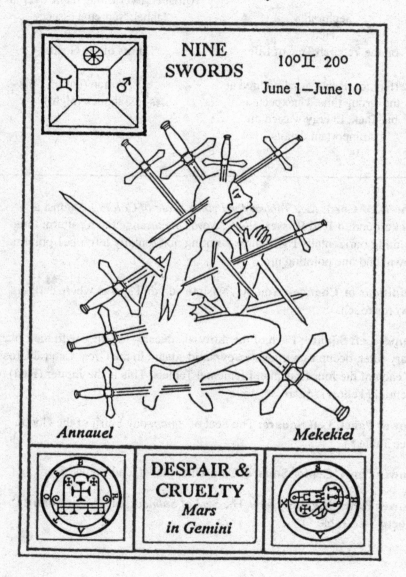

NINE SWORDS

10° ♊ 20°

June 1—June 10

Annauel

Mekekiel

DESPAIR &
CRUELTY
*Mars
in Gemini*

Mars Rules 10°–20° Gemini June 1–June 10	*Shemhamphorash Angels:
	Annauel: Joyful service
Sephirah 9	Mekekiel: Vivifying
Yesod	
on the Yetzirah Tree of Life	*Spirits of the Goetia:
Mental anguish. Nothing furthers. Both the acceptance of martyrdom and unrelenting revenge.	#8 Barbatos (day) #44 Shax (night)

The *TCM* Card: *(See Table 4 for Prince Scale of Colors.)* Against a background of very **Dark Purple**, a naked woman with long **Red** hair crouches in fear, looking upward in profile. Her body is pierced through with nine Swords of various lengths.

Additions or Changes: You may add blood where the Swords enter and exit her body.

Upper Left Square: Each of the thirty-six decans, together with their planetary ruler, occupies a truncated pyramid square in the Great Central Cross of each of the four Enochian Elemental Tablets. This is the Mars (**Blue**) in Gemini (**Yellow**) square.

Lower Panel, Left Square: The Seal of *Barbatos*, day Spirit of the Goetia (see Table 5).

Lower Panel, Center Square: Card Title, Planet, and Zodiac Sign.

Lower Panel, Right Square: The Seal of *Shax*, night Spirit of the Goetia (see Table 5).

Ten of Swords

Ruin

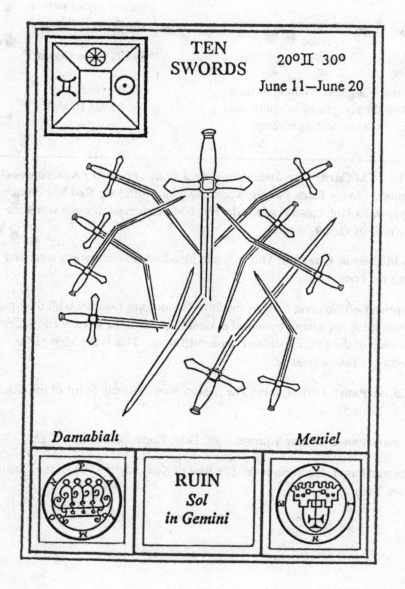

TEN
SWORDS

20° ♊ 30°

June 11—June 20

Damabiah

Meniel

RUIN
Sol
in Gemini

Sol Rules 20°–30° Gemini June 11–June 20	*Shemhamphorash Angels:
Sephirah 10 Malkuth on the Yetzirah Tree of Life	Damabiah: Fountain of Wisdom Meniel: Nourishing all *Spirits of the Goetia:
Madness. Disaster that may signal the end of delusion.	#9 Paimon (day) #45 Viné (night)

The *TCM* Card: *(See Table 4 for Prince Scale of Colors.)* Against a muddied background of **Citrine, Olive, Russet,** and **Black,** ten broken Swords clutter the card.

Additions or Changes: You may add blood and poison dripping from the blades and tips of the Swords.

Upper Left Square: Each of the thirty-six decans, together with their planetary ruler, occupies a truncated pyramid square in the Great Central Cross of each of the four Enochian Elemental Tablets. This is the Sol (**Red**) in Gemini (**Yellow**) square.

Lower Panel, Left Square: The Seal of *Paimon*, day Spirit of the Goetia (see Table 5).

Lower Panel, Center Square: Card Title, Planet, and Zodiac Sign.

Lower Panel, Right Square: The Seal of *Viné*, night Spirit of the Goetia (see Table 5).

Two of Disks

Harmonious Change

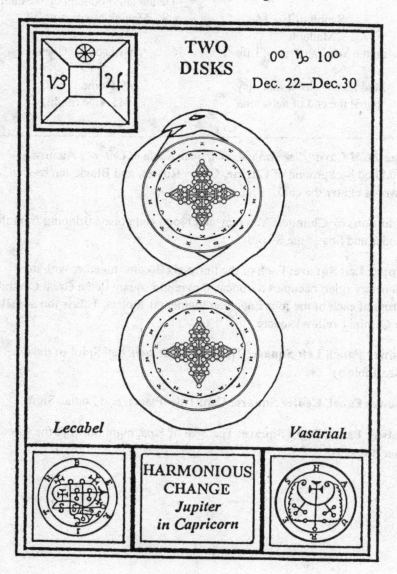

TWO DISKS

0° ♑ 10°

Dec. 22—Dec. 30

Lecabel

Vasariah

HARMONIOUS CHANGE

Jupiter in Capricorn

Jupiter Rules 0°–10° Capricorn
December 22–December 30

Sephirah 2
Chokmah
on the Assiah Tree of Life

Change.
First manifestation of Earth.
Perpetual change maintains
stability.

*Shemhamphorash Angels:

Lecabel: Teacher
Vasariah: Upright

*Spirits of the Goetia:

#28 Berith (day)
#64 Haures (night)

The *TCM* Card: *(See Table 4 for Princess Scale of Colors.)* Against a background of **White** flecked **Red, Blue,** and **Yellow,** two large Disks, on over the other, are encircled in a figure eight by a **Green** snake.

Additions or Changes: You may wish to replace the Disks with your own personal pantacle design.

Upper Left Square: Each of the thirty-six decans, together with their planetary ruler, occupies a truncated pyramid square in the Great Central Cross of each of the four Enochian Elemental Tablets. This is the Jupiter (**Red**) in Capricorn (**Green**) square.

Lower Panel, Left Square: The Seal of *Berith*, day Spirit of the Goetia (see Table 5).

Lower Panel, Center Square: Card Title, Planet, and Zodiac Sign.

Lower Panel, Right Square: The Seal of *Haures*, night Spirit of the Goetia (see Table 5).

Three of Disks

Material Works

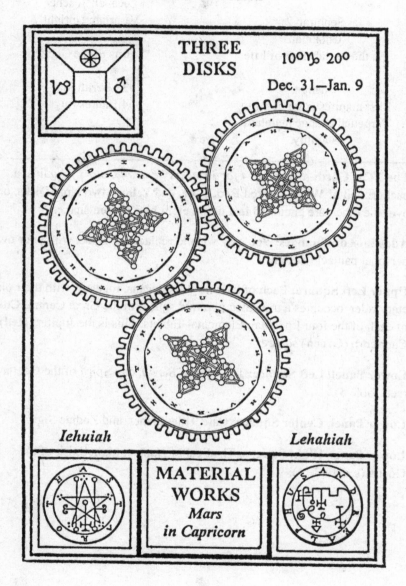

THREE
DISKS

10° ♑ 20°

Dec. 31–Jan. 9

Iehuiah

Lehahiah

**MATERIAL
WORKS**
*Mars
in Capricorn*

Mars Rules 10°–20° Capricorn December 31–January 9 Sephirah 3 Binah on the Assiah Tree of Life Constructive energy. Crystallization of forces. Job. Concentrated effort rewarded now or in the future.	*Shemhamphorash Angels: Iehuiah: Omniscient Lehahiah: Merciful *Spirits of the Goetia: #29 Astaroth (day) #65 Andrealphus (night)

The *TCM* Card: *(See Table 4 for Princess Scale of Colors.)* Against a background of **Grey**-flecked **Pink**, three **Pink** Disks (with cog teeth) join to form a simple gear.

Additions or Changes: You may wish to replace the Disks with your own personal pantacle design.

Upper Left Square: Each of the thirty-six decans, together with their planetary ruler, occupies a truncated pyramid square in the Great Central Cross of each of the four Enochian Elemental Tablets. This is the Mars (**Blue**) in Capricorn (**Green**) square.

Lower Panel, Left Square: The Seal of *Astaroth*, day Spirit of the Goetia (see Table 5).

Lower Panel, Center Square: Card Title, Planet, and Zodiac Sign.

Lower Panel, Right Square: The Seal of *Andrealphus*, night Spirit of the Goetia (see Table 5).

Four of Disks

Earthly Power

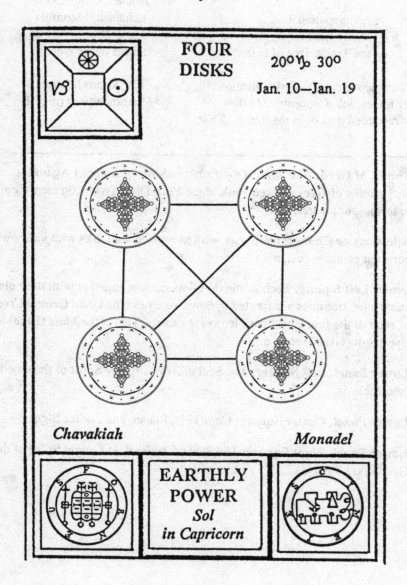

FOUR DISKS

20° ♑ 30°

Jan. 10—Jan. 19

Chavakiah

Monadel

EARTHLY POWER
Sol
in Capricorn

Sol Rules 20°–30° Capricorn January 10–January 19 Sephirah 4 Chesed on the Assiah Tree of Life Unaggressive mastery over purely material circumstances. Security withing protective walls. Law and order.	*Shemhamphorash Angels: Chavakiah: To be rejoiced in Monadel: Honorable *Spirits of the Goetia: #30 Forneus (day) #66 Cimeis (night)

The *TCM* Card: *(See Table 4 for Princess Scale of Colors.)* Against a background of deep **Azure**-flecked **Yellow**, four Disks are arranged in a perfect square.

Additions or Changes: You may wish to replace the Disks with your own personal pantacle design.

Upper Left Square: Each of the thirty-six decans, together with their planetary ruler, occupies a truncated pyramid square in the Great Central Cross of each of the four Enochian Elemental Tablets. This is the Sol (**Red**) in Capricorn (**Green**) square.

Lower Panel, Left Square: The Seal of *Forneus*, day Spirit of the Goetia (see Table 5).

Lower Panel, Center Square: Card Title, Planet, and Zodiac Sign.

Lower Panel, Right Square: The Seal of *Cimeis*, night Spirit of the Goetia (see Table 5).

Five of Disks
Material Trouble

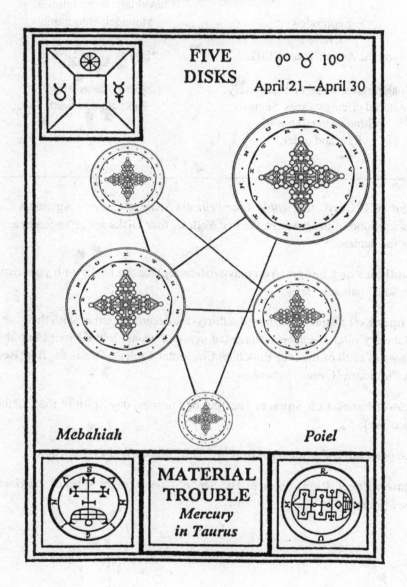

FIVE
DISKS

0° ♉ 10°
April 21—April 30

Mebahiah

Poiel

MATERIAL
TROUBLE
*Mercury
in Taurus*

The _TCM_ Card: _(See Table 4 for Princess Scale of Colors.)_ Against a background of **Red**-flecked **Black,** five Disks of different sizes form an averse pentagram.

Additions or Changes: You may wish to replace the Disks with your own personal pantacle design.

Upper Left Square: Each of the thirty-six decans, together with their planetary ruler, occupies a truncated pyramid square in the Great Central Cross of each of the four Enochian Elemental Tablets. This is the Mercury (**Yellow**) in Taurus (**Green**) square.

Lower Panel, Left Square: The Seal of _Samigina_, day Spirit of the Goetia (see Table 5).

Lower Panel, Center Square: Card Title, Planet, and Zodiac Sign.

Lower Panel, Right Square: The Seal of _Räum_, night Spirit of the Goetia (see Table 5).

Six of Disks

Material Success

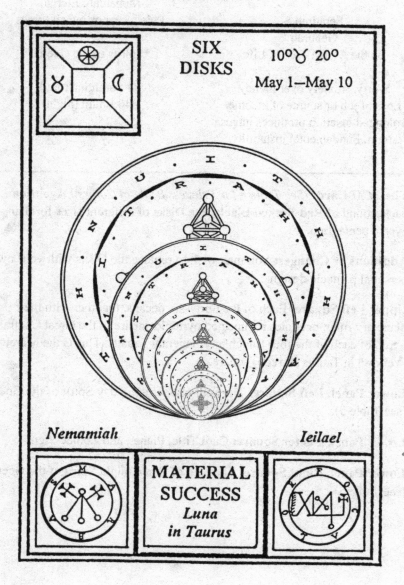

SIX
DISKS

10° ♉ 20°
May 1—May 10

Nemamiah

Ieilael

MATERIAL
SUCCESS
*Luna
in Taurus*

Moon Rules 10°–20° Taurus	*Shemhamphorash Angels:
May 1–May 10	
	Nemamiah: Lovable
Sephirah 6	Ieilael: Hearer of lamentations
Tiphareth	
on the Assiah Tree of Life	*Spirits of the Goetia:
Investment of labor or resources	#5 Marbas (day)
results in high yields. A settling	#41 Focalor (night)
down. Temporary success.	

The *TCM* Card: *(See Table 4 for Princess Scale of Colors.)* Against a background of **Golden Amber,** a pattern of six Disks (versions of the Ace of Disks) seem to grow before us. They have **White** eleven-sided bodies ringed in dark **Amber**.

Additions or Changes: You may wish to replace the Disks with your own personal pantacle design.

Upper Left Square: Each of the thirty-six decans, together with their planetary ruler, occupies a truncated pyramid square in the Great Central Cross of each of the four Enochian Elemental Tablets. This is the Moon (**Green**) in Taurus (**Green**) square.

Lower Panel, Left Square: The Seal of *Marbas*, day Spirit of the Goetia (see Table 5).

Lower Panel, Center Square: Card Title, Planet, and Zodiac Sign.

Lower Panel, Right Square: The Seal of *Focalor*, night Spirit of the Goetia (see Table 5).

Seven of Disks

Success Unfulfilled

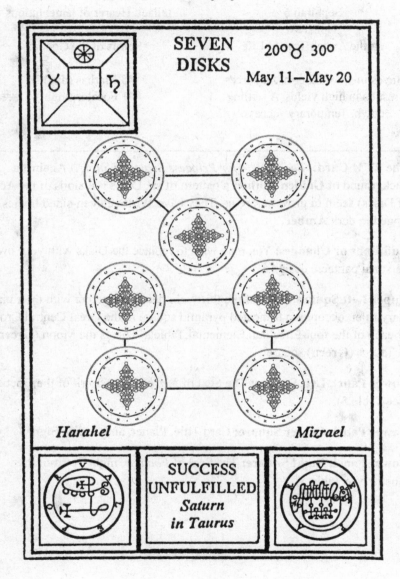

SEVEN DISKS

20° ♉ 30°

May 11—May 20

Harahel

Mizrael

SUCCESS UNFULFILLED
Saturn in Taurus

<table>
<tr><td>

Saturn Rules 20°–30° Taurus
May 11–May 20

Sephirah 7
Netzach
on the Assiah Tree of Life

Expected profits turn to loss or
even liabilities.

</td><td>

*Shemhamphorash Angels:

Harahel: Permeating all
Mizrael: Rising up the oppressed

*Spirits of the Goetia:

#6 Valefor (day)
#42 Vepar (night)

</td></tr>
</table>

The *TCM* Card: *(See Table 4 for Princess Scale of Colors.)* Against a background of **Olive**-flecked **Gold**, a pattern of seven Disks forms the geomantic figure Rubeus.

Additions or Changes: You may wish to replace the Disks with your own personal pantacle design.

Upper Left Square: Each of the thirty-six decans, together with their planetary ruler, occupies a truncated pyramid square in the Great Central Cross of each of the four Enochian Elemental Tablets. This is the Saturn (**Yellow**) in Taurus (**Green**) square.

Lower Panel, Left Square: The Seal of *Valefor*, day Spirit of the Goetia (see Table 5).

Lower Panel, Center Square: Card Title, Planet, and Zodiac Sign.

Lower Panel, Right Square: The Seal of *Vepar*, night Spirit of the Goetia (see Table 5).

Eight of Disks

Prudence

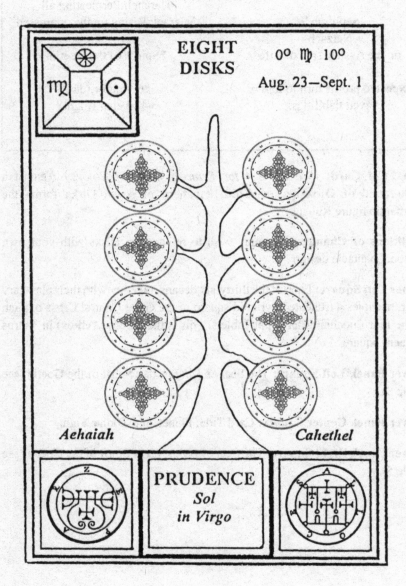

EIGHT
DISKS

0º ♍ 10º
Aug. 23—Sept. 1

Aehaiah

Cahethel

PRUDENCE
Sol
in Virgo

Sol Rules 0°–10° Virgo August 23–September 1 Sephirah 8 Hod on the Assiah Tree of Life "Saving for a rainy day." Plant your garden and wait. Retiring as a positive maneuver.	*Shemhamphorash Angels: Aehaiah: Long suffering Cahethel: Adorable *Spirits of the Goetia: #16 Zepar (day) #52 Alloces (night)

The *TCM* Card: *(See Table 4 for Princess Scale of Colors.)* Against a background of **White** flecked with **Yellowish-Brown**, eight Disks sprout from both sides of a **Dark-Brown** tree trunk.

Additions or Changes: You may wish to replace the Disks with your own personal pantacle design.

Upper Left Square: Each of the thirty-six decans, together with their planetary ruler, occupies a truncated pyramid square in the Great Central Cross of each of the four Enochian Elemental Tablets. This is the Sol (**Red**) in Virgo (**Green**) square.

Lower Panel, Left Square: The Seal of *Zepar*, day Spirit of the Goetia (see Table 5).

Lower Panel, Center Square: Card Title, Planet, and Zodiac Sign.

Lower Panel, Right Square: The Seal of *Alloces*, night Spirit of the Goetia (see Table 5).

Nine of Disks

Material Gain

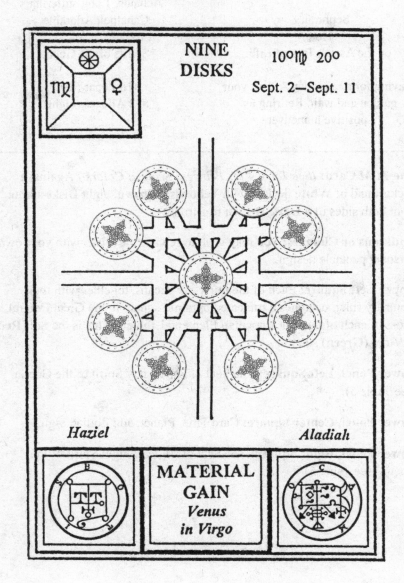

NINE
DISKS

10° ♍ 20°

Sept. 2—Sept. 11

Haziel

Aladiah

MATERIAL
GAIN
*Venus
in Virgo*

Venus Rules 10°–20° Virgo September 2–September 11 Sephirah 9 Yesod on the Assiah Tree of Life Considerable increase in fortune. Reap what you've sown and relax. Popularity. Good luck and good management. Inheritance.	*Shemhamphorash Angels: Haziel: Merciful Aladiah: Profitable *Spirits of the Goetia: #17 Botis (day) #53 Camio (night)

The *TCM* Card: *(See Table 4 for Princess Scale of Colors.)* Against a background of **Citrine**-flecked **Azure**, eight Disks emanate from a ninth central Disk (as if the Supernal Triads of four Trees of Life all share a single Kether in common).

Additions or Changes: You may wish to replace the Disks with your own personal pantacle design.

Upper Left Square: Each of the thirty-six decans, together with their planetary ruler, occupies a truncated pyramid square in the Great Central Cross of each of the four Enochian Elemental Tablets. This is the Venus (**Green**) in Virgo (**Green**) square.

Lower Panel, Left Square: The Seal of *Botis*, day Spirit of the Goetia (see Table 5).

Lower Panel, Center Square: Card Title, Planet, and Zodiac Sign.

Lower Panel, Right Square: The Seal of *Camio*, night Spirit of the Goetia (see Table 5).

Ten of Disks

Wealth

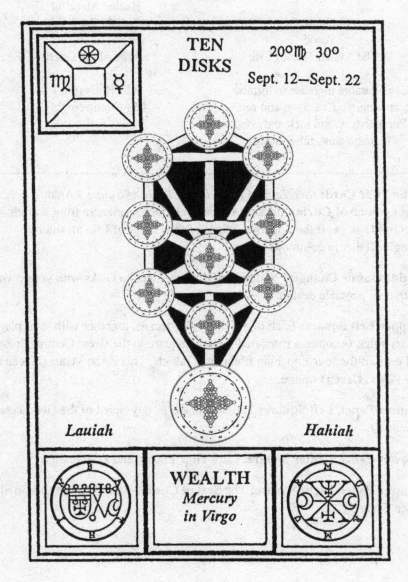

TEN DISKS

20° ♍ 30°

Sept. 12—Sept. 22

Lauiah

Hahiah

WEALTH
Mercury
in Virgo

Note: The Ten of Disks and the Princess of Disks (the Court Card equivalent) represent the "climax of the descent into Matter." Together they hold the key to jump-starting an entirely new cycle of creation.

Mercury Rules 20°–30° Virgo September 12–September 22	*Shemhamphorash Angels:
Sephirah 10 Malkuth on the Assiah Tree of Life	Lauiah: Meet to be exalted Hahiah: Refuge *Spirits of the Goetia:
Material prosperity. Recycle wealth by acquisitions and philanthropy. If properly applied, true wisdom and perfect happiness.	#18 Bathin (day) #54 Murmur (night)

The *TCM* Card: *(See Table 4 for Princess Scale of Colors.)* Against a background of **Black**-rayed **Yellow,** ten Disks form a Tree of Life. The tenth (lowest) Disk is larger than the other nine. The crosses in the Disks are **Green,** and the outer rings are **Yellow**.

Additions or Changes: You may wish to replace the Disks with your own personal pantacle design.

Upper Left Square: Each of the thirty-six decans, together with their planetary ruler, occupies a truncated pyramid square in the Great Central Cross of each of the four Enochian Elemental Tablets. This is the Mercury (**Yellow**) in Virgo (**Green**) square.

Lower Panel, Left Square: The Seal of *Bathin*, day Spirit of the Goetia (see Table 5).

Lower Panel, Center Square: Card Title, Planet, and Zodiac Sign.

Lower Panel, Right Square: The Seal of *Murmur*, night Spirit of the Goetia (see Table 5).

Small Cards Hold It All Together

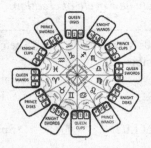

The Small Cards are the important *essential workers* of the tarot universe. We've just spent a lot of time studying the elemental and planetary attributes of these thirty-six cards, but their influence is not limited to the elemental factory floor of the *Lesser Arcana*. In fact—in addition to the rental agreement they have with their Court Card landlords—each of the thirty-six Small Cards is deputized by an even *higher authority* in the *Greater Arcana* whose influence literally trumps the myopic demands of their elementary Court Cards.

Recall that the twelve Signs of the Zodiac are grouped in two ways:

> First by the four elements: three *Fire* Signs, three *Water* Signs, three *Air* Signs, and three *Earth* Signs

> And then by three Qualities: four *Cardinal* Signs, four *Fixed* Signs, and four *Mutable* Signs

The nine Small Cards of each suit have inherited the genes of *both* these groupings:

> The **Twos-Threes-Fours** of each elemental suit are assigned to the **Cardinal** Signs of the Zodiac (Aries, Cancer, Libra, and Capricorn).

> The **Fives-Sixes-Sevens** of each elemental suit are assigned to the **Fixed** Signs of the Zodiac (Leo, Scorpio, Aquarius, and Taurus).

> The **Eights-Nines-Tens** of each elemental suit are assigned to the **Mutable** Signs of the Zodiac (Sagittarius, Pisces, Gemini, and Virgo).

It's as simple as that. But to keep these hardworking Small Cards firmly at work as the foundation of your house of cards, I want you to perform a very simple exercise.

Exercise 5

PART ONE.
CASTING THE MAGIC CIRCLE OF SMALL CARDS

For this exercise you will need the thirty-six Small Cards and the twelve Astrological Trump Cards.

Note: For the second part of this exercise, you will also need your pitch pipe.

1. Seat yourself comfortably in the center of the floor. (You might want to sit on a folded blanket or cushion.)

2. Gather the thirty-six Small Cards. Kiss them, and divide them by suit into four stacks: Wands, Cups, Swords, and Disks.

3. Arrange the cards in each stack in 2–10 order.

4. Using Figure 34 as your guide, carefully lay out all thirty-six cards in a circle around you to form a Small Card Zodiac wheel. Starting to your left, and moving *counterclockwise*, arrange them like this:

    Two, Three, Four of Wands (Aries)—Five, Six, Seven of Disks (Taurus)—Eight, Nine, Ten of Swords (Gemini)

    Two, Three, Four of Cups (Cancer)—Five, Six, Seven of Wands (Leo)—Eight, Nine, Ten of Disks (Virgo)

    Two, Three, Four of Swords (Libra)—Five, Six, Seven of Cups (Scorpio)—Eight, Nine, Ten of Wands (Sagittarius)

    Two, Three, Four of Disks (Capricorn)—Five, Six, Seven of Swords (Aquarius)—Eight, Nine, Ten of Cups (Pisces)

5. Neatly adjust the cards so that your completed circle is round, tidy, and balanced.

6. Now take your twelve Astrological Trump Cards and starting with the Emperor/Aries lay each of the twelve Trumps over the three Small Cards they rule:

   Emperor/Aries, Hierophant/Taurus, Lovers/Gemini, Chariot/Cancer, Lust/Leo, Hermit/Virgo, Justice/Libra, Death/Scorpio, Art/Sagittarius, Devil/Capricorn, Star/Aquarius and Moon/Pisces

7. Look around at your circle and try to sense how each three resident Small Cards might represent three different phases or facets of their Trump's particular powers and energies. Make up a little story if you need to. Here's an example using the three resident cards for Aries, the Emperor:

   - Two of Wands, Dominion—The Emperor seizes control (initial phase).

   - Three of Wands, Virtue—The Emperor administrates control (established phase).

   - Four of Wands, Perfected Work—The Emperor enforces control and strives to preserve control (crystallized phase).

8. In addition to these observations, try to sense how the influences of the assigned *planet* help determine the Small Card's character and personality and divinatory meaning. Let's again use the three Small Cards of Aries as our example:

   - Two of Wands, Dominion—Mars is assigned to this decan. The Mars Trump is the Tower. Consider how the energies and dynamics of the Emperor and the Tower blend to create the character and personality of the Two of Wands and why it is called Dominion.

   - Three of Wands, Virtue—The Sun is assigned to this decan. The Sun Trump is the Sun. Consider how the energies and dynamics of the Emperor and the Sun (the Sun King) blend to create the character and personality of the Three of Wands and why it is called Virtue.

- Four of Wands, Perfected Work—Jupiter is assigned to this decan. The Jupiter Trump is Fortune. Jupiter/Zeus is the king of the Olympian gods. Consider how the energies and dynamics of the Emperor and Jupiter's Fortune blend to create the character and personality of the Four of Wands and why it is called Perfected Work.

9. When you have the time, analyze the remainder of the Small Cards in this way. It will be helpful if you keep a journal of your observations.

PART TWO

If possible, leave your magick circle of Small Cards in place for the following meditation.

Meditation 8

Attunement Meditation upon Completion of the Thirty-Six Small Cards

Hopefully, you will be able to remain seated in the center of your magical circle of Small Cards and Astrological Trumps to perform this attunement meditation. As we did in earlier exercises, you will be vibrating appropriate musical notes for this exercise, so you will need your pitch pipe or another device to produce the proper note.

1. Be seated in the middle of your Small Card and Trump Circle.

2. Take two or three cleansing breaths and clap twelve times (3-3-3–3-3-3–3-3-3–3-3-3).

3. Locate and pick up the Emperor card and the Two, Three, Four of Wands. Arrange them in your hand face up so that the Emperor rests on top, followed by the Two, Three, Four of Wands.

4. Hold the four cards to you heart. Blow a **C** on your pitch pipe. Close your eyes, take a deep breath, and forcefully intone "HAH" until your breath is exhausted. Repeat three times. You should feel the familiar lightheaded glow around your head and body. Use this glow to

magically charge the cards and install them within your inner house of cards.

5. Locate and pick up the Hierophant card and the Five, Six, Seven of Disks. Arrange them in your hand as before.

6. Hold the four cards to you heart. Blow a **C sharp** on your pitch pipe. Close your eyes, take a deep breath, and forcefully intone "WAH" until your breath is exhausted. Repeat three times. Use your glow to magically charge the cards and install them within your inner house of cards.

7. Locate and pick up the Lovers card and the Eight, Nine, Ten of Swords. Arrange them in your hand as before.

8. Hold the four cards to you heart. Blow a **D** on your pitch pipe. Close your eyes, take a deep breath, and forcefully intone "ZAH" until your breath is exhausted. Repeat three times. Use your glow to magically charge the cards and install them within your inner house of cards.

9. Locate and pick up the Chariot card and the Two, Three, Four of Cups. Arrange them in your hand as before.

10. Hold the four cards to you heart. Blow a **C sharp** on your pitch pipe. Close your eyes, take a deep breath, and forcefully intone "CHAH" until your breath is exhausted. Repeat three times. Use your glow to magically charge the cards and install then within your inner house of cards.

11. Locate and pick up the Lust card and the Five, Six, Seven of Wands. Arrange them in your hand as before.

12. Hold the four cards to you heart. Blow a **D sharp** on your pitch pipe. Close your eyes, take a deep breath, and forcefully intone "TAH" until your breath is exhausted. Repeat three times. Use your glow to magically charge the cards and install them within your inner house of cards.

13. Locate and pick up the Hermit card and the Eight, Nine, Ten of Disks. Arrange them in your hand as before.

14. Hold the four cards to you heart. Blow **F** on your pitch pipe. Close your eyes, take a deep breath, and forcefully intone "YAH" until your breath

is exhausted. Repeat three times. Use your glow to magically charge the cards and install them within your inner house of cards.

15. Locate and pick up the Justice card and the Two, Three, Four of Swords. Arrange them in your hand as before.

16. Hold the four cards to you heart. Blow **F sharp** on your pitch pipe. Close your eyes, take a deep breath, and forcefully intone "LAH" until your breath is exhausted. Repeat three times. Use your glow to magically charge the cards and install within your inner house of cards.

17. Locate and pick up the Death card and the Five, Six, Seven of Cups. Arrange them in your hand as before.

18. Hold the four cards to you heart. Blow **G** on your pitch pipe. Close your eyes, take a deep breath, and forcefully intone "NAH" until your breath is exhausted. Repeat three times. Use your glow to magically charge the cards and install them within your inner house of cards.

19. Locate and pick up the Art card and the Eight, Nine, Ten of Wands. Arrange them in your hand as before.

20. Hold the four cards to you heart. Blow **G sharp** on your pitch pipe. Close your eyes, take a deep breath, and forcefully intone "SAH" until your breath is exhausted. Repeat three times. Use your glow to magically charge the cards and install them within your inner house of cards.

21. Locate and pick up the Devil card and the Two, Three, Four of Disks. Arrange them in your hand as before.

22. Hold the four cards to you heart. Blow **A** on your pitch pipe. Close your eyes, take a deep breath, and forcefully intone "AYAH" until your breath is exhausted. Repeat three times. Use your glow to magically charge the cards and install them within your inner house of cards.

23. Locate and pick up the Star card and the Five, Six, Seven of Swords. Arrange them in your hand as before.

24. Hold the four cards to you heart. Blow **B flat** on your pitch pipe. Close your eyes, take a deep breath, and forcefully intone "TZAH" until your breath is exhausted. Repeat three times. Use your glow to magically charge the cards and install them within your inner house of cards.

25. Locate and pick up the Moon card and the Eight, Nine, Ten of Cups. Arrange them in your hand as before.

26. Hold the four cards to you heart. Blow **B** on your pitch pipe. Close your eyes, take a deep breath, and forcefully intone "Quah" until your breath is exhausted. Repeat three times. Use your glow to magically charge the cards and install them in within your inner house of cards.

27. Congratulations! You have charged and consecrated all seventy-eight cards of the Tarot of You.

CHAPTER 11

The House of Cards

While there are many ways to arrange twenty-two cards, I have chosen to follow the developmental stages outlined in the Sepher Yetzirah and illustrated by the Cube of Space. I have numbered the Trumps from 0 to 21—the Fool through the Universe.

The architecture of layout is shown on page 301, and I have elucidated the cards and positioning.

The triangular peak of the roof is formed by the three *Mother Letter Cards*. As in the Cube of Space, they spring from the black void of 21 (Universe) and Saturn. (You will recall that Saturn is the central point from which emanate all the other letters, Trumps, and landmarks on the Cube of Space.)

0 Aleph (Fool) extends infinitely up and down.

12 Mem (Hanged Man) extends infinitely east and west.

20 Shin (Aeon) extends infinitely north and south.

The next level is formed by six of the seven *Double-Letter Cards* (minus Saturn who is busy reabsorbing the whole shebang). These six Trumps represent the six extremities that the Three Mother Letters created when they each extended in opposite directions.

1 Beth (Magus) Mercury, above

2 Gimel (High Priestess) Luna, below

3 Daleth (Empress) Venus, east

10 Kaph (Fortune) Jupiter, west

15 Peh (Tower) Mars, north

19 Resh (Sun) Sun, south

The next level is formed by the twelve Trumps representing the Zodiac teetering in perfect balance upon the fulcrum of 8 or 11—depending on how you wish to number the Lamed (Justice card).

The main body of the house is formed by the four Aces and the sixteen Court Cards. It is flanked on the left and right by walls containing the thirty-six Small Cards arranged in the order they are assigned to the zodiacal year:

> Starting at the top of the left wall with Aries's Two of Wands and ending at the bottom with Virgo's Ten of Disks, continuing at the top of the right wall with Libra's Two of Swords, and ending at the bottom right with Pisces's Ten of Cups

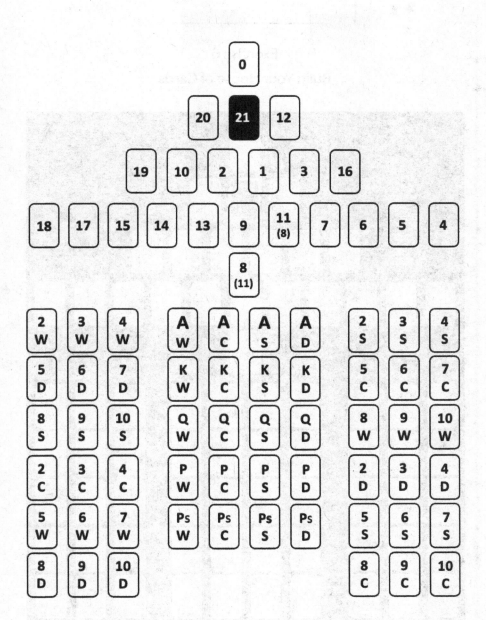

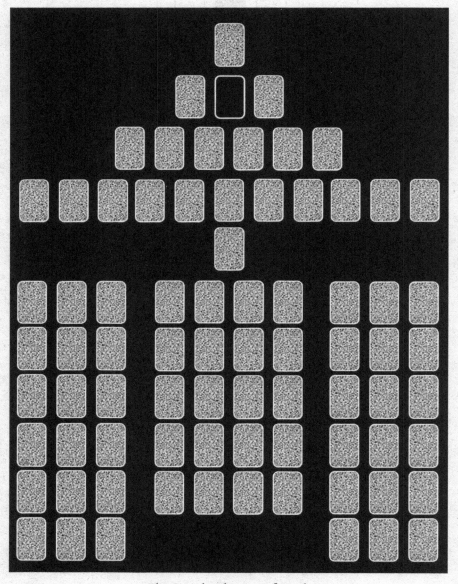

The Completed House of Cards

THE TAROT ARCHITECT

EPILOGUE

The Job Is Yours

As above, so below.
In Earth as it is in Heaven.
The path once laid the journey is inevitable.

In the prologue to this little book, I began with a simple question: "Have you ever tried to build a house of cards?"

I went on to share a silly boyhood memory that was intended, not so much as a device to edify *you*, but as a literary trick to draw *me* through the fourth-wall membrane of writer's block and into the captive-audience venue of shared consciousness with you.

Thank you for your attention, and for allowing me to monopolize the conversation for a few hours. I've done my best to make our time together as pleasant as possible, while at the same time hopefully nudging you out of your comfort zone and into new dimensions of spiritual growth.

Now it's fair for you to ask: "Is my house of cards finished?"

No, but I'm still working on it. This book is my latest effort.

For fifty years, tarot has been for me the only magical tool comprehensive enough to work exactly as advertised. It is my magic wand, my Holy Grail, my Excalibur, my shield, my temple, my filing cabinet, my dictionary, and my microphone. Tarot is the language I use to try to explain the universe to myself. It is the cosmic Grand Hotel whose foundations are formed in the infernal depths and whose penthouse suites rise above the clouds of heaven.

I confess, my life isn't perfect, and I'm not perfectly happy or satisfied with myself or the world around me. My house of cards is as fragile and unstable as anyone's. But the artisan is only as effective as their mastery of the tools of the craft, and if my life, my loves, my work, my level of illumination aren't yet everything they could be, if the edifice of my Great Work remains unfinished, I can't blame my tools, only my imperfect mastery of their use.

It's enough for me to remember that each time my house of cards tumbles down around me it simply means there's more work to be done.

I've accepted the job offer.

I hope you have too.

APPENDIX 1

Simple Divinatory Meanings

The Greater Arcana (Trumps)

0—THE FOOL

Beginning of the Great Work, innocence; a fool for love; divine madness. Reason is transcended. Take the leap. Gain or loss through foolish actions.

I—THE MAGUS

Communication; Conscious Will; the process of continuous creation; ambiguity; deception. Things may not be as they appear. Concentration; meditation; mind used to direct the Will.
Manipulation; crafty maneuverings.

II—THE HIGH PRIESTESS

Symbol of highest initiation; link between the Archetypal and Formative Worlds. An initiatrix. Wooing by enchantment. Possibility. The Idea behind the Form. Fluctuation. Time may not be right for a decision concerning mundane matters.

III—THE EMPRESS

The Holy Grail. Love unites the Will. Love; beauty; friendship; success; passive balance. The feminine point of view. The door is open. Disregard the details and concentrate on the big picture.

IV—THE EMPEROR

Creative wisdom radiating upon the organized man and woman. Domination after conquest; quarrelsomeness; paternal love; ambition. Thought ruled by creative, masculine, fiery energy. Stubbornness; war; authority; energy in its most temporal form. Swift impermanent action over confidence.

V—THE HIEROPHANT

The Holy Guardian Angel. The uniting of that which is above with that which is below. Love is indicated, but the nature of that love is not yet to be revealed. Inspiration; teaching; organization; discipline; strength; endurance; toil; help from superiors.

VI—THE LOVERS

Intuition. Be open to your own inner voice. A well-intended, arranged marriage. An artificial union; analysis followed by synthesis; indecision; instability; superficiality.

VII—THE CHARIOT

Light in the darkness. The burden you carry may be the Holy Grail. Faithfulness; hope; obedience; a protective relationship; firm, even violent adherence to dogma or tradition. Glory; riches; enlightened civilization; victory; triumph; chain of command.

VIII—JUSTICE

Equilibrium; karmic law; the dance of life; all possibilities. The woman satisfied. Balance; weigh each thought against its opposite. Lawsuits; treaties. Pause and look before you leap.

IX—THE HERMIT

Divine seed of all things. By silence comes inspiration and wisdom. Wandering alone; temporary solitude; creative contemplation; a virgin. Retirement from involvement in current events.

X—FORTUNE

Continual change. In the midst of revolving phenomena, reach joyously the motionless center. Carefree love; wanton pleasure; amusement; fun; change of fortune, usually good.

XI—LUST

Understanding; the Will of the New Aeon; passion; sense smitten with ecstasy. Let love devour all. Energy independent of reason. Strength; courage; utilization of magical power.

XII—THE HANGED MAN

Redemption, sacrifice, annihilation in the beloved; martyrdom; loss; torment; suspension; death; suffering.

XII—DEATH

End of a cycle; transformation; raw sexuality. Sex is death. Stress becomes intolerable. Any change is welcome. Time; age; unexpected change; death.

XIV—ART

Transmutation through union of opposites. A perfect marriage exalts and transforms each partner. The scientific method. Success follows complex maneuvers.

XV—THE DEVIL

"Thou hast no right but to do thy will." Obsession; temptation; ecstasy found in every phenomenon; creative action, yet sublimely careless of result; unscrupulous ambition; strength.

XVI—THE TOWER

Escape from the prison of organized life; renunciation of love; quarreling. Plans are destroyed. War; danger; sudden death.

XVII—THE STAR

Clairvoyance; visions; dreams; hope; love; yearning; realization of inexhaustible possibilities; dreaminess; unexpected help; renewal.

XVIII—THE MOON

The Dark Night of the Soul; deception; falsehood; illusion; madness; the threshold of significant change.

XIX—THE SUN

Lord of the New Aeon. Spiritual emancipation. Pleasure; shamelessness; vanity; frankness. Freedom brings sanity. Glory; riches; enlightened civilization.

XX—THE AEON

Let every act be an act of Worship; let every act be an act of Love. Final decision; judgement. Learn from the past. Prepare for the future.

XXI—THE UNIVERSE

Completion of the Great Work; patience; perseverance; stubbornness; serious meditation. Work accomplished.

The Lesser Arcana

WANDS

ACE OF WANDS

Primordial energy as yet unmanifest. Seed of the Will. Masculine archetype. Natural force.

KNIGHT OF WANDS

He is active, generous, fierce, sudden, impetuous. If ill-dignified, he is evil-minded, cruel, bigoted, brutal.

QUEEN OF WANDS

Adaptability, steady force applied to an object, steady rule, great attractive power, power of command, yet liked. Kind and generous when not opposed. If ill-dignified, obstinate, revengeful, domineering, tyrannical, and apt to turn against another without a cause.

PRINCE OF WANDS

Swift, strong, hasty; rather violent, yet just and generous; noble and scorning meanness. If ill-dignified, cruel, intolerant, prejudiced, and ill-natured.

PRINCESS OF WANDS

Brilliance, courage, beauty, force, sudden in anger or love, desire of power, enthusiasm, revenge. If ill-dignified, she is superficial, theatrical, cruel, unstable, domineering.

TWO OF WANDS

Dominion. First manifestation of Fire. Ideal will, independent and creative. Control over circumstances.

THREE OF WANDS

Pride, arrogance, self-assertion. Established force, strength, realization of hope. Completion of labor. Success after struggle. Pride, nobility, wealth, power, conceit. Rude self-assumption and insolence. Generosity, obstinacy, etc.

FOUR OF WANDS

Settlement, arrangement, completion. Perfection or completion of a thing built up with trouble and labor. Rest after labor, subtlety, cleverness, beauty, mirth, success in completion. Reasoning faculty, conclusions drawn from previous knowledge. Unreadiness, unreliable and unsteady through overanxiety and hurriedness of action. Graceful in manner, at times insincere, etc.

FIVE OF WANDS

Quarreling and fighting. Violent strife and boldness, rashness, cruelty, violence, lust, desire, prodigality and generosity, depending on whether the card is well- or ill-dignified.

SIX OF WANDS

Gain. Victory after strife. Love; pleasure gained by labor; carefulness, sociability and avoiding of strife, yet victory therein; also insolence and pride of riches and success, etc. The whole is dependent on the dignity.

SEVEN OF WANDS

Opposition, yet courage. Possible victory, depending on the energy and courage exercised; valor; opposition, obstacles and difficulties, yet courage to meet them; quarreling, ignorance, pretense, wrangling, and threatening; also victory in small and unimportant things and influence upon subordinates.

EIGHT OF WANDS

Hasty communications and messages; swiftness. Too much force applied too suddenly. Very rapid rush, but quickly passed and expended. Violent, but not lasting. Swiftness, rapidity, courage, boldness, confidence, freedom, warfare, violence; love of open air, field sports, gardens, and meadows. Generous, subtle, eloquent, yet somewhat untrustworthy; rapacious, insolent, oppressive. Theft and robbery. According to dignity.

NINE OF WANDS

Strength, power, health, recovery from sickness. Tremendous and steady force that cannot be shaken. Herculean strength, yet sometimes scientifically applied. Great success, but with strife and energy. Victory, preceded by apprehension and fear. Health good, and recovery not in doubt. Generous, questioning and curious; fond of external appearances; intractable, obstinate.

TEN OF WANDS

Cruelty, malice, revenge, injustice. Cruel and overbearing force and energy, but applied only to material and selfish ends. Sometimes shows failure in a matter and the opposition too strong to be controlled, arising from the person's too great selfishness at the beginning. Ill will, levity, lying, malice, slander, envy, obstinacy; swiftness in evil and deceit, if ill-dignified. Also generosity, disinterestedness, and self-sacrifice, when well-dignified.

CUPS

ACE OF CUPS

It symbolizes fertility—productiveness, beauty, pleasure, happiness, etc.

KNIGHT OF CUPS

Graceful, poetic, Venusian, indolent, but enthusiastic if roused. Ill-dignified, he is sensual, idle, and untruthful.

QUEEN OF CUPS

She is imaginative, poetic, kind, yet not willing to take much trouble for another. Coquettish, good-natured, and underneath a dreamy appearance. Imagination stronger than feeling. Very much affected by other influences, and therefore more dependent upon dignity than most symbols.

PRINCE OF CUPS

He is subtle, violent, crafty and artistic; a fierce nature with calm exterior. Powerful for good or evil but more attracted by the evil if allied with apparent Power or Wisdom. If ill-dignified, he is intensely evil and merciless.

PRINCESS OF CUPS

Sweetness, poetry, gentleness, and kindness. Imaginative, dreamy, at times indolent, yet courageous if roused. When ill-dignified, she is selfish and luxurious.

TWO OF CUPS

Marriage, love, pleasure. Harmony of masculine and feminine united. Harmony, pleasure, mirth, subtlety; but if ill-dignified, folly, dissipation, waste, silly actions.

THREE OF CUPS

Plenty, hospitality, eating and drinking, pleasure, dancing, new clothes, merriment. Abundance, plenty, success, pleasure, sensuality, passive success, good luck and fortune; love, gladness, kindness, liberality.

FOUR OF CUPS

Receiving pleasure or kindness from others, but some discomfort therewith. Success or pleasure approaching their end. A stationary period in happiness, which may, or may not, continue. It does not mean love and marriage so much as the previous symbol. It is too passive a symbol to represent perfectly complete happiness. Swiftness, hunting and pursuing. Acquisition by contention; injustice sometimes; some drawbacks to pleasure implied.

FIVE OF CUPS

Disappointment in love, marriage broken off, unkindness of a friend; loss of friendship. Death, or end of pleasure; disappointment, sorrow, and loss in those things from which pleasure is expected. Sadness, treachery, deceit; ill will, detraction; charity and kindness ill-requited; all kinds of anxieties and troubles from unsuspected and unexpected sources.

SIX OF CUPS

Beginning of wish, happiness, success, or enjoyment. Commencement of steady increase, gain and pleasure; but commencement only. Also affront, detection, knowledge, and in some instances contention and strife arising from unwarranted self-assertion and vanity. Sometimes thankless and presumptuous; sometimes amiable and patient. According to dignity as usual.

SEVEN OF CUPS

Lying, promises unfulfilled; illusion, deception, error; slight success at outset, not retained. Possible victory, but neutralized by the supineness of the person: illusionary success, deception in the moment of apparent victory. Lying, error, promises unfulfilled. Drunkenness, wrath, vanity. Lust, fornication, violence against women, selfish dissipation, deception in love and friendship. Often success gained, but not followed up. Modified as usual by dignity.

EIGHT OF CUPS

Success abandoned; decline of interest. Temporary success, but without further results. Thing thrown aside as soon as gained. Not lasting, even in the matter in hand. Indolence in success. Journeying from place to place. Misery and repining without cause. Seeking after riches. Instability.

NINE OF CUPS

Complete success, pleasure and happiness, wishes fulfilled. Complete and perfect realization of pleasure and happiness, almost perfect; self-praise, vanity, conceit, much talking of self, yet kind and lovable, and may be self-denying therewith. High-minded, not easily satisfied with small and limited ideas. Apt to be maligned through too much self-assumption. A good and generous, but sometimes foolish nature.

TEN OF CUPS

Matter settled; complete good fortune. Permanent and lasting success and happiness, because inspired from above. Not so sensual as "Lord of Material Happiness," yet almost more truly happy. Pleasure, dissipation, debauchery, quietness, peacemaking. Kindness, pity, generosity, wantonness, waste, etc., according to dignity.

SWORDS

ACE OF SWORDS

It symbolizes "invoked," as contrasted with natural force: for it is the Invocation of the Sword. Raised upward, it invokes the divine crown of spiritual brightness, but reversed it is the invocation of demonic force and becomes a fearfully evil symbol. It represents, therefore, very great power for good or evil, but invoked; and it also represents whirling force and strength through trouble. It is the affirmation of Justice upholding divine authority; and it may become the Sword of Wrath, Punishment, and Affliction.

KNIGHT OF SWORDS

He is active, clever, subtle, fierce, delicate, courageous, skillful, but inclined to domineer. Also to overvalue small things, unless well-dignified. If ill-dignified, deceitful, tyrannical, and crafty.

QUEEN OF SWORDS

Intensely perceptive, keen observation, subtle, quick and confident; often persevering, accurate in superficial things, graceful, fond of dancing and balancing. If ill-dignified, cruel, sly, deceitful, unreliable, though with a good exterior.

PRINCE OF SWORDS

Full of ideas and thoughts and designs, distrustful, suspicious, firm in friendship and enmity; careful, observant, slow, overcautious. Symbolizes Alpha and Omega; he slays as fast as he creates. If ill-dignified: harsh, malicious, plotting; obstinate, yet hesitating; unreliable.

PRINCESS OF SWORDS

Wisdom, strength, acuteness; subtlety in material things; grace and dexterity. If ill-dignified, she is frivolous and cunning.

TWO OF SWORDS

Quarrel made up, yet still some tension in relations: actions sometimes selfish, sometimes unselfish. Contradictory characters in the same nature; strength through suffering, pleasure after pain. Sacrifice and trouble, yet strength arising therefrom, symbolized by the position of the rose, as though the pain itself had brought forth beauty. Arrangement, peace restored; truce; truth and untruth; sorrow and sympathy. Aid to the weak; justice; unselfishness; also a tendency to repetition of affronts on being pardoned; injury when meaning well; given to petitions; also a want of tact and asking questions of little moment; talkative.

THREE OF SWORDS

Unhappiness, sorrow, and tears. Disruption, interruption, separation, quarreling; sowing of discord and strife, mischief-making, sorrow and tears; yet mirth in platonic pleasures; singing, faithfulness in promises, honesty in money transactions, selfish and dissipated, yet sometimes generous; deceitful in words and repetitions; the whole according to dignity.

FOUR OF SWORDS

Convalescence, recovery from sickness; change for the better. Rest from sorrow, yet after and through it. Peace from and after war. Relaxation of anxiety. Quietness, rest, ease and plenty, yet after struggle. Goods of this life; abundance; modified by dignity as usual.

FIVE OF SWORDS

Defeat, loss, malice, spite, slander, evil-speaking. Contest finished and decided against the person; failure, defeat, anxiety, trouble, poverty, avarice, grieving after gain; laborious, unresting; loss and vileness of nature; malicious, slanderous, lying, spiteful and tale-bearing. A busybody and separator of friends, hating to see peace and love between others. Cruel, yet cowardly, thankless and unreliable. Clever and quick in thought and speech. Feelings of pity easily roused, but unenduring.

SIX OF SWORDS

Labor, work, journey by water. Success after anxiety and trouble; self-esteem, beauty, conceit, but sometimes modesty therewith; dominance, patience, labor, etc.

SEVEN OF SWORDS

Journey by land; in character untrustworthy. Partial success. Yielding when victory is within grasp, as if the last reserves of strength were used up. Inclination to lose when on the point of gaining through not continuing the effort. Love of abundance; fascinated by display; given to compliments, affronts, and insolences and to spy upon others. Inclined to betray confidences, not always intentionally. Rather vacillatory and unreliable.

EIGHT OF SWORDS

Narrow, restricted, petty, a prison. Too much force applied to small things; too much attention to detail at the expense of the principal and more important points. When ill-dignified, these qualities produce malice, pettiness, and domineering characteristics. Patience in detail of study; great care in some things, counterbalanced by equal disorder in others. Impulsive; equally fond of giving or receiving money or presents; generous, clever, acute, selfish and without strong feeling of affection. Admires wisdom, yet applies it to small and unworthy objects.

NINE OF SWORDS

Illness, suffering, malice, cruelty, pain. Despair, cruelty, pitilessness, malice, suffering, want, loss, misery. Burden, oppression, labor; subtlety and craft, dishonesty, lying and slander. Yet also obedience, faithfulness, patience, unselfishness, etc., according to dignity.

TEN OF SWORDS

Ruin, death, defeat, disruption. Almost a worse symbol than the Nine of Swords. Undisciplined, warring force, complete disruption and failure. Ruin of all plans and projects. Disdain, insolence, and impertinence, yet mirth and jollity therewith. A marplot, loving to overthrow the happiness of others; a repeater of things; given to much unprofitable speech, and of many words. Yet clever, eloquent, etc., according to dignity.

DISKS

ACE OF DISKS

It represents materiality in all senses, good and evil, and is, therefore, in a sense, illusionary. It shows material gain, labor, power, wealth, etc.

KNIGHT OF DISKS

Unless very well-dignified he is heavy, dull, and material. Laborious, clever, and patient in material matters. If ill-dignified, he is avaricious, grasping, dull, jealous; not very courageous, unless assisted by other symbols.

QUEEN OF DISKS

She is impetuous, kind, timid, rather charming, greathearted, intelligent, melancholy, truthful, yet of many moods. If ill-dignified, she is undecided, capricious, changeable, foolish.

PRINCE OF DISKS

Increase of matter. Increases good or evil, solidifies; practically applies things. Steady, reliable. If ill-dignified, he is selfish, animal and material, stupid. In either case slow to anger, but furious if roused.

PRINCESS OF DISKS

She is generous, kind, diligent, benevolent, careful, courageous, persevering, pitiful. If ill-dignified, she is wasteful and prodigal.

TWO OF DISKS

Pleasant change; visit to friends. The harmony of change; alternation of gain and loss, weakness and strength; ever-changing occupation; wandering, discontented with any fixed condition of things; now elated, then melancholy; industrious, yet unreliable; fortunate through prudence of management, yet sometimes unaccountably foolish; alternatively talkative and suspicious. Kind, yet wavering and inconsistent. Fortunate in journeying. Argumentative.

THREE OF DISKS

Business, paid employment, commercial transaction. Working and constructive force, building up, creation, erection; realization and increase of material things; gain in commercial transactions, rank; increase of substance, influence, cleverness in business, selfishness. Commencement of matters to be established later. Narrow and prejudiced. Keen in matters of gain; sometimes given to seeking after impossibilities.

FOUR OF DISKS

Gain of money or influence; a present. Assured material gain: success, rank, dominion, earthy power, completed but leading to nothing beyond. Prejudicial, covetous, suspicious, careful and orderly, but discontented. Little enterprise or originality. According to dignity as usual.

FIVE OF DISKS

Loss of profession; loss of money; monetary anxiety. Loss of money or position. Trouble about material things. Labor, toil, land cultivation; building, knowledge and acuteness of earthly things; poverty; carefulness, kindness; sometimes money regained after severe toil and labor. Unimaginative, harsh, stern, determined, obstinate.

SIX OF DISKS

Success in material things, prosperity in business. Success and gain in material undertakings. Power, influence, rank, nobility, rule over the people. Fortunate, successful, liberal, and just. If ill-dignified, may be purse-proud, insolent from excess, or prodigal.

SEVEN OF DISKS

Unprofitable speculations and employments; little gain for much labor. Promises of success unfulfilled (shown, as it were, by the fact that the rosebuds do not come to anything). Loss of apparently promising fortune. Hopes deceived and crushed. Disappointment, misery, slavery, necessity, and baseness. A cultivator of land, yet a loser thereby. Sometimes it denotes slight and isolated gains with no fruits resulting therefrom, and of no further account, though seeming to promise well.

EIGHT OF DISKS

Skill; prudence; cunning. Overcareful in small things at the expense of great. Penny wise and pound foolish. Gain of ready money in small sums; mean, avaricious; industrious; cultivation of land; hoarding; lacking in enterprise.

NINE OF DISKS

Inheritance; much increase of goods. Complete realization of material gain, good, riches; inheritance; covetous, treasuring of goods, and sometimes theft and knavery. The whole according to dignity.

TEN OF DISKS

Riches and wealth. Completion of material gain and fortune; but nothing beyond; as it were, at the very pinnacle of success. Old age, slothfulness; great wealth, yet sometimes loss in part; heaviness; dullness of mind, yet clever and prosperous in money transactions.

Court Cards—I Ching Hexagrams

17. FOLLOWING (QUEEN OF WANDS)

To prepare to rule, first learn to serve. If you're a true ruler, it will seem like a rest.

18. WORK ON WHAT HAS BEEN SPOILED (DECAY)
(PRINCESS OF SWORDS)

What somebody ruined, somebody can fix. Study the cause. Fix it. Then watch it for a while to make sure it works.

27. THE CORNERS OF THE MOUTH (*NOURISHMENT*)
(PRINCESS OF WANDS)

Observe what comes out of the mouth and what goes into it. You are what you eat—and what you say.

28. PREPONDERANCE OF THE GREAT (QUEEN OF SWORDS)

Things are fast reaching the breaking point. Revolution is not required, but start creating a transition strategy.

31. INFLUENCE (WOOING) (QUEEN OF DISKS)

Mutual attraction. Courtship, not seduction. The man's on his knees, but the woman is in control. Be happy to give people your advice, but don't act like a know-it-all.

32. DURATION (KNIGHT OF SWORDS)

Marriage. The courtship is over. The man gets off his knees (the woman is still in control). Living force and energy—enduring because it is flexible—moving yet stable like the stars.

41. DECREASE (PRINCESS OF CUPS)

A downturn in the economy—less stuff—less time—less energy. Don't get mad. Become simpler. Make it an art form.

42. INCREASE (PRINCE OF WANDS)

An upturn in the economy—more stuff—more time—more energy. It won't last forever, so do great things while you can. Start by imitating great deeds.

51. THE AROUSING (SHOCK, THUNDER) (KNIGHT OF WANDS)

Boo! Scared you didn't it? It scared everyone else too! Ha ha. That's only natural. When you've got your poop together, you should never really be afraid.

52. KEEPING STILL, MOUNTAIN (PRINCESS OF DISKS)

Find a quiet place away from people and noises. Forget your body for a while. Go inside and meet yourself. Keep focused on the present situation. Thinking beyond that will only bum you out and waste your time.

53. DEVELOPMENT (GRADUAL PROGRESS) (PRINCE OF DISKS)

Slow but sure. No need to be hasty. Be patient. Proceed gradually, one step at a time. Progress remains stable and strong by growing slowly.

54. THE MARRYING MAIDEN (KNIGHT OF CUPS)

Watch your step. You're pretty damned low on this totem pole. You won't be able to force anything. Bite the bullet and keep your eye on the prize.

57. THE GENTLE (THE PENETRATING WIND) (PRINCE OF SWORDS)

Success through small, subtle, but persistent means. Don't freak people out by acting unexpectedly. Gently prepare them for you actions.

58. THE JOYOUS, LAKE (QUEEN OF CUPS)

Joy springs from deep happiness. Be friendly and cheerful; it's contagious. Enjoy gatherings with happy and intelligent friends. Have fun and learn from one another.

61. INNER TRUTH (PRINCE OF CUPS)

The purity and strength of the truth inside you inspires all—even to good-for-nothing jerks and morons. Flush your prejudices down the toilet and put yourself for a moment in the other guy's shoes.

62. PREPONDERANCE OF THE SMALL (KNIGHT OF DISKS)

Keep your expectations low. Don't expect big things to come out of this. Concentrate on the little stuff. Keep it simple and unpretentious. Do the correct thing in the correct way at the correct time.

Court Card / Small Card Dates

Mar. 11 to Apr. 10   **Queen of Wands**

    Mar. 11 to Mar. 20   Ten of Cups

    Mar. 21 to Mar. 30   Two of Wands

    Mar. 31 to Apr. 10   Three of Wands

Apr. 11 to May 10   **Prince of Disks**

    Apr. 11 to Apr. 20   Four of Wands

    Apr. 21 to Apr. 30   Five of Disks

    May 1 to May 10   Six of Disks

May 11 to June 10   **Knight of Swords**

    May 11 to May 20   Seven of Disks

    May 21 to May 31   Eight of Swords

    June 1 to June 10   Nine of Swords

June 11 to July 11   **Queen of Cups**

    June 11 to June 20   Ten of Swords

    June 21 to July 1   Two of Cups

    July 2 to July 11   Three of Cups

July 12 to Aug. 11   **Prince of Wands**

    July 12 to July 21   Four of Cups

    July 22 to Aug. 1   Five of Wands

    Aug. 2 to Aug. 11   Six of Wands

Aug. 12 to Sept. 11   **Knight of Disks**

    Aug. 12 to Aug. 22   Seven of Wands

    Aug. 23 to Sept. 1   Eight of Disks

    Sept. 2 to Sept. 11   Nine of Disks

Sept. 12 to Oct. 12   **Queen of Swords**

    Sept. 12 to Sept. 22   Ten of Disks

    Sept. 23 to Oct. 2   Two of Swords

    Oct. 3 to Oct. 12   Three of Swords

Oct. 13 to Nov. 12   **Prince of Cups**

    Oct. 13 to Oct. 22   Four of Swords

    Oct. 23 to Nov. 1   Five of Cups

    Nov. 2 to Nov. 12   Six of Cups

Nov. 13 to Dec. 12   **Knight of Wands**

    Nov. 13 to Nov. 22   Seven of Cups

    Nov. 23 to Dec. 2   Eight of Wands

    Dec. 3 to Dec. 12   Nine of Wands

Dec. 13 to Jan. 9   **Queen of Disks**

    Dec. 13 to Dec. 21   Ten of Wands

    Dec. 22 to Dec. 30   Two of Disks

    Dec. 31 to Jan. 9   Three of Disks

Jan. 10 to Feb. 8   **Prince of Swords**

    Jan. 10 to Jan. 19   Four of Disks

    Jan. 20 to Jan. 29   Five of Swords

    Jan. 30 to Feb. 8   Six of Swords

Feb. 9 to Mar. 10   **Knight of Cups**

    Feb. 9 to Feb. 18   Seven of Swords

    Feb. 19 to Feb. 28   Eight of Cups

    Mar. 1 to Mar. 10   Nine of Cups

APPENDIX 2

Correspondence Tables for the Trump Cards

Table 1. The Mother Letters

Hebrew Letter & Number			Element & Trump	Four Color Scales *King *Queen *Prince *Princess	Position on Cube	Qabalistic Intelligence	Musical Note
א	A	Aleph 1	Air **0** **Fool**	K- Bright Pale Yellow Q- Sky Blue P- Blue/Emerald Green Ps- Emerald, Flecked Gold	Up-Down	Scintillating Intelligence	E
מ	M	Mem 40	Water **XII** **Hanged Man**	K- Deep Blue Q- Sea Green P- Deep Olive Green Ps- White, Flecked Purple	East-West	Stable Intelligence	G#
ש	Sh	Shin 300	Fire (& Spirit) **XX** **Aeon**	K- Orange Scarlet Q- Vermilion P- Scarlet, Flecked Gold Ps- Vermilion, Flecked Crimson & Emerald	North-South	Perpetual Intelligence	C

Table 2. The Double Letters

Hebrew Letter & Number			Planet & Trump	Four Color Scales *King *Queen *Prince *Princess	Position on Cube	Qabalistic Intelligence	Musical Note
ב	B	Beth 2	Mercury **I** **Magus**	K- Yellow Q- Purple P- Grey Ps- Indigo, Rayed Violet	Above	Intelligence of Transparency	E
ג	G	Gimel 3	Luna **II** **High Priestess**	K- Blue Q- Silver P- Cold Pale Blue Ps- Silver, Rayed Sky Blue	Below	Uniting Intelligence	G#
ד	D	Daleth 4	Venus **III** **Empress**	K- Emerald Green Q- Sky Blue P- Early Spring Green Ps- Bright Rose, Rayed Pale Green	East	Illuminating Intelligence	F#
כ	K	Kaph 20	Jupiter **X** **Fortune**	K- Violet Q- Blue P- Rich Purple Ps- Bright Blue, Rayed Yellow	West	Intelligence of Conciliation	Bb
פ	P F	Peh 80	Mars **XVI** **Tower**	K- Scarlet Q- Red P- Venetian Red Ps- Bright Red, Rayed Azure or Emerald	North	Active or Exciting Intelligence	C
ר	R	Resh 200	Sun **XIX** **Sun**	K- Orange Q- Golden Yellow P- Rich Amber Ps- Amber Rayed Red	South	Collecting Intelligence	D
ת	Th T	Tav 400	Saturn (& Earth) **XXI** **Universe**	K- Indigo Q- Black Ps- Blue Black K- Black-Flecked Yellow	Center	Administrative Intelligence	A

Table 3. The Simple Letter Trumps.

Hebrew Letter & Number			Zodiac & Trump	Four Color Scales *King* Queen *Prince *Princess	Position on Cube	Qabalistic Intelligence	Musical Note
צ* הּ*	Tz X	Tzaddi 90 *or Heh see Star	Aries IV Emperor	K- Scarlet Q- Red P- Brilliant Flame Ps- Glowing Red	North-East Edge	Constituting Intelligence	Bb *(Tz)* C *(Heh)*
ו	V W U O	Vav 6	Taurus V Hierophant	K- Red Orange Q- Deep Indigo P- Deep Warm Olive Ps- Rich Brown	South-East Edge	Triumphal Intelligence or Eternal Intelligence	C#
ז	Z	Zain 7	Gemini VI Lovers	K- Orange Q- Pale Mauve P- New Yellow Leather Ps- Reddish-Grey	East-Above Edge	Disposing Intelligence	D
ח	Ch H	Cheth 8	Cancer VII Chariot	K- Amber Q- Maroon P- Rich, Bright Russet Ps- Dark Greenish-Brown	East-Below Edge	Intelligence of the House of Influence	C#
ט	T	Teth 9	Leo XI Lust	K- Yellow Q- Deep Purple P- Grey Ps- Reddish-Amber	North-Above Edge	Intelligence of All Activities of the Spiritual Being	D#
י	Y I J	Yod 10	Virgo IX Hermit	K- Yellowish-Green Q- Slate Grey P- Greenish-Grey Ps- Plum	North-Below Edge	Intelligence of Will	F

Hebrew Letter & Number			Zodiac & Trump	Four Color Scales *King* Queen *Prince *Princess	Position on Cube	Qabalistic Intelligence	Musical Note
ל	L	Lamed 30	Libra **VIII** **Justice**	K- Emerald Green Q- Blue P- Deep Blue-Green Ps- Pale Green	North-West Edge	Faithful Intelligence	F#
נ	N	Nun 50	Scorpio **XIII** **Death**	K- Green Blue Q- Dull Brown P- Very Dark Brown Ps- Livid Indigo Brown	South-West Edge	Imaginative Intelligence	G
ס	S	Same-kh 60	Sagittarius **XIV** **Art**	K- Blue Q- Yellow P- Green Ps- Dark Vivid Blue	West-Above Edge	Intelligence of Probation or Tentative	G#
ע	Au O U	Ayin 70	Capricorn **XV** **Devil**	K- Indigo Q- Black P- Blue-Black Ps- Cold Dark Grey	West-Below Edge	Renovating Intelligence	A
ה צ*	H	Heh 5 *or Tzaddi see Em-peror	Aquarius **XVII** **Star**	K- Violet Q- Sky Blue P- Bluish Mauve Ps- White, Tinged Purple	South-Above Edge	Natural Intelligence	C (*Heh*) Bb (*Tz*)
ק	Q	Qoph 100	Pisces **XVIII** **Moon**	K- Crimson Q- Buff, Flecked Silver-White P- Pinkish Brown Ps- Stone Color	South-Below Edge	Corporeal Intelligence	B

Enochian Tablet of Union

Aces and Court Cards on the Enochian Tablet of Union
(Spirit Tablet)

	Ace Spirit	Prince Air	Queen Water	Princess Earth	Knight Fire
Swords Air	E	X	A	R	P
Cups Water	H	C	O	M	A
Disks Earth	N	A	N	T	A
Wands Fire	B	I	T	O	M

Endnotes

Prologue

1. A qabalistic in-joke in reference to the magician's marriage to the Holy Guardian Angel.

2. William Shakespeare. *Julius Caesar* in *The Complete Works of Shakespeare* (New York: Longman, 1997), Act I, Scene ii.

3. "Now first I understand what he, the sage, has said: The world of spirits is not shut away; Thy sense is closed, thy heart is dead!" Johann Wolfgang Goethe, *Faust* (New York: Knopf, 1941).

4. The "Perfect Ashlar" of Freemasonry.

What to Expect

1. "Founded by Dr. Paul Foster Case in 1922, Builders of the Adytum is a Mastery School and training order based on the Western Mystery tradition. B.O.T.A. members receive weekly lessons in Tarot, Qabalah, Gematria, Astrology, Alchemy, and other related disciplines." From "Builders of the Adytum—an Authentic Mystery School," *bota.org*, accessed October 2024.

2. These images were the creation of Dr. Paul Foster Case and artist Jessie Burns Parke. The general formats of the B.O.T.A. cards owe much to that of the famous deck created earlier in the century by Golden Dawn initiates Arthur Edward Waite and artist Pamela Colman Smith.

3. I should point out that in 1969 artist-magician Jerry Kay designed and published his own uncolored *The Book of Thoth Tarot* (Los Angeles: XENO Publications, 1969) and encouraged the owners to color in and personalize their own decks.

BOOK I

Chapter 1

1. Lon Milo DuQuette, *Tarot of Ceremonial Magick,* Next Millennium ed. (Omaha, NE: Magical Omaha, 2019), *magicalomaha.com,* 1.

2. Ibid.

3. Aleister Crowley, *Thoth Tarot Deck* (Stamford, CT: US Games Systems, Inc., 2008).

4. Arthur Edward Waite and Pamela Colman Smith, *Rider-Waite Tarot Deck* (Stamford, CT: US Games Systems, Inc., 1971).

5. Paul Foster Case, *Builders of the Adytum Tarot Cards* (Stamford, CT: US Games Systems, Inc., 1997).

6. Chick and Sandra Tabatha Cicero, *Golden Dawn Magical Tarot* (Minneapolis, MN: Llewellyn Publications, 2010).

7. When I use the terms *standard tarot deck* or *fundamental structure*, I am referring to a deck of *twenty-two* numbered **Trumps** and *four* suits each made up of *four* **Aces**, *four* **Court Cards**, and *nine* Pips or **Small Cards**.

8. Yes, this is not a typo. I said *genetically*, as in *genes and DNA*.

9. Qabalah (spelled here with a *Q*) usually refers to the application of qabalistic principles practiced by nonsectarian students of the Western hermetic arts and mysteries. Spelled *Kabbalah* it usually relates to the more traditional Jewish/scriptural applications. Christian mystics, especially those of the Renaissance period, spelled it *Cabala*.

Chapter 2

1. $1 + 2 + 3 + 4 = 10$.

2. In the *Thoth Tarot* and *Tarot of Ceremonial Magick*, the Yod-Heh-Vav-Heh order of the Court Cards is Yod-Knight, Heh-Queen, Vav-Prince, Heh Princess. In the Waite-Smith tarot decks the order is Yod-King, Heh-Queen, Vav-Knight, Heh-Page.

3. To traditional Jewish Kabbalists, sacred scriptures mean primarily the Torah, aka the Pentateuch or the first five books of Moses in the Bible. But true to transcendental qabalistic wisdom, any text (or indeed, any*thing*) can serve as sacred scripture. "Look hard enough at anything and you will eventually see everything," as Rabbi Lamed Ben Clifford said.

4. Exodus 6:1: "Then said יהוה (Yod Heh Vav Heh) unto Moses, Now shalt thou see what I will do to Pharaoh."—a very dramatic and memorable verse that demonstrated the awesome power of God.

5. No one can forget in Charlton Heston's movie Moses stretching out his rod to part the Red Sea and bellowing "Behold His [Her/Its/Their] mighty hand!"

6. They tried to divide the One God into two and three parts but couldn't do much better than thinking about God as just a more complicated singularity.

7. Yes, I said *kiss* the card, with your lips. This initial intimate gesture will begin the process of integrating the spiritual essence of each card within yourself and, at the same time, imbue the card with a portion of your living DNA.

8. Qabalists also view the Yod part of the soul as being the Yechidah (the inmost unity of the soul), and the Chiah (the Life Force itself), and together assign them to Kether and Chokmah.

9. There are actually five Elements: Fire, Water, Air, Earth, and Spirit. Spirit is the key Element that simultaneously binds the Four Elements together and pushes them apart so they do not lose their essential nature. This dynamic is exhibited in tarot in several ways; for instance, the four Elemental suits of the Lesser Arcana (Fire/Wands, Water/Cups, Swords/Air, and Disks/Earth) are held together and separated by Greater Arcana Trumps.

Chapter 3

1. My favorite translation is Aryeh Moshe Eliyahu Kaplan, *Sepher Yetzirah: The Book of Creation* (York Beach, MA: Weiser, 1997).

2. Please keep in mind even the most respected translators of the Sepher Yetzirah admit that the source texts from which they worked contain organizational inconsistencies and evidence of corruption. Hermetic qabalists of the 19th and 20th centuries, particularly the tarot adepts of the Golden Dawn, noted what appeared to them to be certain blinds and obvious aberrations and freely adjusted certain planetary and zodiacal letter assignments to reflect modern and universally accepted astrological standards. We will be using these forms as well.

3. *Sephiroth* plural; *sephirah* singular.

4. Words, the *third helper* that the Sepher Yetzirah tells us assisted in creating the universe, are important to other aspects of qabalistic study and not immediately relevant to our discussion of tarot.

5. When I use the term *Yourhead* in reference to Number 10 (Malkuth) on the Tree of Life, I am more or less referring to one's everyday consciousness and perception of three-dimensional / time / space objective reality.

6. *Ain* (Nothing), *Ain Soph* (Limitless Nothing), *Ain Soph Aur* (Limitless Light).

7. What this fairy tale is trying to describe isn't an event that happened "in the past" but instead a process that is occurring in an eternal *now*. The author's occasional use of the past tense is only a clumsy, but unavoidable, literary device.

8. One of the qabalistic epithets for Kether is "The Smooth Point."

9. The Chinese philosopher Lao Tzu, the founder of Taoism, began his classic *Tao Te Ching* by explaining all this in breathtakingly few words: "The *nameless (#1)* is the *origin* of Heaven and Earth. The *named (#2, etc.)* is the *mother* of the myriad creatures."

10. In the same way One initially did when it reflected itself to create Two.

11. Qabalists sometimes differ on the use of words *macrocosm* and *microcosm* as the terms relating to the Tree of Life. Some prefer to label the macrocosm sephiroth 1-2-3 (the Supernal Triad) and the microcosm sephiroth 4–10. Both views (and various others) are equally valid and workable within their own self-referential context. The definitions we will use are those most familiar to many modern tarot qabalists.

12. My use of the terms *god* and *god names* in reference to the divine characters and powers of the sephiroth should not be confused with the all-encompassing singularity of the Primal One.

13. Every Hebrew letter represents a number. Consequently, every word, name, and sentence resonates to the vibratory frequency of a specific number.

14. The Aeon (Trump XX), and its Hebrew letter ש, Shin, also does double duty representing both the Primitive Elements of Fire and Spirit.

15. What this fairy tale is trying to describe isn't an event that happened "in the past" but a process occurring in *an eternal npw*. The author's occasional use of the past tense is only a clumsy, but necessary, literary device.

16. In qabalistic Tree of Life terms, Saturn is 3 (Binah), and Saturn's father, Uranus, is 2 (Chokmah) in the Supernal Triad.

17. You might be thinking this is sort of like the situation Number Three on the Tree of Life might have found itself in before the Supernal Triad finally allowed itself to be reflected.

18. Aleister Crowley, *The Book of Thoth* (York Beach, ME: Weiser, 1974).

19. Traditional initiation mystery.

20. M. David Litwa, ed./trans., *Emerald Tablet* (Cambridge, MA: Cambridge University Press, 2018), *www.cambridge.org*.

Chapter 4

1. Please be mindful that there is a difference between the Three Primitive Elements (Air/Fool/א [Aleph], Water/Hanged Man/מ [Mem], and Fire/Aeon/ש [Shin]) and the Four (Five) Elements (Fire, Water, Air, Earth, and *Spirit), which we associate with the material universe.

Element *Earth* is a composite and somewhat an elemental aberration, enjoying a unique status like that of Malkuth (the tenth sephiroth) and the Court Card Princesses. In the Greater Arcana, the Universe card does double duty representing both Saturn and Earth.

2. When I ask you to say something out loud, I really want you to do it. Hearing yourself make an affirmation places the words in a deeper part of your brain and opens additional memory circuits.

3. Sepher Yetzirah, chapter V, section 16.

BOOK II

A Little Background Information

1. Trionfos displayed colorful images of characters, concepts, biblical events, gods of antiquity, political and ecclesiastical personages, etc., each assigned a level of importance relative to the others and positioned in order of their importance in a *triumphal* parade.

2. Modern tarot decks have four Court Cards per suit rather than the three Court Cards of modern playing cards.

3. A Turkish card game brought to Western Europe prior to the 14th century that used a deck of fifty-two cards structured similarly to a deck of modern playing cards—four suits, each with three Court Cards and ten Pips.

4. The four Elements of the Lesser Arcana (Fire, Water, Air, Earth) are elemental aspects of the four fundamental forces of existence expressed in the Qabalah as the four letters of the Tetragrammaton (Yod Heh Vav Heh). These four Elements are not the same as the three "Primitive" Elements of the Greater Arcana represented by the three Mother Letters: Primitive Air (Aleph), Primitive Water (Mem), and Primitive Fire (Shin).

5. The four Court Cards also follow the Yod Heh Vav Heh designations.

6. Aleister Crowley, in his *Thoth Tarot*, would rename the old King "Knight." *Tarot of Ceremonial Magick* does the same.

7. Aleister Crowley, in his *Thoth Tarot*, would rename the old Knight "Prince." *Tarot of Ceremonial Magick* does the same.

8. Aleister Crowley, in his *Thoth Tarot*, would rename the old Page "Princess." *Tarot of Ceremonial Magick* does the same.

Introduction to the Cards

1. Qabalistic World of Yetzirah (the Formative World).

2. Qabalistic Part of the Soul, Neshamah (the Soul Intuition).

3. Qabalistic World of Assiah (the Material World).

4. Lon and Constance DuQuette, *Tarot of Ceremonial Magick Tarot Deck* (Omaha, NE: Magical Omaha, 2018), *magicalomaha.com*.

Chapter 1

1. Notice that I describe the steps of qabalistic evolution in the present tense. That is because the steps of creation aren't events that occurred in the past, but a continuous process.

2. Dharana is an early phase of concentration whereby the object of focus is held in one's mind without consciousness wavering from it.

Chapter 2

1. An important distinction must be made between the *four* Primitive Elements (Earth, Air, Water, Fire) that are expressed in the Greater Arcana and the four Natural Elements (Fire, Water, Air, Earth) that are expressed in the four suits of the Lesser Arcana.

2. The four Kerubic beasts (Lion, Eagle, Angel, Bull) are representatives of the four Elemental Fixed Signs of the Zodiac: Leo/Fire, Scorpio/Water, Aquarius/Angel, and Taurus/Earth. They will appear also in Trump X, Fortune.

Chapter 3

1. You may wish to make it an octave higher or lower than the E of the Magus.

Chapter 4

1. Note: The Golden Dawn assigned the Hebrew letter Heh to the Emperor and the letter Tzaddi to the Star. Aleister Crowley and the *TCM* reversed this assignment.

2. Note: The traditional order of the Trumps placed the Leo card (Lust/Strength) as Key XI and the Libra card (Justice) as Key VIII. The Golden Dawn tarot deck reversed it. Aleister Crowley and the *TCM* returns to the original sequence.

3. Traditional titles: Strength or Fortitude.

4. Note: The traditional order of the Trumps placed the Leo card (Lust/Strength) as Key XI and the Libra card (Justice) as Key VIII. The Golden Dawn tarot deck reversed it. Aleister Crowley and the *TCM* returns to the original sequence.

5. Note: The Golden Dawn assigned the Hebrew letter Tzaddi to the Star and the letter Heh to the Emperor. Aleister Crowley and the *TCM* reversed this assignment.

Chapter 5

1. See Figure 4 in Book I, chapter 3, p. 19.

2. Lon Milo DuQuette, *Enochian Vision Magick,* 2nd ed. (York Beach, ME: Weiser Books, 2019).

Chapter 6

1. Paraphrased from Aleister Crowley: Liber B vel Magi sub Figura I.

Chapter 7

1. Sorry, the Princesses do not get to rule days of the year like the rest of her family. See chapter 5.

2. Qabalists might try to assign the eight trigrams to the eight corners of the Cube of Space.

3. For your convenience, the degrees and the dates of the year they represent are printed on the card forms of Astrological Court Cards and the Small Cards of the *Tarot of Ceremonial Magick.*

Chapter 9

1. For your convenience, all this information is printed in several places of each Small Card of the *Tarot of Ceremonial Magick.*

Bibliography

Achad, Frater (Charles Standfield Jones). *Q.B.L.: Being A Qabalistic Treatise on the Nature and Use of the Tree of Life.* York Beach, ME: Weiser Books, 2005.

Case, Paul Foster. *The Tarot: A Key to the Wisdom of the Ages.* New York: Tarcher Perigee, 2006.

Chang, T. Susan. *36 Secrets: A Decanic Journey Through the Miner Arcana of the Tarot.* Addlestone, Surrey, UK: Anima Mundi Press, 2021.

Chang, T. Susan, and M. M. Meleen. *Tarot Deciphered: Decoding Esoteric Symbolism in Modern Tarot.* Woodbury, MN: Llewellyn Worldwide, 2021.

Crowley, Aleister. *The Book of Thoth: A Short Essay on the Tarot of the Egyptians, Being the Equinox, Volume II, No. V.* Facsimile edition. York Beach, ME: Weiser Books, 2017.

———. *Magick: Liber ABA, Book Four.* York Beach, ME: Weiser Books, 1997.

———. *The Qabalah of Aleister Crowley.* New York: Weiser Books, 1973. Retitled *777 and Other Qabalistic Writings of Aleister Crowley* 1977 in the fifth printing, 1977. Reprinted York Beach, ME: Weiser Books, 1990.

DuQuette, Lon Milo. *The Book of Ordinary Oracles.* York Beach, ME: Weiser Books, 2005.

———. *The Chicken Qabalah of Rabbi Lamed Ben Clifford.* York Beach, ME: Weiser Books, 2001.

———. *Enochian Vision Magick: A Practical Guide to the Magick of Dr. John Dee and Edward Kelley.* York Beach, ME: Weiser Books, 2019.

———. *I-Ching of Mi Lo: Magical Antiquarian Curiosity Shoppe.* York Beach, ME: Weiser Books. 2012.

———. *The Key to Solomon's Key: Is This the Lost Symbol of Masonry?* San Francisco: CCC, 2010.

———. *The Magick of Aleister Crowley: A Handbook of the Rituals of Thelema (Weiser Classics Series).* York Beach, ME: Weiser Books, 2022.

———. *Son of Chicken Qabalah.* York Beach, ME: Weiser Books, 2018.

———. *Understanding Aleister Crowley's Thoth Tarot.* York Beach, ME: Weiser Books, 2017.

Greer, Mary K., and Benebell Wen. *Tarot for Your Self: A Workbook for the Inward Journey,* 35th Anniversary ed. York Beach, ME: Weiser Books, 2019.

Hulse, David Allen. *The Key of It All: An Encyclopedic Guide to the Sacred Languages & Magickal Systems of the World: Book Two: The Western Mysteries).* Woodbury, MN: Llewellyn Worldwide, 1996.

Kaplan, Aryeh Moshe Eliyahu. *Sefer Yetzirah.* York Beach, ME: Weiser Books, 1997.

Pollack, Rachel. *Seventy-Eight Degrees of Wisdom: A Tarot Journey to Self-Awareness (A New Edition of the Tarot Classic).* York Beach, ME: Weiser Books, 2019.

Regardie, Israel. *The Tree of Life: An Illustrated Study in Magic.* Edited and annotated by Chic Cicero and Sandra Tabatha Cicero. Woodbury, MN: Llewellyn Worldwide, 2001.

Townley, Kevin. *The Cube of Space: Container of Creation.* Boulder, CO: Archive Press, 1993.

Wang, Robert. *The Qabalistic Tarot Book: A Textbook of Mystical Philosophy.* Samford, CT: US Games Systems, 2017.

Wen, Benebell. *I Ching, The Oracle.* Berkeley, CA: North Atlantic Books, 2025.

Wilhelm, Richard, and Cary, Robert Baynes. *The I Ching, or Book of Changes (Bollingen Series XiX).* Princeton, NJ: Princeton University Press, 1967.

Zalewski, Pat. *Kabbalah of the Golden Dawn. Lulu.com,* 2023.

About the Author

Lon Milo DuQuette is a bestselling author and lecturer, whose books on magick, tarot, and the Western Mystery traditions have been translated into twelve languages. He is currently the US Deputy Grand Master of Ordo Templi Orientis and is on the faculty of the Omega Institute in Rhinebeck, New York, and the Maybe Logic Academy. Among his many books are *The Chicken Qabalah, The Magick of Aleister Crowley, Understanding Aleister Crowley's Thoth Tarot,* and *My Life with the Spirits.* He lives in Sacramento, California, with his wife Constance. Visit him on the web at *lonmiloduquette.com.*

The cards used to illustrate *The Tarot Architect* are the uncolored version of Lon and Constance DuQuette's *Tarot of Ceremonial Magick* published by

Magical Omaha
3141 North 93rd Street
Omaha, NE 68134
magicalomaha.com

To Our Readers

Weiser Books, an imprint of Red Wheel/Weiser, publishes books across the entire spectrum of occult, esoteric, speculative, and New Age subjects. Our mission is to publish quality books that will make a difference in people's lives without advocating any one particular path or field of study. We value the integrity, originality, and depth of knowledge of our authors.

Our readers are our most important resource, and we appreciate your input, suggestions, and ideas about what you would like to see published.

Visit our website at *redwheelweiser.com*, where you can learn about our upcoming books and free downloads, and also find links to sign up for our newsletter and exclusive offers.

You can also contact us at *info@rwwbooks.com* or at

Red Wheel/Weiser, LLC
65 Parker Street, Suite 7
Newburyport, MA 01950